Riding the Mutual Aid Bus and Other Adventures in Group Work

ALSO PUBLISHED BY
WHITE HAT COMMUNICATIONS:

BOOKS

Days in the Lives of Social Workers
edited by Linda May Grobman

Days in the Lives of Gerontological Social Workers
edited by Linda May Grobman and Dara Bergel Bourassa

More Days in the Lives of Social Workers
edited by Linda May Grobman

The Field Placement Survival Guide
edited by Linda May Grobman

Is It Ethical? 101 Scenarios in Everyday Social Work Practice
by Thomas Horn

An Introduction to the Nonprofit Sector:
A Practical Approach for the Twenty-First Century
by Gary M. Grobman

The Nonprofit Handbook
by Gary M. Grobman

The Nonprofit Management Casebook
by Gary M. Grobman

MAGAZINE
The New Social Worker—The Magazine for Social Work
Students and Recent Graduates

VISIT OUR WEB SITES
www.socialworker.com
www.socialworkjobbank.com
www.whitehatcommunications.com
www.daysinthelivesofsocialworkers.com

NETWORK WITH US
www.facebook.com/newsocialworker
www.facebook.com/whitehatcommunications
www.twitter.com/newsocialworker
http://www.linkedin.com/groups?gid=3041069

Riding the Mutual Aid Bus and Other Adventures in Group Work

A "Days in the Lives of Social Workers" Collection

Linda May Grobman
Jennifer Clements

Editors

With a foreword by
Steven Kraft, MSW, JD
Past President, International Association
for Social Work With Groups

White Hat **Communications**

Harrisburg, Pennsylvania

Riding the Mutual Aid Bus and Other Adventures in Group Work
A "Days in the Lives of Social Workers" Collection

Edited by Linda May Grobman and Jennifer Clements

Published by:

White Hat **Communications**

Post Office Box 5390
Harrisburg, PA 17110-0390 U.S.A.
717-238-3787 (voice)
717-238-2090 (fax)
http://www.socialworker.com

The editors can be contacted by e-mail at: *lindagrobman@socialworker.com*

Note: The names and identities of social work clients mentioned in this book have been carefully disguised in accordance with professional standards of confidentiality.

Listing of a resource in this book does not imply endorsement.

Cover photo credit: Thomas Perkins/BigStockPhoto.com

Library of Congress Cataloging-in-Publication Data

Riding the mutual aid bus and other adventures in group work : a "days in the lives of social workers" collection / Linda May Grobman, Jennifer Clements, editors ; with a foreword by Steven Kraft.
   p. cm.
Includes bibliographical references.
ISBN 978-1-929109-33-3
1. Social group work–United States. 2. Social workers–United States. 3. Social case work–United States. I. Grobman, Linda May. II. Clements, Jennifer.
HV45.R5155 2013
361.40973–dc23
            2012028051

Riding the Mutual Aid Bus and Other Adventures in Group Work
A "Days in the Lives of Social Workers" Collection

Table of Contents

About the Editors

Linda May Grobman, ACSW, LSW, is the founder, publisher, and editor of **THE NEW SOCIAL WORKER**®, the magazine for social work students and recent graduates, and editor of the **Days in the Lives of Social Workers** book series. She has practiced social work in mental health and medical settings, and is a former interim executive director of the Pennsylvania and Georgia state chapters of the National Association of Social Workers. She received her MSW and BM (Music Therapy) degrees from the University of Georgia, and is a graduate of the Music for Healing and Transition Program.

Jennifer Clements, Ph.D., LCSW, is currently an associate professor of social work at Shippensburg University of Pennsylvania. She is Vice President of the International Association for Social Work With Groups and a passionate group worker. She has worked in child welfare practice for 15 years, where she has led numerous groups with children and adolescents.

About the Contributors

Golnaz Agahi, MPH, LCSW, is a clinical program manager at Kaiser Permanente Psychiatry Department and a part-time lecturer at the University of Southern California. She has more than 15 years of experience working in public health and social services settings. Her past work, research, and publications have addressed alcohol and drug prevention and treatment, high-risk and homeless youth services, gang prevention and intervention, and crisis intervention. She received dual master's degrees in public health and social work from San Diego State University.

Patricia Berendsen, RMFT, RSW, SEP, is a psychotherapist in private practice and an adjunct faculty in London, Ontario, Canada. She formerly worked as a clinician with the Centre for Children and Families in the justice system. She is an AAMFT/ OAMFT Approved Supervisor and Somatic Experiencing Practitioner. Patricia has published and presented extensively in the areas of trauma, integrating the body into psychotherapy, strengths-based therapeutic practices, incorporating spirituality in clinical work, creating positive team culture in social services, and "keeping the soul in our work."

Robert Blundo, Ph.D., LCSW, is a professor in the School of Social Work at the University of North Carolina Wilmington. He teaches strengths-based and solution-focused practice with individuals, families, and groups at the undergraduate and graduate levels. He established the Strengths Collaborative, which works to bring strengths-based practice to his region and state through trainings, consultations, and presentations. He is also director of the Solution-Focused Practice, Training, and Research Group, which is part of the Strengths Collaborative.

Wendy Bunston, BSW, MaFT, GCertOrgDyn, GDipInfMH, is a senior clinical social worker in the Integrated Mental Health Service at the Royal Children's Hospital, Melbourne, Australia. She also has a master's degree in family therapy and further post-graduate qualifications in organizational dynamics and infant mental health.

Tom Caplan, MSW, is a social worker in private practice who works with individuals, couples, families, and groups. He is an adjunct professor at McGill University School of Social Work and director and supervisor of the McGill Domestic Violence Clinic. He is also a designated expert in domestic violence for the Quebec Court System.

Christina M. Chiarelli-Helminiak, MSW, is a doctoral student at the University of Connecticut School of Social Work, where she teaches graduate courses in the MSW program. Ms. Chiarelli-Helminiak led the development of a children's advocacy center providing community-based services in rural north Georgia. She received her BA in social work from Shippensburg University and her MSW from Marywood University, where she was the first social work student to receive the Sister M. Eva Connors Peace Medal.

Michael G. Chovanec, Ph.D., LICSW, is an associate professor at St. Catherine University/University of St. Thomas School of Social Work in St. Paul, MN. He has been a clinician for more than 30 years and currently works part time as coordinator and group facilitator for a county domestic abuse program that he helped develop in 1988. He is licensed as a clinical social worker and a marriage and family therapist in Minnesota.

Jennifer Clements, Ph.D., LCSW, is currently an associate professor of social work at Shippensburg University of Pennsylvania. She is Vice President of the International Association for Social Work With Groups.

Elizabeth P. Cramer, Ph.D., LCSW, ACSW, is a professor in the School of Social Work at Virginia Commonwealth University. Her primary practice and scholarship areas are lesbian and gay issues, domestic violence, and group work. Dr. Cramer is the editor of the book, *Addressing Homophobia and Heterosexism on College Campuses,* and she serves on the editorial board of the *Journal of Gay and Lesbian Social Services.*

Charles C. Daniels, Jr., MSW, received the Herb Sneider Memorial Group Student of the Year Award for 2011-2012 from the Massachusetts Chapter of the Association for the Advancement of Social Work With Groups. Charles is the CEO and founder of Fathers' Uplift, an organization that works with fathers in overcoming barriers that prevent them from being engaged in their children's lives through support groups and activities that promote civic engagement.

Ashley D. Davis, Ph.D., LICSW, is an assistant professor of social work at Wheelock College in Boston, MA, where she teaches courses on social research and social work practice with children and families. Her research interests include cultural competence, intergroup dialogue, and intersectionality theory in social work education. She treats couples and families from diverse backgrounds in her private practice.

Nicole Dubus, MSW, LICSW, Ph.D., is a licensed clinical social worker with nearly 25 years of clinical experience as a group worker. She is currently in private practice and is an assistant professor in the social work department at Wheelock College in Boston MA.

Andy Dunlap, Ph.D., LCSW, is a clinical social worker who teaches at Shippensburg University and has worked extensively in college counseling. His research focuses on changes in the coming out process over time.

Marci Mayer Eisen, MSW, works at the Jewish Federation of St. Louis as Director of the Millstone Institute for Jewish Leadership. She previously worked at the Jewish Community Relations Council (JCRC) and spent the majority of her career at the Jewish Community Center (JCC). A 1981 graduate of the Wurzweiler School of Social Work, Yeshiva University, Marci received a Certificate in Nonprofit Management and Leadership from the University of Missouri–St. Louis in 2010. Marci has proudly supervised more than 25 MSW students over the years.

Denise M. Ellis, Ph.D., MSW, received her Ph.D. and master's degrees in social work from Fordham University and her bachelor's degree in social work from York College of the City University of New York (CUNY). She is a full-time faculty member in the Department of Social Work at Kean University in Union, NJ, where she teaches graduate students. Prior to working in academia, she worked as a psychiatric social worker with individuals, families, and groups in several outpatient departments of psychiatry in New York. She enjoys spending time with her family, dancing, and traveling.

Sue Foley, B. Soc. Stud., MSW, MA, M.Ed., graduated in social work in 1975 from the University of Sydney, Australia. She is a councillor of the International Society for Prevention of Child Abuse and Neglect. She has worked in the areas of child protection, treatment of trauma and mental health, and is currently the coordinator the Child and Adolescent Telepsychiatry Outreach Services at the hospital where she is employed. She loves to travel and to stretch the boundaries!

Jim Frentrop, MSW, LCSW, is a graduate of the University of Missouri in Kansas City (UMKC) School of Social Work, and is a clinical social worker at a therapeutic day treatment school in Kansas City, where he conducts many group, individual, and family therapy sessions. He also enjoys research, writing, teaching, and being a field instructor for practicum students in social work or counseling degree programs. Additionally, he enjoys spending time with his family or in his woodworking shop.

Margot Wilson Jurgensen, MSW, LCSW, attended Rutgers University and completed her master's at Indiana University in 1996. She is a Board Certified Professional Christian Counselor, AACC, and currently in private practice as a counselor and a coach, in Carmel, IN. She has worked as an elder care manager, in a mental health agency, and in a hospice, and has developed several women's groups.

Sharon A. Lacay, LMSW, is a graduate of Stony Brook University's School of Social Welfare. She has held various positions working with youth and families in an effort to promote positive emotional and behavioral health. She plans to continue her clinical work and empower clients by researching and developing creative and trauma informed interventions for at-risk populations.

Kenna Liatsos, MSW, Ph.D., has 25 years of experience working with young children in public schools. In addition, her professional work has been dedicated to families with a child with a life-threatening illness and bereaved children. She received her Ph.D. from Simmons College. She currently works part time with Cranberry Hospice and Palliative Care in Plymouth, MA, and teaches graduate social work courses at Simmons College and Bridgewater State University.

Denice Goodrich Liley, Ph.D., ACSW, LCSW, is an associate professor at Boise State University, School of Social Work. Dr. Liley is a licensed clinical social worker who specializes in gerontology and end-of-life care.

Kim Lorber, Ph.D., LCSW, MSW, is a social worker and associate professor specializing in group work with caregivers of older adults, seniors, bereavement, and people living with HIV/AIDS. She is the convener of the gerontology minor at Ramapo College of New Jersey. In addition, Dr. Lorber is an HIV/AIDS researcher who works with artists and craftspeople through Worldesigns, Incorporated, in South Africa and Thailand, helping to create income opportunities for unemployed or underemployed individuals living in poverty and infected or affected by HIV/AIDS.

Andrew Malekoff, LCSW, is Executive Director/CEO for North Shore Child and Family Guidance Center, where he has worked since 1977. He is Editor-in-Chief of the professional journal *Social Work With Groups: A Journal of Community and Clinical Practice* and author of the critically acclaimed textbook, *Group Work With Adolescents: Principles and Practice.* He is a board member of the Association for the Advancement of Social Work With Groups and has taught at Adelphi and New York University and presented to audiences across the U.S. and Canada.

Tracy A. Marschall, MSW, is an assistant professor of social work at the University of Indianapolis. She holds an MSW from Indiana University and completed doctoral work at the University of Illinois at Champaign-Urbana. In addition to teaching courses on interpersonal and group practice, child welfare, families, and research, her primary research interests include diverse family systems, divorce, custody, and therapeutic supervised visitation.

Kyle McGee, II, LMSW, is a faculty advisor and adjunct lecturer at the Silberman School of Social Work at Hunter College. His 15 years of experience include working with young adults and homeless adults with chronic mental illness and chemical dependency. Mr. McGee has particular interest and research work with providing effective group work practice to individuals residing in New York City homeless shelters and Drop-In Centers. He has also developed curricula and incorporated the use of music and drumming into his practice with groups.

Tuyen D. (Trent) Nguyen, Ph.D., has taught undergraduate and graduate courses in the areas of psychology, counseling, sociology, social work, health sciences, and human services. He is the editor of *Domestic Violence in Asian American Communities* and *Many Paths, One Purpose: Career Paths for Social Work and Human Services Majors.* He has published 30 research articles focusing on intimate partner abuse, Asian American youth identity development, and depression among the elderly population. Professor Nguyen has worked with juvenile delinquents since the early 1990s.

Christine Lynn Norton, Ph.D., LCSW, assistant professor of social work at Texas State University-San Marcos, received her Ph.D. in social work from Loyola University Chicago. She has a Master of Arts in social service administration from the University of Chicago and a Master of Science in experiential education from Minnesota State University-Mankato. Dr. Norton has run groups with adolescents in a variety of practice settings, including therapeutic wilderness programs, juvenile justice, youth and family counseling, schools, and youth mentoring and educational empowerment programs.

Rachel Odo, LCSW, is a clinical social worker with a specialty in acute, chronic, and life-threatening illness. She works as a consultant lecturing and presenting workshops on a range of topics for healthcare professionals, patients, and caregivers, and has served as a moderator in the online support program at CancerCare, Inc. for more than six years.

Emma Giordano Quartaro, DSW, ACSW, LCSW, established and chaired the nationally accredited baccalaureate social work program and the Multidisciplinary Certificate in Gerontology program at Seton Hall University in South Orange, New Jersey. Dr. Quartaro was awarded the Gerontologist of the Year by the Society on Aging, the Mirror of Justice of the Women's Faculty Association, and the Ann Klein Advocate of the Community Health Law Project. Groups of all kinds are her passion and the optimal well-being of persons with disabilities her professional mission.

Elaine S. Rinfrette, Ph.D., LCSW-R, worked for 19 years in outpatient mental health with a special interest in trauma. She is currently a tenure track assistant professor at Edinboro University of Pennsylvania Department of Social Work and facilitator of a group for women with gynecologic cancer.

Ogden W. Rogers, Ph.D., LCSW, ACSW, is professor and chair of the Department of Social Work at the University of Wisconsin-River Falls. He has practiced social work in emergency medicine, community psychiatry, and disaster services. He has a small black dog named Lily.

Mitchell Rosenwald, Ph.D., LCSW, is an associate professor of social work at Barry University. His favorite social work modality is group work, and he has presented and published nationally on group work. Dr. Rosenwald is also the president of the National Association of Social Workers, Florida Chapter.

Rochelle E. Rottenberg, MSW, LISW, graduated in 1981 with a master's in social work from Hunter College in New York City, where she specialized in group work and aging. She worked at the Educational Alliance (a settlement house on the lower East Side) running group services for the senior center. In 1989, she moved to Minnesota, where she did resettlement and acculturation work with recently arrived Russian émigrés, many of whom were older adults. In 1995, she became a field faculty liaison at the School of Social Work at St Catherine University/University of St Thomas.

Kristen Marie (Kryss) Shane, MSW, LSW, LMSW, earned her BS at The Ohio State University and her MSW at Barry University. She holds social work licenses in Ohio and New York. Her professional foci are in the areas of LGBTQI issues and elder issues. She has aided in the introduction of Gay Straight Alliances in high schools, participated in the National Equality March in Washington, DC, rallied for non-discrimination laws, conducted professional trainings on making agencies and companies more inclusive, and continues to actively advocate for LGBTQI rights.

Marge Shirilla, MSW, LCSW, is an associate professor in the School of Social Work at Dalton State College. She has led psychotherapy groups on inpatient units and in outpatient settings at psychiatric and general medicine hospitals, community mental health centers, and hospices. She has witnessed the power of group therapy with clients who are in recovery from substance abuse and trauma; people who are struggling with the grief generated by the loss of a loved one; and women in a group focused on a variety of issues, including those related to power, self-assertion, and realizing full potential as a woman.

Christopher M. Sims, MSW, LCSW, lives in Chico, California, and practices clinical social work within a variety of settings and populations. He is deeply appreciative of the field and those with whom and for whom he works and their contributions to his professional and personal development.

Johanna Slivinske, MSW, LSW, teaches social work courses in the Department of Social Work of Youngstown State University, including Social

Work and Disability, Human Behavior and Lifespan Development, Human Behavior and Environmental Influences, Field Work Seminar, and Cultural Diversity. She is also a therapist at PsyCare, working with children, adolescents, and adults. She has extensive experience in working with individuals with disabilities and is the former Coordinator of Disability Services at Youngstown State University. She is the author of *Storytelling and Other Activities for Children in Therapy.*

Steven Soifer, Ph.D., MSW, is Professor and Chair, University of Memphis Department of Social Work. He was formerly an associate professor at the University of Maryland School of Social Work. He is also co-founder and CEO of the International Paruresis Association, co-founder/co-director of the Shy Bladder Center, and secretary of the American Restroom Association.

Moshe Sonnheim, DSW, ACSW, retired from Bar Ilan University School of Social Work in Israel as a senior lecturer. He has 50 years experience in practicing, supervising, and teaching social work methods. He earned his MSW in social group work at the University of Pennsylvania School of Social Work and his DSW from the School of Applied Social Sciences at Case Western Reserve University. He is the author of *The Andragogic Learning Center: A Field Study in Social Work Education.*

Juliet Sternberg, LMSW, is founder and practice director at Hope Veterinary Clinic. She obtained her MSW degree from Fordham University in 2002. Prior to launching Hope Veterinary Clinic, Juliet had 10 years of experience in mental health and geriatric case management and counseling. Working with clients who had pets persuaded her of the positive impact that companion animals have on the needs and well-being of humans. She founded Hope Veterinary Clinic in 2002 with her veterinarian partner, Kristine Young.

Relando Thompkins, MSW, is a social justice worker interested in conflict resolution, improving intergroup relations, and using peace as nonviolent action. Through service, conflict resolution through non-violent communication, and social action, he works to build more equitable and inclusive communities and increase intercultural understanding. Relando also maintains a blog entitled *Notes from an Aspiring Humanitarian (N.A.H.).* By exploring social identities through written word, film and video, and other forms of media, he hopes to continue to expand and enrich conversations about social issues that face our society.

Gregory J. Tully, Ph.D., MSW, is an associate professor at West Chester University. Previously, he taught at Barry University, Iona College, New York University, and the Silberman School of Social Work. His practice expertise is in the areas of family victimization, child abuse, HIV/AIDS, juvenile probation, and organizational leadership coaching. Dr. Tully's scholarship includes numerous presentations, articles in peer-reviewed journals, and the editing of a group work book, as well as a special issue of a social work with groups journal. He is currently the president of the International Association for Social Work With Groups (IASWG).

Lucille Geiser Tyler, MSW, is a retired assistant dean from the University of Maryland School of Social Work. She is a trainer/consultant for the Nurturing Parenting Programs (since 1988) and developed the first family camp in 1993. With a practice background in child welfare, she has facilitated therapeutic groups for adolescents, support groups for foster parents, and psychoeducational groups for parents.

Kay E. Whitehead, MSW., LCSW, CT, completed her MSW at Indiana University School of Social Work in 1996. She is a Certified Thanatologist with the Association for Death Education and Counseling and is trained in EMDR. She has used her skills in hospice, group development, teaching, and offering retreats for the bereaved. Kay is currently in private practice in Indianapolis, Indiana.

Foreword

IIIIIIIIIIIIIIIIIIIIIIIIIIIIIIIIIIIIIIIII

by Steven Kraft, MSW, JD, Past President
International Association for
Social Work With Groups (IASWG)

As the outgoing president of the International Association for Social Work With Groups (formerly the Association for the Advancement of Social Work With Groups), I am particularly enthusiastic to see this project come to fruition. *Riding the Mutual Aid Bus and Other Adventures in Group Work* is a book that captures the passion, skills, values, and principles of the social group work method. It is especially satisfying because it represents a collaboration of the IASWG, the editors, and the contributors. As you read it, you will appreciate the significant role of the "clients" in this collaboration, as well. The concept of mutual aid is operationalized throughout the book in the descriptions of and dialogues within the various group processes. One gets a clear sense that social group work skill is aimed at helping clients help each other.

The power in this book lies in its concreteness. One sees the group in action. One hears the dialogue. The reader laughs, cries, and celebrates with the participants—workers and clients alike. The worker as a person emerges, not simply as the applier of principles of practice. The helping power of relationships among the clients and with the workers is evident throughout.

In these 44 chapters, we get an appreciation for the wide range of fields of practice in which social group work is utilized. We see work with families, with infants, with children, adolescents, adults, and seniors. We see client systems with an array of challenges, from loneliness to paruresis; from substance abuse to sexual abuse; from personal development to community and agency development. While we learn about the uniqueness of each client system, the stories never fail to demonstrate they are about a method more than a field of practice—a method that values democracy, humility, respect for difference, and the capacity of all people as helping agents.

I have had the privilege of working with Jen Clements, one of the editors, as we were both members of the Board of Directors of the IASWG. Jen's energy, enthusiasm, intelligence, and commitment to the social group work method emerge in the way this book is put together. Her students at Shippensburg University in Pennsylvania are fortunate to be exposed to her. I was also especially excited that we would work with Linda Grobman. Linda is an incredible social worker, and through her work in publications has made a significant impact on our profession. The stories of all the *Days in the Lives of Social Workers* books are so powerful and accessible. They have changed many a student's feelings about social work practice.

The contributors to this remarkable compilation are distinguished. Some are distinguished by their reputations and positions. For example, Andrew Malekoff is the editor of the journal *Social Work With Groups* and the executive director of one of the great social service agencies, North Shore Child and Family Guidance Association. Greg Tully is the incoming president of IASWG and professor of social work at West Chester University. Others are distinguished by the power of their work. You simply have to open any chapter in the book and read about another example of fantastic group work.

This book is a must read for all social workers who want to feel proud of their profession and for anyone else who has ever wondered what social workers really do.

Steven Kraft, MSW, JD
July 2012

Introduction

IIIIIIIIIIIIIIIIIIIIIIIIIIIIIIIIIIIIIIIIIIIIIIIIIIIIIIIIIIIIIIIIIIIIIIIIIIIIIIIIIIIIIIIIIIIIIIIIIIIIIIIIIIIIIIIIIIIIIIIIIIIIIIIIIIIIIII

Groups come in all kinds. Therapy groups. Support groups. Task groups. Psychoeducational groups. Online groups. Play groups. Experiential groups. Art groups. Drumming groups. Co-facilitated groups. Child groups. Adult groups. Family groups. The list goes on.

Regardless of what setting you are in, if you are a social worker, you will work with groups at some time in your career. Some social workers look forward to this. Others find it a bit overwhelming at first.

The International Association for Social Work With Groups (IASWG) is an international organization that was formed for the sole purpose of supporting social workers in working with groups. Many of those involved in the association have made it their life's work to specialize in the use of groups in social work practice. I was excited to be approached last fall by Jennifer Clements, a current member of the IASWG board of directors, with a proposal that we collaborate to develop this collection of stories about group work.

This book is one of several in the *Days in the Lives of Social Workers* series. In this series, my co-editors and I have collected real-life stories that illustrate what it is like to be a professional social worker in a variety of settings, with a variety of populations, and using a variety of practice methods. Through these stories, it is easy to see how rewarding a career in social work can be, and specifically in this volume, how beneficial the use of groups can be to social workers and their clients.

You may have a picture in your mind of what a social work group looks like. It probably has people sitting in a circle, talking about their feelings. There certainly are many groups described in this book that fit that image of a traditional group. However, we also introduce you to groups that take place on a bus or a train, in a public restroom, in cyberspace, or on a zipline 40 feet in the air!

Each story takes us into the life of a particular social worker and shares practice wisdom about a time when that social worker worked with a group. Ogden Rogers gives us a glimpse into the world of critical incident stress debriefing (CISD), Steven Soifer

19

introduces us to the issue of shy bladder (paruresis) and how a graduated exposure group helps, and Kyle McGhee shows how the saying "marching to the beat of a different drum" applies to group work. Rachel Odo brings us into the "connected" world of today with her discussion of online cancer support groups, and Elaine Rinfrette illustrates how a group can surprise a social worker by presenting something different from what was initially thought. These are just a few examples of what you will find in the pages of this book.

We have organized the book generally by age of group members, types of groups, and populations. However, we have not put the chapters into categories as such, because there is quite a bit of overlap among the issues presented in the stories. They cannot just be put in one "box" each. Some of the common themes we found were the use of a "check-in" at the beginning of groups, use of co-facilitators, and similar stages of development among groups. As you read the book, see if you can find other common themes, as well as differences, among the various groups.

Each chapter includes questions to think about. Besides being fascinating reading, each story teaches lessons to help you think about ways to be a better social worker with groups. We encourage you to think about ways these lessons might apply with groups you are working with in your social work practice or field placement.

We have included an appendix that lists resources that may be of interest to you as you develop your skills as a group worker. Finally, we offer a second appendix that includes the full text of the IASWG Standards for Social Work Practice With Groups, which will serve as a guide in your group work practice.

My hope is that the stories in this book will bring to life the theories you have read about groups, and that you will become excited about trying group work yourself. It can be quite an adventure!

Linda May Grobman, ACSW, LSW
July 2012

I am thrilled to be a part the development of this book. My journey as a group worker began in the same way that many of you reading this book can relate. I was an undergrad social work student, and I took a class with an incredible professor, Dr. Carolyn Knight, who taught about the unique qualities of social work with groups. The concept of facilitating so that members can help members was so novel yet so familiar to me. Some of the best experiences I have had as a social worker have been in the circle of group work.

Although the use of groups is familiar and common in social work practice, the training is lacking. Schools of social work that once had group work tracks and concentrations now have just one course on group work. Students are thrown into groups unprepared and unable to take full advantage of the magic of group work. I knew that it could be extremely powerful to have stories of social workers sharing what they do in groups, what works, what mistakes have been made, and lessons learned from those mistakes. As a professor at Shippensburg University, I teach group work classes to our undergrad and graduate students. The theory and concepts are being taught, but I knew that the stories would be a powerful addition to the students' learning. As a professor and a learner, I enjoy the art of storytelling. In fact, the mutual aid bus chapter will be familiar to many of my past students, as it really illustrates a moment of success in practice, along with a mistake to learn from, as well.

I have been serving on the board of the International Association for Social Work With Groups (IASWG) for about five years now. I was introduced to this organization in 2004 by my mentor, Dr. Knight. This professional organization has been key to my group work development and leadership. The organization has been growing, and at this writing, there are members all over the world in more than 24 countries. As of May 2012, the organization's name changed from AASWG to IASWG to reflect the growing international membership. This is to point out that you will see IASWG and AASWG used interchangably throughout the book.

It was through the IASWG that the idea for this book first developed. Having used Linda Grobman's fantastic *Days in the Lives of Social Workers* books in other classes, I offered up to our board the idea of a *Days in the Lives* version for group work. With the board's full blessing, I approached Linda, who has been nothing but supportive. There are 44 incredible chapters in this book. By reading each one, you will have a greater perspective on social work with groups. The diversity of the chapters, fields of practice, types of group, and populations will give you a greater idea of the power of group work. As incredible as the stories are in this book, they are not all-inclusive. You will find that there are areas not covered or discussed. This is because the stories included must be limited to what can fit in a book. As you read, you will understand that the power of group work certainly cannot be contained in just one book.

Will you have a group work story to share some day? We certainly hope so!

Jennifer Clements, Ph.D., LCSW
July 2012

Acknowledgments

‖‖

The editors would like to thank the International Association for Social Work With Groups (IASWG, formerly AASWG) for its participation in the development of this book. The IASWG supported the idea of the book from the beginning, helped in recruiting social workers to write chapters, allowed us to include the Standards for Social Work Practice With Groups in Appendix B, provided reviewers for early versions of the manuscript, and more.

We would like to thank the many social workers who responded to our call for submissions, which was distributed through the AASWG mailing list; BPD-L list; MSW-L list; SOCWORK list; and *The New Social Worker's* mailing lists, Facebook page, and other social media networks. There were so many interesting and inspiring manuscripts, and it was difficult to narrow it down to the 44 we have included.

This book was possible only with the participation of the social workers who took time out of their busy days to write about what happens during those days, and we thank them for the work they do and for their contributions to this book.

Linda would like to thank the many social work educators and students who have read and used the previous volumes in the *Days in the Lives of Social Workers* series, and who have taken the time to give her their input. Their comments helped shape the new content in each subsequent edition and volume.

Thank you to Steven Kraft, past president of IASWG, for his support of this book and for writing the foreword. We would also like to thank the IASWG Commission on Social Work Education members, especially Carol Cohen and Mark Macgowan, for their help and support of this book.

Thanks go to Linda's husband, Gary Grobman, for his meticulous proofreading, editorial input, and support of this endeavor.

Linda thanks Jennifer Clements for coming to her with the idea for this book and for all of her group work expertise that went into making this a valuable contribution to the group work and social work literature. She also thanks Gary and their son, Adam, for their support of this and all of her many projects.

Jennifer would like to thank Linda Grobman for her support of this incredible opportunity to share the power of group work through the stories in this edition. She would also like to thank her own personal group that includes her husband, Paul, and children Maya, Calyn, and Kai. She is supported daily by their love and laughter, and she is forever grateful. The entire Department of Social Work and Gerontology at Shippensburg University have been nothing but encouraging. The IASWG has made a significant impact on her life personally and professionally. The connections made have been life-changing. She has never worked in a more supportive and powerful community than when in a circle of group workers.

Linda May Grobman
Jennifer Clements
July 2012

Chapter 1
Somewhere Else

IIIIIIIIIIIIIIIIIIIIIIIIIIIIIIIIIIIIIIIIIIIIIIIIIIIIIIIIIIIIIIIIIIIIIIIIIIIIIII

by Moshe Sonnheim, DSW, ACSW

Joey was always "somewhere else." When his mother called, he didn't answer. When his father commanded, he didn't hear. When his teacher punished, he didn't obey.

He was always "somewhere else." This was what brought him and his parents to the Base Child Guidance Center. I saw before me an Army Colonel, his somewhat distraught-looking wife, and a cherubic, but stiff-faced seven-year-old dragged along between his parents. Warily, Joey sat opposite me, eyeing the toys and games in my office.

I had barely welcomed them when Joey's father poured out their problems.

"This child is always somewhere else. He doesn't pay attention to anyone. He's in a world of his own. Look at him—little stoneface!"

He continued, "His mother is too easy on him. She gives him everything he wants, but I have to discipline him." Tears began to appear in his wife's eyes. Joey remained stolid. "Every morning, I inspect him before he goes to school. Is he dressed neatly, hair combed, schoolbag ready. And what does his mother do? She makes his lunch and kisses him goodbye."

As he paused for an instant, I turned to his wife and asked her reaction. With trembling voice and wet eyes, she answered, "The Colonel is right. Joey is very difficult. He was such a cute baby, but as he grew older, he became more stubborn. He wasn't really bad; he just seemed to shut us out. We love him, but it's hard. He doesn't hug or kiss us, barely talks to us, and doesn't listen to us or his teacher."

She dabbed her eyes with the Kleenex I offered her; her husband sat rigid. In Joey, however, there was a flicker of feeling as his eyes moved toward her.

"Joey, why do you think you are here?" I asked gently, but pointedly.

"'Cause I don't listen," his face still stolid, but with a tremulous voice. "And why do you think you don't listen?" "I don't know." "How about if we try to find out together—you, me, and your Mommy and Daddy? I see you like the toys and games I have here. Would you like to come here once a week to play with them and talk to me?"

Joey's face relaxed a bit. His eyes lit up, and he gave a firm "yes" with a sideward look at his parents.

"And, you know what?" I added. "Would you like to be in a play group with boys your own age?" A bit less enthusiastically, Joey agreed.

"Now, Joey, would you like to play with things in this room—whatever you want?" He leaped from his chair and headed straight for the "hostility toys" (punching bag, plastic guns, hammer board, and toy soldiers).

Meanwhile, I "contracted" with his parents for an initial period of six months, and suggested that perhaps, they, too, would like to participate in a parents' group.

"Why?" asked the Colonel. "Joey is the problem, and besides, I'm very busy with my men." His wife, however, welcomed the idea. "Oh, Joe, maybe we can help each other in the group. Besides, it will be a night out for us." Reluctantly, the Colonel agreed, and Joey, his parents, and I embarked on a journey to "somewhere."

My first meeting alone with Joey was a "feeling-out" time for both of us. I knew from the psychologist's report that Joey was a "passive-aggressive, angry child of above average intelligence." But I wanted to see for myself, with a minimum of interaction and a maximum of permissiveness.

Joey, for his part, was wary of this new adult in his life. Without a word, he began to play.

He clashed the soldiers with sounds of war. He pounded the pegs into their holes, he fired every toy gun loudly, and he pounded the punching bag mercilessly. Board games and books were not for him.

After half an hour of frenzied activity, Joey slowed down enough for me to ask him what else he wanted to do, because we only had a little bit more time before our meeting ended. Joey didn't seem to hear me, and he made no attempt to clean up, so I "helped" him a bit.

As he prepared to leave, he picked up a toy machine gun to "practice at home" for next week. Gently, but firmly, I explained to him that everything had to remain in the room so that other children could play with them, but I assured him that it would be here again for him next week. Grudgingly, he agreed, and his mother arrived to collect him.

Joey's entrance to the group was more stressful. Two of the boys had problems similar to his. Another boy was "very devious," and the fourth boy was literally "starved" for attention (positive or negative). The noise level was high as they struggled for "hostility" weapons and happily "shot" each other to death. Toward session's end, I focused their energy on the punching bag, which I held while they took turns pummeling it. Frequently, "by accident," they missed the bag and hit me, wary of my reaction (which was gentle, but firm).

To close the meeting calmly, I asked a volunteer to place a plate of cookies on the table so that each boy could take three cookies and talk about what we did today. Joey volunteered, and while I was replacing the jar, a strident cry arose from the table—one boy had eaten all the cookies! So much for a "calm" ending! They had not yet learned "controls from within." Together, however, we decided how to prevent a recurrence of such behavior.

Concurrently, the parents' group had begun. Five sets of their parents—husbands in uniform and wives well-dressed—took turns complaining about their children's behavior. Joey listened to no one. Billy stole food from the table. Jackie goaded other children to misbehave. "We give them everything, and they appreciate nothing."

"How do you deal with their behavior?" I asked. Mutual recriminations between husband and wife ensued, followed by mutual help suggestions. The group process was taking shape. Individual strengths moved the group forward. "Maybe, Joe, you should ease up on the morning inspection." "Maybe, Mary, you should define what you mean by 'appreciation.'"

The Colonel and his wife related to these points in their individual meeting with me. But they remained on an intellectual level, citing the literature they had read on child-rearing. There were, however, hints of relationship problems between them.

Meanwhile, the children were improving more rapidly than their parents. Joey's face became more expressive, his voice loud and clear, his actions more aggressive. He enjoyed coming to me and to the group. "Why?" I asked him. "'Cause I can do things here without Daddy and Mommy always yelling at me."

Joe and Mary were also loosening up. Inspections became less stringent. Joe attended meetings in civvies, and he even cracked some jokes. But they still had a way to go. Joe couldn't understand why my advice to spend homework time with Joey still didn't work. "I told Joey that you said we have to spend an hour on homework every day exactly at 1800 hours." I replied that I didn't mean a rigid regimen like Morning Inspection.

Meanwhile, I noticed that Mary was dressing rather seductively for group meetings, and especially for our individual meetings. Simultaneously, she and Joe were shifting focus from Joey to themselves. With ironic anger, Mary said, "The great Colonel watches TV late into the night. I go early to bed, alone, and he sleeps when I wake."

Their problem was not unique, and the parents' group began to make the connection between conjugal and parent-child relations.

Five months had passed, and I felt I had sufficient control in the children's group to risk more demanding activities. I brought out the dart board. I lined the boys up, one behind the other. I warned them to be careful when throwing the steel-tipped dart. I warned them to take turns.

Excitedly, but carefully, they queued up. Joey was third in line, followed by Jackie. All went well. Suddenly, however, I felt a sharp sting in my back. A strident cry burst from the group. "Joey did it, Joey did it." Some of the boys started to attack him. Jackie had a satisfied grin on his face. Joey trembled with fear (and guilt?).

What to do? With a bit of pain and a bit of anger (toward them and me), I made a split-second response—the dart in my back could wait. Jackie could wait. I held Joey close to me, protecting and reassuring him. His small body relaxed as I told him and the others, "These things happen, and we'll talk about it now."

Meanwhile, they looked curiously at my back and the dart protruding from it. Billy ran to bring the psychiatrist, who was, after all, a physician! Recalling his medical training, Dr. Newman opined that the puncture was superficial, did not penetrate deeply, and thereupon removed the dart, and cleansed the wound antiseptically.

Then, the boys and I talked. They had, indeed, matured as a group and as individuals. Except for Jackie, the traumatic experience enabled them to express feelings openly and sensitively without fear of inappropriate adult response. Jackie, however, still had the need to act surreptitiously. It was he who "egged" Joey on to aim the dart in my direction as I tried to move away from guiding the previous boy in line.

From this point on, group meetings became calmer, and more balanced in regard to quiet activities such as reading, drawing, and talking as opposed to aggressive activities.

The parents' group also progressed. Discussions were more focused, with less mutual flirting, and with more sharing of positive experiences with their children and with each other.

Joe and Mary were more relaxed in their individual meetings with me. Joe ceased being "The Colonel," and he and Mary allowed themselves to be the basically uncertain, but loving couple and parents they were.

The time for ending was approaching. As usual, in such cases, there are conscious and unconscious attempts to prolong the relationship. Joey, especially, tested me. He was again "somewhere else."

"It's okay, Joey, I know you like being here with me and with the group, and I like being with you and the other boys, but you don't need me now." We talked about his progress, and planned an ice cream trip to the PX for our last meeting.

On that day, Joe, in civvies, brought Joey to my office. Somewhat embarrassingly, Joey burst from his father's hands and jumped into my arms. Joe understood, and, joined by Mary, returned to collect Joey after the meeting.

Hand-in-hand, they walked away.

Wiping my eyes, I returned to my office, awaiting the next child and parents.

Think About It

1. What do you think was the rationale behind asking the parents to participate in a parents' group?

2. If your client hit you with a dart, as depicted in this story, what would you do? What do you think of the writer's reaction?

Chapter 2
Journey Into the Land of Groups: How Groups Found Me!

||||||||||||||||||||||||||||||||||||||||||||||||||||||||||||||||||||||||||||||||||||||||||||||||||||||||||||||||||||

by Patricia Berendsen, RMFT, RSW, SEP

I didn't plan on being a group social worker. I guess you could say groups found me. Being drawn to group work happened as most things usually do...by being at the right place at the right time.

I invite you to accompany me as I share with you my professional journey into the "land of group work." If you accept this invitation, you will be a witness to two significant experiences that have had a positive impact on my career as a social worker working within Children and Youth Mental Health Services in Ontario, Canada. The first is pioneering a group process for young girls, and the second is engaging in collaboration with the secondary school education system involving teenaged female youth in trouble with the law.

Groovy Girls Group

When I was a clinical team leader of a large multi-disciplinary team in a residential children's mental health setting, my responsibilities included program development, clinical case supervision, and direct clinical intervention. Three young girls who were between 10 and 12 years of age in the mixed gender residential program were having significant issues. They were acting out by stripping down to their birthday suits (aka naked) in front of male staff. They were urinating in cups and then throwing the contents at staff. They were pretty much out of control.

31

The day after this event, two other clinicians and I met with the girls to debrief what had happened. We framed their actions as "protesting" and that they were "turning up the volume" so that adults would listen. We inquired as to what they wanted us to hear. They said they wanted more attention. They wanted fewer demands and more kindness and warmth. They wanted what was happening right now—sitting down, and being listened to—not being blamed and in trouble. They wanted something just for them. So the inception of the infamous "Groovy Girls Group" began the following week.

This quick turnaround for the start of the group demanded a lot of preparation—meeting with the residential team to see what their opinion was on beginning a group (which they were in complete support of), consulting and obtaining necessary permissions from legal guardians and Children's Aid Workers, ensuring that a group room was available, and so forth. Once we had the go-ahead, we let the girls know that we would be seeing them every Tuesday from 9:30-10:30 a.m. for 10 weeks. They were ecstatic! We, on the other hand, were shaking in our boots! We were nervous.

I worked on a clinical team with two other female clinicians. Together, we conceptualized the groups, with each group having a theme such as emotions, power, anger, friendship, or something similar. The group rules were simple: stick together, no hurts (physical or name calling), and have fun! We designed and utilized structured games and exercises to activate and then settle their arousal systems with the intention of introducing emotional regulation experiences. A snack/story time with healthy food choices and warm and fuzzy blankets that the girls could "snuggle up" in during the story time was the highlight of the group process. We also planned a time when we would "give compliments" to the girls at the end of the group. Every group began and ended with singing the same opening and closing songs. Each song emphasized the girls' names and acknowledged their presence in the group.

The surprising reward was seeing the enthusiasm of the girls each week. They were constantly talking about the "Groovy Girls" group in settings like the on-campus school and in the residence. They proudly talked about their participation in group during case management planning meetings. It was clear that something "special" was going on, and as facilitators, we were intent on following their lead.

Team collaboration and synergy was what made the group experience so successful. To this day, although we all work in different capacities, we regard the "groovy girl" time as a highlight of our careers. We took time after each group to openly evaluate what had occurred and our role in the groups. Since we had the ability and required permissions granted to videotape each session, we were able to critically evaluate ourselves. This was essential to the ongoing development of the quality of each group. We would make adjustments based on the feedback from the girls' behavior as well as from one another. Oftentimes, we laughed and laughed until we had tears running down our faces about some of the antics that occurred during group or the things the girls blurted out. What I enjoyed the most was the camaraderie that we experienced as a unit. We were able to play to each other's strengths and compensate for each other's weaker areas. The ease and authenticity of our interactions was the glue that held the group together. We were modeling for the young girls in our groups how to be in relationship with one another as women.

Sometimes, we weren't sure if we were really making any "progress." However, our compass, our north star, was that initial debriefing meeting when we listened to the request of the girls to have a space that was "their own" and to have more attention. Their behavior, although challenging at times, seemed to be responding to the Groovy Girls group. We were being asked to "trust the process."

An unexpected outcome was that we had no idea how much these groups would transform us. We had to "dig deep" to respond to the transference and countertransference that occurred within the group. Each of us had very nurturing personalities, and two of us were mothers. These characteristics made the plight of these young "motherless" girls difficult to sit with. The girls would often express that they wished we were their mothers. There were also times in the groups when the girls wanted to be cuddled by us during the story time, revealing their early neglect and desire for comfort. These were risks that we chose to take. We continued to trust that their want for nurturance would be met by our attunement and by being responsive to their needs. We were grateful that we were videotaping groups should any allegations arise.

The girls showed up eagerly every week, and we ended our 10-week journey with an extended group time that allowed for their favorite activities, much-loved stories, and "best of" film clips from our videotaped sessions for them to view. Of course, we had a very special pizza snack and a frozen ice cream cake for dessert! We were also able to get donations of "Groovy Girl" dolls, and each participant was given a doll as a reminder of the group.

The rest is history. We provided ongoing groups that accommodated a gender-specific group model. Groups began with highly traumatized boys as well as the continuation of Groovy

Girls groups. Our repertoire of group facilitators was expanded to include a team psychologist and child and youth workers from the residential program. Concrete criteria were developed to assist us with charting and recording progress. We enlisted the help of our team psychologist to structure a quantitative research model for the groups. Initial research showed promising outcomes. The culmination of our work was a presentation about our groups at a joint Children's Mental Health and Children's Aid Society Provincial Conference given by the executive director of our agency and me.

These groups, as effective as they were, were time and personnel intensive. There were many pressures to consider reducing the one-to-one staffing pattern. However, as we were working with such a highly traumatized clinical population, we strongly advocated for ongoing one-to-one staffing. We could not have done it without the support of the residential team and the agency at large. Moreover, the strong collaboration of my peers and our working well as a team largely contributed to the success of the groups. As the acronym for TEAM states, *Together Everyone Achieves More.*

Salon de Thé

When an opportunity in my professional life opened up for me to work as a clinician with young offenders, I was excited. I wondered how my interest in group work would develop with a new population. The young women ages 14-18, many of whom were gang-involved, were in secure custody. They had committed serious offenses and were quite guarded. Needless to say, they were not always the most receptive audience and often not open to counseling. As they were in a secure setting, they had an on-site school. Fortunately, they had a wonderful teacher who saw beyond the academic needs of these young women and was seeking to collaborate with me, a clinician who provided clinical support to the youth.

The school curriculum required students to participate in a discussion forum in order to be evaluated on their oral communication skills. This was creatively accomplished through a Salon de Thé. Initially, salons were popularized in the 17th and 18th centuries. They were a gathering of like-minded people that posited to facilitate philosophical and literary discussions. It was hoped that knowledge would be gained through conversation. In the spirit of the French historical salons, we focused on current and relevant themes such as strong female role models, people who were "different," and people who were down and out and made a comeback. As many of the girls struggled with literacy, the genre of film was used rather than novels for the Salon de Thé. Every other week, a movie was selected by either the teacher or me, viewed by the class, and then discussed at the Salon. A formal atmosphere was created with a table complete with a colorful tablecloth and napkins. Regular and herbal tea was served from unique tea pots. Hot chocolate was also available for those who did not like tea. Bone china tea cups and saucers, along with home-baked goodies and fruit, made this a most festive and unique occasion...none like any other. For new residents, the Salon de Thé was an interesting surprise. Many had never tried tea (especially herbal), nor had they ever used a china tea cup and saucer before!

This was truly a collaborative venture. Attending the Salons were the teacher, child and youth workers from the unit, student interns, myself as a clinician, as well as the residents of the secure custody setting. Discussion was prompted by slips of paper placed in an old fashioned cookie tin that contained phrases or words that pertained to the film. Each person took a turn and picked a slip of paper and was asked to comment on it. Their remarks could be related to the movie, their life, or their views of that particular topic or quote.

The beauty of this group experience was seeing the vulnerability of the girls who often projected a crusty and rough exterior. Many would end up sharing aspects of their neglectful traumatic histories. Some would cry as they revealed their personal views as no one had sought to hear them before. Folks who were shy found the courage to speak. They could voice their truth as they came to trust the group environment. The safety and containment of the group process allowed for disagreements to occur. These conflicts were not easy, nor were they comfortable, yet they were invaluable life lessons. Not surprisingly, the girls didn't ever want to miss a Salon!

A unique encounter that ties my two group experiences together happened when I walked into the secure custody setting one day. One of the girls looked vaguely familiar to me. She was sitting on the sofa eating toast in a way that was oddly recognizable. Her demeanor was standoffish and her gaze was avoidant. As was customary in my role, I ventured closer to make some casual conversation with her. She did so reluctantly. After a few moments, I was sure that this was Natasha (not her real name), who had been in the original Groovy Girls group. I suggested to her that we may have met before, when she was in residence at another facility a few years earlier. She immediately jumped up, the remnants of her toast flying everywhere, and shouted with surprise, "The Groovy Girls!" She proceeded to give me a huge hug in front of all her peers. She was so excited to see me again (although I would have preferred it had not been in a custody setting). We were able to spend some time reminiscing about the group. Natasha shared that she had moved several times and that her Groovy Girl doll had gone with her everywhere. She said that the Groovy Girls group was one of the best things she ever did!

When it came time to participate in the Salon de Thé, Natasha was thrilled to know that I would be joining the group. She shared enthusiastically her heartfelt appreciation for people who had been in her life and had made a difference. She talked about how meeting me again had given her hope for the future and rekindled some positive memories that she had forgotten about. I, in turn, was amazed at how life can come full circle. The plaque on my office wall comes to mind. "You never know the difference you'll make in a child's life...for a moment or for a lifetime!"

Lessons I Have Learned From Group Practice

- Clients are our teachers. Ask and learn from them.
- Dare to actively trust the voice of the client(s).
- Be willing to be vulnerable with your colleagues so that you can become the best clinician you can be.
- Think outside the box. Look for ways to creatively collaborate with different systems and professional disciplines.
- Outcomes might be difficult to measure. Small gains are gains nonetheless.
- Trust the process. *Really* trust the process.
- Group work is fun, exhilarating, exhausting, and definitely worth every ounce of energy.

Think About It

1. What role does attunement play in group process? Do you think attunement is necessary in group process? Why or why not?

2. What challenges have you encountered with transference and countertransference in your group process? How have you managed this?

3. Discuss how the collaboration between group facilitators can be the "glue" of a group?

4. What is your view of physical contact in a therapeutic group context?

Additional Reading Resources

Berendsen, P. (2010, Spring). Connection is key: What's love and belonging got to do with it? *Child and Family Professional, 13* (1), 7-10.

Freeman, J., Epston, D., & Lobivits, D. (1997). *Playful approaches to serious problems: Narrative therapy with children and their families.* New York: W.W. Norton and Company.

Garvin, C. D., Gutierrez, L. M., & Galinsky, M. J. (Eds.). (2004). *Handbook of social work with groups.* New York: Guilford Publications.

Kim Berg, I., & Steiner, T. (2003). *Children's solution work.* New York: W.W. Norton and Company.

Satir, V. (1976). *Making contact.* Berkeley, CA: Celestial Arts.

Vanderheyden (Berendsen), P. (2007, Summer). It's the small things that matter. *Child and Family Journal, 10* (2), 69-71.

Vanderheyden (Berendsen), P. (2006, Spring). I dare you: Our client's challenge to us. *Child and Family Journal, 9* (1), 44-45.

Chapter 3
Group Worker's Heaven

by Jim Frentrop, MSW, LCSW

I enjoy group therapy so much that I call my workplace "Group Worker's Heaven." I have found the group to be a powerful place to help my clients experience healing, growth, support, and camaraderie. My clients are K-12 students in a therapeutic day-treatment school whose behaviors, disabilities, or trauma histories make it difficult to function in a mainstream school. I am one of several clinical social workers responsible for conducting 60 minutes of therapy per student per week. We do a combination of individual and group therapy.

Our school is divided into small classrooms with six to 10 students, a teacher, and a paraprofessional. I call them "ready-made therapy groups." We have freedom to develop numerous types of groups, such as psychoeducational groups, process groups, behavioral therapy groups, support groups, and a host of others. Groups may be open-ended or short-term topical groups. We may hold groups in the classroom or form pull-out groups of selected students from several classrooms. We may use off-the-shelf curricula, customize it to meet specific needs, or develop our own using evidence-based materials. We can choose from an endless list of topics, such as anger management, bullying prevention, drugs, or social skills. I call my workplace "Group Worker's Heaven" because the opportunities for social work with groups are unlimited.

My daily schedule contains mostly planned therapy sessions. I have weekly individual sessions scheduled for every student on my caseload. I also have weekly scheduled groups, family therapy sessions, supervision, and staff meetings. Every student has a treatment plan that describes his or her goals for change and specific objectives for meeting these goals. My job in therapy is to help guide the client in the change process.

A daily activity that consumes much of my time is unplanned crisis management. My students might enter a crisis cycle at any given time, for a variety of reasons. I need to triage each crisis and determine how to best handle the situation. Sometimes the crisis trumps my scheduled activities. Most of my students understand when I have to postpone a session to help someone else with a crisis. After all, the next crisis I get pulled into may be theirs.

As is true for many social workers, every intervention I conduct with a student, be it planned or unplanned, has to be documented to show whether or not our students are making progress toward their goals (and to show I do something to earn a paycheck). For each 60-minute session, I may spend 10 to 20 minutes entering a progress note into the student's electronic record or dealing with action items from the session. For every group session, I need to enter a progress note in each group member's electronic record. Documentation can be a significant daily effort. I usually try to do my documentation at the end of the day. If I wait too long, it piles up quickly, and I forget things that need to be recorded.

Every day is different in my workplace. I can look back on any given day and identify good things that happened, as well as some things I would do differently. Since group work is the topic of this chapter, I will share a few stories of some successful groups I have facilitated, as well as some that weren't so successful. Success is a subjective measure. In group therapy, success is determined by the process as much as the end result (Yalom, 1995).

The most common type of group I conduct is a psychoeducational group, which is one in which I teach a topic, or a skill, or share information with the group. I recently led a psychoeducational group on bullying. It was a 6- to 8-session curriculum I found online (Operation Respect, 2012) and customized to meet my group's specific needs. Because this group had a scheduled beginning and ending, we would see it morph through a series of developmental phases: forming, storming, norming, performing, and adjourning (Tuckman, 1965). Just looking at the catchy names should give you an idea of what to expect in each phase.

During the first session, the "forming" stage of our group, I asked group members to share examples of words that were hurtful and made them feel bullied. I explained I would write their responses on a flip chart. The first student, a middle school girl, said she felt bullied when she was called "the b-word." I said, "Oh, you mean bitch?" and wrote it on the flip-chart. Mild laughter ensued. ("Ha ha, he said bitch out loud!") The next student stated he felt bullied when people used "the f-word." I said, "Oh, you mean f...." Uh, anyhow, I said the word and wrote it on the flip-chart. More laughter from the group. Although saying these words out loud would be frowned upon in most environments, I allow my students to use their familiar "street language" during therapy. By meeting them at their level, I build a stronger alliance, which is one of the greatest predictors of group success, according to Yalom (1995).

I now had the group's attention. We continued this exercise for a few minutes. Then I asked the group to list words that make them feel respected...and continued with the curriculum. If you don't get the group's attention early on, it's a challenge to proceed to more mature stages of group development. The second session of my group was a bit stormy, because the kids expected to do something fun like use dirty words again, but instead I prodded them into more serious discussions. Eventually, we normalized and had productive sessions, then adjourned with ice cream sundaes for our final session. As with any therapeutic relationship, groups require appropriate closure and termination. This had been a fun group, and I wanted it to have a fun ending.

Another type of group I frequently conduct is the process group, which deals with issues in the here-and-now. In a process group, I play the role of facilitator or moderator. I was recently asked to conduct a process group in a classroom to help the teacher announce he was transferring to another school. Many of our students struggle with attachment and loss as a result of significant trauma in their young lives. These students had a close bond with their teacher. We would need to plan this group carefully to create a therapeutic and emotionally safe environment for our students to process their emotions. I asked the teacher and paraprofessional to help predict which students might become tearful or angry. I asked a few colleagues to be available for support. We needed to be mindful that the actions of any one member may have a significant impact on the overall group.

We kicked off our process group with a ritual called check-in. We went around the room and asked each group member to share how they felt on a scale of one to 10. This process creates a good transition away from academic activities and establishes the mindset of group sharing. My students tend to like this routine and will grumble if I attempt to start group without it. After check-in, I always remind the group of our mantra, "emotional safety," to encourage open and honest sharing and discourage any kind of repercussion or ridicule. Then I remind them of the confidentiality rule, "What we say in group stays in group." It's important to lay this groundwork before every group session to maintain trust and openness.

After check-in, I invited the teacher to share his news with the class. When he finished, I invited group members to share their feelings. One by one, they shared, each emotion as different as the person expressing it. As facilitator, I didn't say much, I simply listened as each student spoke in turn, maintained eye contact, nodded, reflected back what I heard them say, and thanked them for sharing. As we predicted, some students were tearful and some were angry. But the process was successful in that there was a healthy sharing of feelings and camaraderie as group members discovered common emotions. Plans were made to discuss grief and loss in upcoming sessions. In our process group, we had created an emotionally safe environment, and our students used that environment for a remarkable showing of resilience and mutual support. This was the group process at its finest. In the end, both the process and results were positive.

One of my favorite genres of group therapy is bibliotherapy. This simply means reading a story and discussing it. Reading an engaging story often has a calming effect on a classroom of students. I enjoyed being a volunteer reader when my own children were in a mainstream elementary school, and knew that younger children enjoy being read to. I was quite surprised when my older students and students with low attention spans listened intently as I read to them. Reading seems to capture their attention, so I can engage them in meaningful discussions. Group members can identify with characters in a story and gain insight into their own situations. I have had great luck finding stories by searching the Internet for keywords such as "therapeutic stories for adolescents." There are books for sale, but I also find a plethora of free downloadable stories. I have also written my own short stories to address specific issues, developing fictional characters and placing them in situations my students can relate to. Maybe someday I'll publish them in a book. A common question at the start of group is, "What story are we going to read today?"

Sometimes I have little or no time to prepare for a group session. Some of my best groups have been process groups in which I walked in with no agenda, and led a group discussion on what's happening in the here-and-now. Often, during check-in, a student will bring up an issue and I will lead the group in sharing their thoughts about the issue in a helpful and supportive way. On the other hand, there have been times when I spent hours preparing psychoeducational material for a 30-minute session, only to have it all go out the window within the first 30 seconds. I learned the hard way to always have a "Plan B" and "Plan C" when going into a group session. Therapeutic games and social skills games, such as the Ungame or Emotional Bingo, are helpful items to have when you need a spur-of-the-moment group idea. Another ready-made group idea is listening to calming, meditative music while reading guided-imagery stories or coloring mandalas.

Perhaps my worst group work nightmare was a group I was assigned to conduct after school. I was given a group of kids at the same time I was handed a book of psychoeducational group lesson plans. The kids would have preferred to have been on the playground, and they didn't hesitate to tell me this. The curriculum was one-size-fits-all, was not a good fit for them, and I had been given no time to familiarize myself with it or customize it to meet their needs. After about 10 minutes of grumbling, we were able to pull together some ice-breaker games to keep the kids entertained while we regrouped and customized the curriculum for future sessions. No prep time plus no flexibility equaled no success that evening. The next morning, I would have a rather spirited discussion with my supervisor.

The school of hard knocks has taught me important lessons about leading groups. I am rarely successful conducting a group with a rigid agenda and no room for flexibility, or trying to play the role of authoritarian. In these cases, a dominant group member usually will arise and challenge me to a power struggle. When students feel powerless in the group, they will do everything they can to feel powerful. This does not usually end well for me, or for them. During group therapy, I am not just a group leader; I am also a group member. In individual therapy, a therapist may be viewed as someone with a certain amount of wisdom or authority, but a therapist in a group session is seen in a more egalitarian, transparent role (Yalom, 1995).

Basic social work skills of engagement, active listening, probing, using open-ended questions, reflecting, and reframing are invaluable for a group practitioner. I also find a basic understanding of general systems theory helpful in understanding the dynamics of a group. A group will form a system, and group members will form subsystems. They will take on roles and define boundaries, then try to modify those roles and boundaries. When a group member does something different to upset the status quo, others within the system will adjust their behavior to try to influence the wayward member and restore the system to its original state of functioning. This is the concept of homeostasis from general systems theory (Rogers, 2006), and it plays out frequently during group sessions. A group therapist always has one more client than the number of individual group members. The group itself becomes a client–a living, breathing entity.

Personality traits such as warmth, empathy, and genuineness that are helpful for a social worker in general are magnified in importance in the group environment. Other characteristics that are especially helpful for a group practitioner are patience, flexibility, and a sense of humor. Textbooks, grad schools, and seminars only scratch the surface of teaching group-work skills. For me, nothing can replace real-world experience and practice. I also try to keep up with the latest literature in group work through the National Association of Social Workers (NASW) Web site and publications, as well as social media groups such as Social Work With Groups on Facebook. I didn't always love doing group work, and I wasn't always good at it. I still learn something new in every group session, even if what I learn is how *not* to do something.

Every day is unique. Each group is a new experience. At times, walking into a group session is as nerve-wracking as walking on stage to a packed auditorium. Other times, it's as comfortable as sitting in front of the fireplace watching TV and eating popcorn with my family. I love the variety of groups I conduct, and I love the freedom my agency allows me to design groups that meet our clients' needs while allowing us to be creative, and have a little fun. To personally experience the power of the therapeutic group process to help my clients heal and grow is, for me, Group Worker's Heaven.

Think About It

1. If you wanted to develop your own group, what criteria would you use to determine if it was successful?

2. Should adolescent clients be permitted to break an occasional rule (such as using language in group that would be inappropriate outside the group)?

3. The author mentioned a group confidentiality rule: "What we say in group stays in group." How would you react if you found out one of your group members was sharing confidential information outside the group? Is it ever okay to break the confidentiality rule?

4. How would you react if a group member became disruptive during group or tried to engage you in a power struggle?

Additional Reading

Gladding, S. (2002). *Group work: A counseling specialty* (4th ed.). New Jersey: Prentice-Hall.

Rogers, A. T. (2006). *Human behavior in the social environment.* New York: McGraw Hill.

Schwartz, A. (1995). *Guided imagery for groups.* Duluth, MN: Whole Person Associates Inc.

Tuckman, B. (1965). Developmental sequence in small groups. *Psychological Bulletin, 63* (6), 384-399. Retrieved February 6, 2009 from http://dennislearningcenter.osu.edu/references/GROUP%20DEV%20ARTICLE.doc.

Vrancken, S. (2012). *Mandala coloring meditation and music web site.* Retrieved January 2, 2012 from http://mandalacoloringmeditation.com.

Yalom, I. (1995). *The theory and practice of group psychotherapy* (4th ed.). United States: Basic Books, Inc.

Resources

Operation Respect. (2012). *Operation Respect web site.* Retrieved January 2, 2012 from http://operationrespect.org.

Ungame. (2012). *Official web site of the Ungame.* Retrieved January 2, 2012 from http://www.ungame.com.

Chapter 4
When the Group Clicks: Psychoeducation With Adolescent Girls in Crisis

IIIIIIIIIIIIIIIIIIIIIIIIIIIIIIIIIIIIIIIIIIIIIIIIIIIIIIIIIIIIIIIIIIIIIIIIIIIIIIIIIIIIIIIIIIIIIIIIIIIIIIIIIIIIIIIIIIIIII

by Sharon A. Lacay, LMSW

C reativity is a very important word when conducting groups with young adults. I have found that working with young people on a daily basis forces you to dig deep in your toolbox and discover new and interesting ways to engage, connect, and motivate. As with all social work, you never know what you are going to get when you first walk into a room with a client, so you better bring an open mind and lots of ideas!

For several years, I co-facilitated a psychoeducational workshop for adolescent girls in crisis who were dealing with truancy, substance abuse, family violence, and other behavioral and emotional issues. They were referred to our family crisis intervention program through the county's probation office as a chance to obtain the resources and support they needed in hopes to make positive changes and healthier choices in their lives. One of the struggles my colleagues and I would sometimes face was that many of the clients were mandated to be part of the group, which made the initial engagement challenging. It was not uncommon that a client would come into group on the first day, sit in her chair, cross her arms, and state that she had no intention of contributing today or in future sessions. Of course, we respected that decision, but always encouraged participation and continued to provide opportunities for her to change her mind and get involved.

The first day of working with a new group is always interesting. I tend to get anxious and excited in anticipation of what sort of crowd we will have. Several winters ago, it was the start of another session. After everyone arrived and was seated, I smiled, took a deep breath, and began.

"Welcome everyone! Today we are all meeting for the first time, and hopefully during this and the coming weeks, we will really get a chance to know one another."

Briefly, my colleague Jessica and I described the curriculum and went over logistics. We discussed confidentiality and the caveat of our ethical duty to report any disclosures of abuse or harm to self or others. Following this, we turned it over to the group asking, "Does anyone have a concern or something they would like to share before we begin today's activities?"

In response, a meek looking girl, Hannah, raised her hand in the air slightly. "Yes?" I responded. "Welcome. What's on your mind?"

Slowly, she raised her gaze to the group. "I...I don't know why I am here, I'm a good girl. I just don't get along with my mom sometimes." Curiously, I asked if her case manager had told her why she was referred to the group, and she said simply, "No, she just said I had to come."

I've heard this same concern from many group participants in the past. They protest that they don't belong here, and insist with sincerity on being good students, daughters, and girlfriends—which I believe they are. However, it was rare that a participant had zero issues to bring to group and was there by accident. Usually, there was a noted pattern of behavior or an event significant enough to land them a spot in our chairs. I also knew that case managers were diligent about letting clients know why they were a good fit for the group. Instead of confronting Hannah about this, though, I asked the others in the room, "How many of you feel like you don't belong here or shouldn't have to come to group?" Eight of the ten girls sitting in our intimate circle raised their hands.

I smiled at my co-facilitator and she was smiling, too. Jovially, she said, "See? You already have so much in common! Let's see what else you can relate on." This opening to group was the perfect transition to our first activity of the day.

We asked the girls to stand in a large circle. We explained that Jessica or I would recite a statement, and if that statement applied to them, they should step toward the center of the circle waiting until we asked them to step back. We began with simple statements: "Please step forward if you can speak another language...if you've traveled to a different country...if you like school...." The girls followed along, smiling and giggling, as the questions seemed easy and light. "Please step forward if your parents are not together."

This time almost half of the girls stepped forward. They no longer had smiles and looked at each other with repose. "Please step forward if you've ever been bullied...if you've ever bullied someone else...if you've ever done something you are not proud of...if you or someone you know has a substance abuse problem...if you or someone you know has been a victim of dating violence...if you're hurting and feel like no one can help you."

And by the time we got to the fortieth question, "Please step forward if you've ever felt alone," this time, all the girls were standing together in the middle. As we broke up to sit back in the circle, we could feel the tension dissipating.

"How did it feel to be standing up there with everyone else?" we asked the group. They shouted out answers.

"Comforting!"

"Like I wasn't alone."

"I was surprised to see certain people walk forward who I wouldn't expect for certain questions."

"And what do you think the purpose of this activity was?" Jessica asked.

A couple of girls said simultaneously, "To show us that we have stuff in common." Another said, "To make us see that we aren't alone." "Exactly!" Jessica exclaimed. "You will all find out so much about each other and see that everyone has something to bring to the table. Even if you feel like you don't belong here, then try to help someone else with your own experiences."

This is my favorite part of group—when it starts to "click" and people begin to let their guard down because it reminds me why I love social work so much. You get to create relationships and enrich lives with human interaction that may not have been experienced otherwise. Group work has been found to foster healthy socialization, empathy, empowerment, problem solving skills, communication, self reflection, and diversity awareness. It can be paramount in the cultivation of identity, self esteem, and purpose. Particularly with younger populations, psychoeducation is an invaluable tool to engage and develop healthy minds. Helping young women form ideas about who they are and what they believe in is essential to ensuring healthy decision-making. One of the credos we have for group is, "When we respect ourselves, others will, too."

It is now a few weeks after our initial meeting. The girls come in and we hand them a worksheet to complete entitled "The Real Me." It asks each of them to describe how different people perceive them, such as a mother, father, teacher, significant other, and friends.

I begin by asking, "Okay, it looks like everyone is done. Would someone like to share what they wrote first?"

A girl named Abigail starts. She clears her throat and reads from the top of her paper, "When my mother sees me, she sees an irresponsible girl."

"Do you agree with the perception that she has of you?" I ask.

"Well no, she's always on my case about everything."

This piques my curiosity as I wonder if Abigail understands her dilemma, so I ask, "Do you have any idea why she might perceive you as irresponsible?"

"Not really."

I turn to the group, asking if anyone else feels that their parent views them this way and if they may know why. Rachel's eyes light up as she raises her hand, and I signal for her to share. "I feel the same way as Abigail. My parents tell me that I'm irresponsible because I miss curfew a lot, and I forget to do chores." Nodding, Abigail shakes her head in agreement. Recognizing the similarity between their situations, I probe further and ask, "It sounds like you understand how she can view you that way, but how would you want her to view you differently?"

"I want them to see me as independent," says Abigail. "Yeah, me too. I want them to trust me to go out and come back when I want to," Rachel adds.

Facilitating the discussion, I address the room, "Does the group have any ideas on how Rachel and Abigail could get their parents to see them as independent, because just not coming home on time doesn't seem to be working?"

As group facilitators, we always like to redirect solution finding to the group as a whole. One of the first steps in developing esteem and identity is establishing a sense of confidence and purpose. Sometimes to do this, we enable clients to see that they are competent and capable of helping others, and group work is a great strategy to accomplish this.

A few of the other girls raise their hands. Sallyanne goes first. "I used to be in the dog house with my parents, because they caught me sneaking out multiple times. I was grounded for a really long time, and we would fight all the time about it. Eventually I just sat down with them and talked to them about why I was sneaking out, and they told me about why they didn't want me to go out late for safety reasons. I still don't agree with it, but since I've been more open with them, they've been letting me out more."

Jessica praises Sallyanne and asks the group, "What makes communicating with our parents so important?" This leads us into a conversation about qualities we want our loved ones to possess, such as trust, compassion, honesty, and reliability. We allow the girls a chance to articulate their needs and fears about different relationships and communication styles.

As the group progresses over the weeks, there is a noticeable difference in their awareness of self and others. Having opportunities to express themselves, be heard, and be accepted for their great qualities and in spite of their not-so-good ones enables positive identity formation, which is so very important for young people.

Two months later, on the last day of group, I feel both excited and sad. I'm happy that some of the girls really opened up and learned something about themselves, and I am sad that some did not. As part of closing and termination with the group, we have prepared an activity called "My Gift." In the weeks of group, the girls have hopefully learned a lot about each other, too.

We ask each girl to draw a gift for one of the other group members with the instructions that it should depict what she would give her if it could be anything in the world. When it comes time to present the gifts to each other, we all sit in a semi circle and ask Hannah to go first. "I made a gift for Debbie. She often shared that she has low self esteem and depended a lot on her boyfriend and friends to feel good about herself so I want to give her this." She turns around a drawing of a girl standing in front of a mirror. The girl is smiling at her reflection and looks confident and put together. Hannah adds, "I'm giving Debbie the confidence to look at herself and be happy about who she is. I know it's hard, because I don't always like myself, either. But I want her to know that the most important opinion of ourselves is our own."

Now, I have to tell you, I've seen girls give each other some really creative gifts in the past, but this one was beyond words. Jessica and I both fought to hold back our prideful tears. This is what it means to work with young women. These girls have obviously touched each other, and if my only role in it was that our group brought them together, then that is enough for me.

Think About It

1. What are some essential elements in developing healthy and positive peer relationships?
2. Why is confidence building so important when working with groups of young people?
3. Under what circumstances could a group member's behavior become inappropriate or harmful to the group process, and how would you address the situation?

Additional Reading

Malekoff, A. (2004). *Group work with adolescents: Principles and practice* (2nd ed.). New York: Guilford Press.

Northen, H., & Kurland, R. (2001). *Social work with groups* (3rd ed.). New York: Columbia University Press.

Straus. M. B. (2007). *Adolescent girls in crisis: Intervention and hope.* New York: W.W. Norton & Company.

Chapter 5
Social Work 40 Feet in the Air

IIIIIIIIIIIIIIIIIIIIIIIIIIIIIIIIIIIIIIIIIIIIIIIIIIIIIIIIIIIIIIIIIIIIIIIIIIIIIIIIIIIIIIIIIIIIIIIIIIIIIIIIIIIIIIIIIIIIII

by Christina M. Chiarelli-Helminiak, MSW

B eing a social worker has provided me with many opportunities that I never could have imagined as an undergraduate student and even as a graduate student. As a group social worker, I have had the experiences of teaching anger management skills to students, facilitating support groups for parents with children with Attention Deficit Hyperactivity Disorder, and guiding at-risk youth on outdoor adventure programs. By far, though, my favorite experience has been leading an adventure-based counseling (ABC) group for adolescent girls who experienced abuse.

While working at a domestic violence/sexual assault program in the rural, Appalachian mountains, where social services are often sparse, I developed a partnership with the local school districts. Through this partnership, support groups for children whose lives had been affected by violence either directly or as a secondary victim (i.e., witnessing abuse) were offered during the school day. Offering support groups during the school day was often the only way for some of the children to access services, as many families lacked reliable transportation and no public transportation was available. During the time I spent at the schools, I learned of a new prevention program being offered through the local public health district to provide adventure-based counseling for high risk youth. Seeing an opportunity to expand services at the schools, I collaborated with the school guidance counselors and public health staff to develop groups specifically geared toward elementary, middle, and high school students exposed to violence.

The ABC group for adolescent girls who experienced abuse was an expansion of a support group I had already been running for a year with this particular group of students. I felt the girls were starting to grow weary of the typical support group structure, as some had begun to miss our weekly meetings. I discussed the idea of transitioning the format with the group, including the addition of a co-facilitator, necessary to ensure safety of the group. The group members were all excited about the new format, but a bit hesitant about someone they did not know coming in to co-lead the group. Before summer break, we "auditioned" the co-facilitator, and afterward, the whole group felt comfortable bringing in the new person.

During the next school year, the group met weekly at the school. On optimal days, we met outside on the athletics field. On bad weather days, we met in a classroom. During the first meeting, the group members were introduced to the concepts of an ABC group, including safety, goal setting, providing feedback, and no devaluing of self or others. Another important concept was the philosophy of "challenge by choice," meaning a participant was free to determine how far she was willing to challenge herself, but still needed to stay engaged with the group (Schoel & Maizell, 2002).

Over the next few weeks, the group was engaged in communication and problem solving activities. The group began to form a new cohesiveness, and typically quiet members of the group began to share their ideas and suggestions when working on a challenging activity. During one activity called "Mine Field" (Rohnke, 1984), one of the more quiet members of the group found her voice. This particular activity requires members to pair up. One member of the pair is blindfolded and directed to walk through a "mine field" of toys and various other objects by her partner on the side of the field. As her partner was nearing a "mine," the quiet partner spoke up and successfully directed her partner to the other side of the field. After that day, she was more vocal and would go on to become one of the leaders within the group.

As all of the group members had experienced some type of violence in their lives, my co-facilitator and I were very thoughtful about introducing trust activities, especially ones involving touch. We did not want any of the members to feel uncomfortable with being touched by or touching other members of the group, but at the same time, we wanted to introduce the group to safe touch. Such activities allow for the development of trust among group members and set the group up for more challenging activities on a ropes course. We decided to try the "Trust Walk" (Rohnke, 1994) to see how the members would react to touch. The trust walk involves the group standing in a line and placing hands on the shoulder of the person directly in front of them. The member at the very front of the line guides the group around an area, while the rest of the group walks with their eyes closed. The leader of the line must give verbal directions to the group, and the group must listen to the direction of the leader to know which way to go. At first, some of the members were tentative to touch or be touched by another group member. Respecting the challenge by choice philosophy, group members uncomfortable with touch participated by walking alongside the group and ensuring safety. By the end of the activity, all of the members felt comfortable enough to at least join the walk for a short distance. Over the next few weeks, all of the members developed a sense of comfort and felt safe touching and being touched by other group members.

The school had a small ropes course with low elements for the group to use. Low elements are activities on a ropes course that are built low to the ground, such as the "TP Shuffle," a telephone pole laid flat on the ground that the group must all walk across (Rohnke, 1994). By the middle of the school year, the group was taking on more challenging activities on the course, developing leadership skills, and becoming a tight knit group.

An integral part of ABC groups is processing the learning opportunities to address "the what," "the so what," and "the now what" of the experience (Schoel, Prouty, & Radcliffe, 1988). "The what" is related to the activity or challenge given to the group, the rules, and the safety of the group. "The so what" addresses what the challenge meant to the individual and how the experience is internalized. "The now what" is a way to integrate how the experience will be used by the individual in the future. One of my favorite processing tools is having group members find an item from nature they identify with. The item can be used to illustrate their feelings or feedback to give to another group member. During one of the meetings, a group member found a seedling and described how the seedling represented her as a child and the growth she was currently experiencing.

As the facilitator, I participated with the group in games, initiatives, and energizers. I did not, however, participate in elements that would be processed among the group members. This was to ensure that the facilitators did not become a part of the group and allowed the members to own the experience and the ultimate lessons learned.

As the end of the school year drew near, the group was scheduled to take a field trip to a larger ropes course to face their biggest challenges yet. The last activity of the day was the "zipline," essentially a wire cable strung between two telephone poles. The group members were all dressed in harnesses and helmets. One person at a time climbed up the pole to a platform 40 feet up. Once on the platform, the member's harness was hooked into a rope. She then sat down on the edge of the platform, pushed off, and zipped away! The group members all cheered for one another and helped each other get off the rope. All of the members of the group had gone, and it was Margaret's turn.

All year long, Margaret had exhibited leadership skills, was very caring for other group members, and had shown no hesitation in participating in the activities. Margaret slowly climbed the ladder to the platform, where I was waiting. Once on the platform, she began to cry, while down below the group shouted encouraging words. I told Margaret it was okay if she decided not to go—that we could lower her down to the ground—but Margaret was resistant to this idea, as well. Over the next 20 minutes, Margaret continued to cry and discuss how this challenge was like facing her greatest fear—her father who had abused her. Finally, Margaret said, "So, if I can face this challenge, I know I can face my father and stand up to him." And with that, Margaret found the courage to push off the platform and scream and giggle as she zipped away! Once on the ground again, Margaret told the group about what had happened on the platform and how she felt stronger as a person.

The skills I learned as an ABC group facilitator have proven useful in many other areas of my practice as an administrator, multi-disciplinary team leader, and instructor. To this day, my time spent with Margaret 40 feet in the air is one of the most powerful experiences of my social work career.

Think About It

1. What personal and social work skills are necessary when facilitating adventure based counseling?

2. Why was it important for the co-facilitators to carefully consider introducing trust and touch activities to the group?

3. How did Margaret's experience on the platform relate to her relationship with her abusive father?

References

Rohnke, K. E. (1984). *Silver bullets: A guide to initiative problems, adventure games and trust activities.* Dubuque, IA: Kendall/Hunt.

Rohnke, K. E. (1994). *The bottomless bag again?!* (2nd ed.). Dubuque, IA: Kendall/Hunt.

Schoel, J., & Maizell, R. S. (2002). *Exploring islands of healing: New perspectives on adventure based counseling.* Beverly, MA: Project Adventure.

Schoel, J., Prouty, D., & Radcliffe, P. (1988). *Islands of healing: A guide to adventure based counseling.* Hamilton, MA: Project Adventure.

Additional Reading

Gass, M. A. (1993). *Adventure therapy: Therapeutic applications of adventure programming.* Dubuque, IA: Kendall/Hunt.

Luckner, J. L., & Nadler, R. S. (1997). *Processing the experience: Strategies to enhance and generalize learning* (2nd ed.). Dubuque, IA: Kendall/Hunt.

Sugerman, D. A., Doherty, K. L., Garvey, D. E., & Gass, M. A. (2000). *Reflective learning: Theory and practice.* Dubuque, IA: Kendall/Hunt.

Resources

Project Adventure: *http://www.pa.org/*

Chapter 6

Creating Group Norms Around the Campfire: Adventure Based Group Work With Adolescents

IIIIIIIIIIIIIIIIIIIIIIIIIIIIIIIIIIIIIIIIIIIIIIIIIIIIIIIIIIIIIIIIIIIIIIIIIIIIIIIIIIIIIIIIIIIIIIIIIIIIIIIIIIIIIIIIIIIIIIIIIIIIIII

by Christine Lynn Norton, Ph.D., LCSW

I remember sitting on a dusty road at the head of the portage trail in the Boundary Waters Canoe Area Wilderness, waiting for a group of seven "struggling teens" to arrive in a van, straight from the Duluth airport. I was working for Outward Bound's youth-at-risk program, known as Intercept (formerly Ascent), a 28-day therapeutic wilderness program that utilizes adventure-based group work in a wilderness context with teenagers who are struggling with family and school problems, substance abuse, learning disorders, and mental health challenges. Young people from all over the country participate in the program, and my group was expected in from the airport that day to begin the course with an "immersion start." This meant they would come from the airport straight to the trailhead, unpack their bags and repack into our canoeing dry bags, hike the distance of the portage trail to the canoes, and paddle to the campsite.

Getting prepared for this moment, when a group of young people nervously step off the van wondering what exactly their parents signed them up for, requires a ton of logistical planning and preparation. My group co-leader and I spent three full days prior to the course start planning our menus and route, gathering maps, packing our food and equipment, reviewing participants' files and paperwork, and creating a therapeutic and educational curriculum based on participants' goals.

By the time we were done with all of this, we were exhausted! My group co-leader was especially run down, as he was fighting a minor cold, as well. This was my first course, but he had worked for

Outward Bound for years, and didn't feel the level of anxiety that I was feeling, which was a good thing. He was the yin to my yang, and I could tell that we would balance one another's temperaments.

As we sat waiting for the van, we finalized our plan for how we would welcome the group. We both knew that the very first moments with a group are essential to building a lasting rapport and creating a physically and emotionally safe environment. We planned to welcome them off the van with a name game called Group Juggle. Our course director was bringing a bag of Kush balls, Nerf footballs, and even a rubber chicken that the group could toss around and practice one another's names.

Then, we decided on a tone set for the course in which we would frame the course theme, which was "Travel Light." We predicted that they would find this ironic, given that our food packs were almost 80 lbs. each. However, we knew that they would eventually realize that we carried only what we needed on our expedition and didn't carry any unnecessary baggage. We hoped this theme would become a metaphor for their lives, as well.

After the tone set, our plan was to pack and repack, hike down the portage trail to our canoes, and paddle to our campsite, which we had already set up. Once there, we would orient the group to the campsite, help them unpack, and then gather around the campfire to create our group norms. It was ambitious, but we knew we would have plenty of time.

As we sat waiting, we noticed that the sun was getting lower in the sky. The van was late. Very late. No one called, but we knew something was wrong. Finally, at 8:30 p.m., as the northern Minnesota sun was beginning to set, the van drove up. The original van had broken down on the way from the airport, and they had had to call in for a new van. All of this added hours to the trip, giving us very little daylight in which to accomplish our plans for the evening. Given our experience with groups, we knew that our agenda would need to take a back seat to making sure we met the basic needs of the group.

As the group got out of the van, we could tell that the group process had already begun. The group had spent hours in the van together, and had already lived through the van breaking down. The van driver and the course director reported that most of the group was getting along well, but that there were a few dominant personalities that seemed to bring an undercurrent of bullying. The group was also hungry.

As my co-leader gathered some peanut butter and crackers for the group to snack on, I changed plans and took the lead on the tone set. This way, the group had a chance to sit, eat, and listen. Then, with full bellies, we led the group in our name game/ice breaker in the light of dusk, after which we unpacked and repacked their belongings in the Outward Bound gear. By this time, it was dark, which meant we had to attend to making sure each person had a headlamp, and we needed to be especially careful when carrying the heavy packs down the rocky trail at night. My co-leader and I were very directive about safety, making sure to help the teenagers with anything they needed. This immediately created trust, letting the group members know we were there to support them and keep them safe, which is important in the context of adventure based group work in a backcountry setting.

As the group finally reached the end of the portage trail, they were relieved to be able to stop hiking, but their level of anxiety spiked again when they realized they had to paddle at night. All participants were instructed to wear their life vests and reassured that the camp was only a short paddle along the shore. Several group members were subdued, but the big personalities in the group were dominating with inappropriate humor and in-your-face types of attitudes, no doubt trying to minimize their anxiety.

As my co-leader and I got a brief moment together alone in our canoe, we reflected on the group dynamics that were occurring. By this time, it was almost 10:30 p.m., and we knew that after a day of travel, the group was tired. Still, when group members have to actually camp out together in tents, a much more intimate component than traditional group work, it is a MUST for group norms to be in place to maintain appropriate boundaries and physical and emotional safety.

Just as we had agreed to have a group meeting when we got to camp, an argument broke out in one of the canoes. Two girls began yelling at one another for not being able to keep the boat straight. Since we had not even had a chance to teach a paddling lesson, my co-leader and I paddled over and very calmly offered to switch with one of the girls, so that each of them would be in a boat with an experienced paddler. This helped a lot and gave us a chance to calm the situation down and teach a few basic paddle strokes.

It also provided an experiential rationale for why we needed to take time to meet as a group to create group norms before the group went to bed. The group was tired, the mosquitoes were out, and everyone just wanted to go to bed—but given the difficulties of the day and the prospect of having to sleep with a bunch of strangers, the group acquiesced. As the group put their belongings in the tents and I oriented them to camp, my co-leader built a small campfire around which we gathered.

I don't know if you've ever sat around a campfire, but there's something innately calming about staring into the blue, orange, and yellow flames. The light smoke kept the bugs at a minimum, and the group settled into a relatively mellow mood. Once everyone was settled, we once again welcomed group members and thanked them for making the choice to be here. Some of them grumbled, given that they felt coerced by their family or a referring professional. But we rolled with this resistance and reminded them that at any point, they could've bailed. Yet here they were, sitting under the stars in Northern Minnesota, warmed by the light of a campfire.

"So we're all going to be living together as a group for 28 days… well, 27 if you don't count today, which is actually almost over," I said. I went on to explain that in order for everyone to have a positive experience, we would need to create a safe and respectful community. We reviewed the "Laws of the Land," or non-negotiables set forth by Outward Bound, such as no drugs, no sex, no violence— basic rules that if broken would mean having to leave the program. Then, I explained to them that what was even more important than our rules were the things they needed from one another in order to live well together.

I pulled out a new composition notebook that my co-leader and I had decorated with inspiring photos and quotes. This was to be our group journal in which we would write about our journey. At the beginning of this book is where we would write our group norms, or what we called at Outward Bound community standards. At first, the group was very reticent to speak up, but the warmth of the campfire eventually prevailed. "Respect," spoke a quiet but intimidating boy. "No gossip," said one of the girls. "No name calling," another girl said. Eventually, everyone was chiming in, throwing out ideas and further articulating what exactly they meant. As each new idea was presented, we wrote it down in the group journal, finally reading off the entire list, before asking everyone for one final agreement.

To seal this agreement, we asked each group member to sign the group norms in the group journal. We signed, as well. The discussion had been very open and real, and there seemed to be a wave of relief in the air. We had succeeded in creating group norms that would serve to maintain a safe environment in which group members could actually be vulnerable and work on their issues.

As the group members quietly passed the group journal around the circle to sign, I looked at my watch. It was after midnight. A loon called out in the darkness. I looked up at the stars and took a deep breath. "I think it's time for everyone to get some sleep. I think we might stay dry tonight." But before I ended the group meeting, I asked them to take one last long look into the flames of the campfire and quietly read this quote:

> *Now I see the secret of making the best persons, it is to grow in the open air and to eat and sleep with the earth.*

Walt Whitman

Think About It

1. In what stage of group development is this group, and what are some of the attributes of this stage that you notice in this scenario?

2. What did the group leaders do to build rapport between themselves and group members?

3. How important are group norms when starting a new group? Should they be revisited? Revised?

4. How do you think the experiential nature of adventure-based group work affects group cohesion?

Additional Reading

Gass, M., Gillis, L., & Russell, K. (2012). *Adventure therapy: Theory, research, and practice.* New York: Routledge.

Norton, C. L., & Tucker, A. (2010). New heights: Adventure-based group work in social work education and practice. *Groupwork: An Interdisciplinary Journal for Working With Groups, 20* (2), 24-44.

Tucker, A. R. (2009). Adventure based group therapy to promote social skills in adolescents. *Social Work With Groups, 32* (4), 315-329.

Chapter 7
Riding the Mutual Aid Bus

IIIIIIIIIIIIIIIIIIIIIIIIIIIIIIIIIIIIIIIIIIIIIIIIIIIIIIIIIIIIIIIIIIIIIIIIIIIIIIIIIIIIIIIIIIIIIIII

by Jennifer Clements, Ph.D., LCSW

I remember the conversation pretty well. My supervisor called me into his office and said he liked my proposal to begin groups at the center. I was prepared to fight for group work. The center I work at is a 90-day residential treatment program for adolescents in foster care. What kind of residential program do you know that does not do group work? I had so many experiences with group work before I came to this residential facility that I was excited to be at a place where groups were one of the main treatment modes. I looked at the schedule, and groups were nowhere to be found! The reason was simply stated to me that we are too busy to run groups. So when my clinical supervisor was on board, I was thrilled. He told me that the group topics I needed to start with were anger management and independent living skills. My co-worker took the anger management, and I took on the independent living skills group. I grabbed my group work texts and the federal guidelines for independent living and planned out a first session!

The group is co-ed with four adolescent girls and three adolescent boys who are between 16 and 19 years old. I am not so sure I would normally go co-ed in a teen group, but these teens are 30 days or less from discharge, and some of them will be moving to independent or semi-independent living situations, so the need is great. We had our first session, and I worked hard to shift the ownership of the group to the members. They agreed on future topics: budgeting, employment, college/trade school opportunities, transportation, cooking, and hopes and fears. We were all set and in two days we would tackle our first topic: transportation! Our facility is high up on a hill in an urban area. The kids feel as if they are far away from the city, but they are right in the city limits. I get my supervisor to agree to let me take the kids on the city bus and learn the public transportation system.

My day starts off as usual. I begin with a check-in with the overnight staff. I review our level board, which indicates which kid got in trouble and who is doing well and moving up through the behavior level system. It is great to see that all seven of my group members are on Level 4, the highest level in our program. I see several of the teens on my caseload, and they wave or ask me about a request for visitations with their families over the weekend. It is Friday, and the unit is busy. The teens are rushing to get to their classes down the hall. I remind staff that I will need the seven kids for group in an hour. I go upstairs and set up my circle. In each chair, I place a copy of the bus route, bus passes, and maps of the city. Our plan is to ride the bus together to get to McDonald's across town and then return back to the center. The kids arrive to group ready and excited. Everyone agrees to the safety of the trip and that we all stay together. Since we are leaving the center, I have another staff person go with us. We plan our trip, pick the bus transfers, and plan how long we can be at McDonald's before we need to catch the next bus back. The group plans together, and we walk down the hill to catch the Number 3 bus.

The group cohesion is already developing. These seven teens who one week ago did not even talk to each other are laughing and checking in with each other as we travel the city. Once on the bus, the teens are pointing out old neighborhoods and homes of previous foster parents. They make quick friends with the driver and enjoy asking him about his job. I overhear them talking about more personal issues. They share their mixed feelings about wanting to be on their own so badly but wanting someone to care about where they are, too. They talk to each other about leaving friends behind and changing schools. Soon they would be in charge of their lives, but did they want to be?

The group notices the upcoming stop, and we load off the bus and into McDonald's. We check for everyone, buy sodas, and sit down to chat. Tom, one of the older kids in the group, jokes about the taste of freedom as he downs his soda. We have a great talk about hopes and fears, and I mention that they were talking about this on the ride. It is amazing how candid they are with me and with each other. For a small window, they seem to be able to be vulnerable. They can admit to feeling abandoned and scared in this safe circle in the middle of McDonald's. There are so many emotions running around in just a short time span. Rebecca, the youngest of the kids, suggests, as I am closing up our time, that they end with a group hug. We squeeze into that huddle and, for a moment, they are just "regular kids." I feel it, and on the ride home, another kid says it to me. "Ms. Jen, this was a really good day. I forgot all about the center, my meds, and felt just regular today." When I ask him what he thinks about group, he shares, "It's pretty good, Ms. Jen. I'll let you have that one." We get back to the center, and I am on cloud nine. I finish up with my individual and family sessions for the day and make sure all the kids who have home visits scheduled get out the door with their families. As I drive down that long hill, I feel pretty excited about the future of group work at the center.

Monday morning, I head into the residence and review with overnight staff about the weekend and check the behavior board. I don't see any staff free just yet, but I do see the board. ALL SEVEN of the group kids are down to Level 1. I am in shock, and a staff member sees the look on my face. "What happened?" I ask. The staff member says back to me, "Well, you can look at it this way—the kids got a whole lot out of your group Friday."

Apparently, on Friday night, when none of them had family visits and they were all commiserating with each other, plans were set for an AWOL. They all left together, caught the Number 3 bus, went to McDonald's, and came back together.

I have to meet with my supervisor and explain a few things. As my supervisor calls me into his office, I feel sick to my stomach. He starts to sigh and then starts to laugh. He explains that after a group with me, the best kids in our program are now on the lowest level. He agrees with me that there is something impressive about it. Although it was dangerous and scary, it was empowering. We talk about making sure all future groups do not lead to adventures off campus without staff.

As I walk back down to the unit, I cannot help but smile. They knew the consequences of their leaving without permission, but they knew they could do it. They had learned how in group. When they were together they were stronger, happier, a little less alone. We all took a ride on the Mutual Aid Bus. It really is a fantastic ride!

Think About It

1. Self determination and client empowerment are important aspects of social work practice. How do these values play out in a group?

2. Learn and read about the independent living guidelines. What skills are important for young teens transitioning to independent living, and how can those needs be met in a group setting?

Additional Reading

Child Welfare League of America (2005). *Standards of excellence in transition, independent living, and self-sufficiency services.* Retrieved from http://www.cwla.org/programs/standards/standardsintroindependentliving.pdf

Frey, L., Greenblatt, S., & Brown, J. Casey Family Services, (2005). *A call to action: An integrated approach to youth permanency and preparation for adulthood.* Retrieved from The Casey Center for Effective Child Web site: http://www.aecf.org/upload/publicationfiles/casey_permanency_0505.pdf

Chapter 8
The Magic of Group Work: Preparing for Adoption

||||||||||||||||||||||||||||||||||||||||||||||||||||||||||||||||||||||||||||||||||||||||||||||||||||||

by Tracy A. Marschall, MSW

I have a confession: I didn't always like group work. That probably sounds funny coming from someone who has taught group work classes for eleven years and looks forward to convincing each new group of BSW students that social work practice with groups is not just cost-effective and therapeutically beneficial, but really fun, too. I see them exchange looks across the room when I start getting excited as I tell them how they are going to have the opportunity to actually plan and lead a real group with real clients over the course of the semester. I don't miss the occasional eye roll when I get going about how group work is actually magical...yes, I actually say that, and believe it...when it goes well. I know not all students come into groups class thrilled at being thrown into the role of leader, outnumbered, with their new skills on display. My hope is that by the time they finish the course and graduate, they will share my enthusiasm. Most do. But it wasn't always the case.

I always knew I wanted to work with families, particularly in the field of adoption. I lobbied hard for a field placement in an adoption agency and was placed at a very traditional Catholic agency that provided services to all members of what we call the adoption triad: birthfamilies, adoptees, and adoptive families. There were a lot of different opportunities for group work at this agency, and it was used often. Like many students, this was a task I knew I needed experience in, but I was not looking forward to seeing it on my learning plan. I was a little bit bossy, to be honest, and I tended to take over the planning stages of groups, which usually meant others were all too happy to let me run things and handle the bulk of the responsibility. I didn't learn until a lot later that collaborating with others means you need to value their contributions, and that people who feel investment in something will participate more fully. So when my field instructor, an experienced social worker with great clinical skills whom I admired a great deal, announced she'd like my help re-working some group sessions with families interested in adopting, I was pretty conflicted. I was excited to be working with potentially adoptive families, but not very keen on the group format. We decided my first step would be to attend one of the informational meetings myself to observe the existing format and become familiar with the content that needed to be presented.

I arrived early on the morning of the meeting and observed the participants arriving. Most were in pairs: husbands and wives, a few single women, and one woman appeared to have brought a friend. Everyone seemed nervous. A few people spoke quietly, but mainly to their own partners. The seats were arranged in rows, and the agency staff stood at the front of the room. They greeted the participants, and handouts were passed out as each took a turn talking about the different steps in the process, applications, fees, the home study, home visits, and legal issues. What everyone seemed to want to know was how long everything would take. I imagined what they really wanted to ask was how long from that morning would it be before they held their own baby in their arms. Unfortunately, there were no good answers for those questions, because adoption as most of these families understood it was rapidly changing.

For a very long time, adoption was mainly about finding babies for infertile or childless couples. When becoming pregnant outside of marriage was much stigmatized, the practice of adoption was pretty common. Staff at the agency would tell stories about going from house to house on Christmas Day, dropping off babies to thrilled families all day long. It was pretty exciting to think about a time when hundreds of adoptions were creating new families, because we were down to only a handful of adoptions per year. Before now, once your home study was complete, you were added to the list of potential adoptive families, until it became your turn. Occasionally there were exceptions. Some families might strongly want a boy. Others might not be comfortable with the lack of information available regarding a birthmother's possible use of drugs or alcohol or family history. But for the most part, there was some comfort in knowing while the waiting could be agonizing, your number should eventually come up.

In the early 1990s, however, practices were changing. Adoption became less about finding babies for infertile couples and more about finding families for homeless children. New research indicated the ways adoptions were handled in the past, with secrecy and shame and sealed files—what were usually referred to as "closed" adoptions—might not be healthy. At the very least, birth parents were beginning to have increased involvement in the process: helping to select adoptive families for their child, sometimes meeting and interviewing a few selections, and negotiating levels of ongoing participation in the child's life with potential adoptive families. For some, it might be letters and pictures, or gifts, or the willingness to be contacted at some point. For others, birth families and adoptive families were forging new relationships to support the child. Some birthmothers would attend family events and maintain a presence in the child's life indefinitely, hopefully sparing some of the grief, identity issues, and fear experienced by the child and everyone involved. As these practices grew in popularity and the research seemed to indicate favorable outcomes, some of the staff at our agency attended trainings and brought enthusiasm for these changes back to our agency. Although they were met with considerable resistance from some who had been doing things a certain way for a long time, many of the changes were implemented and became policy.

From a social worker's perspective, these changes were exciting and promised better outcomes for everyone involved. But for adoptive families, this changed everything. No longer would they just wait long enough for their families. Now it was possible that a birthmother might not ever choose them. She might want a younger couple. A Catholic couple. A non-Catholic couple. A family that reminded her of her own in some way, or the exact opposite. She might want her child to go to a family who already had children so he or she would have a big brother or sister. Or she might not want her baby to have to compete for the parents' attention. Even though there were never any guarantees, the new changes were going to leave the adoptive families, particularly those who had already been waiting quite a long time, feeling like the rug had been pulled out from underneath them in the cruelest way.

And these were the folks coming into the group I was going to be planning and co-leading with my field instructor. I was convinced after observing the existing session that we really needed to change things. For one thing, three hours is a long time to expect people to sit passively and take in information. Also, in an attempt to be thorough, much of the presentation was pretty tediously straightforward, with a lot of reading and not much variety. When the participants left, they either cornered a staff member to ask questions or left in a hurry. They never talked to each other past an occasional pleasantry or holding the door.

My field instructor and I decided we still needed to deliver the important information, but that creating a therapeutic climate that would support participants through the process was more important than answering every possible question anticipated in the three hours. Some of that could be accomplished in later activities like home visits and private sessions with families. We wanted to select activities to break up the session and break the tension, to allow relationships to form that could be great sources of support and encouragement. I thought part of the problem was that the couples saw each other as potential competition, which prevented them from being vulnerable or expressing concerns or fears. They were good and kind people, but at this point the idea of helping someone else become successful was interpreted to be at odds with their own goal. I wanted to give the spouses a chance to discuss their own concerns with others of their own gender. Might potential moms have different concerns or questions than potential dads? Maybe they didn't feel as if they could express them to each other, but in a group of other men or other women, they might feel more comfortable. We came up with a plan, divided up the preparation responsibilities, and agreed to meet about 45 minutes prior to the beginning of the group.

The day of the session arrived. We descended into the basement where the conference room was and began to set up. We arranged the chairs into groupings with tables for about six people each. As people began to arrive, they came in and took their seats. There is something about joining people already seated at a table that inspires conversation that rows do not. People asked if they could sit down. Some of them made small talk over coffee about the cold weather or how far they had driven to get there. The energy in the room was very different from the day I observed, and I took this as a good sign. My field instructor gave me the "ready" signal, and we introduced ourselves. We went around the room and asked each person to introduce his or her partner to us and include something they admired about them. People were alternately serious and funny about what they shared, and I hoped it helped to build participants up. We then went over the agenda. I thought it was helpful for participants to have an idea of the flow of the morning, so they would know when breaks and formal opportunities for questions were planned, although they could ask at other times, too. We invited suggestions, so participants wouldn't feel as if they were getting on a fast-moving train with no input as to why or where they were going. And we made adjustments based on their feedback, so it wasn't an empty gesture.

My field instructor began by going over some of the policies and the different parts of the process. When we'd given enough information to get them thinking, it was my turn. I asked them to form two groups, with women at one table and men at the other and asked them to take some time identifying thoughts, feelings, or concerns about the adoption process. My field instructor and I each took a group and explained that we would be the "scribes" or the reporters, writing down their responses. I remember working with the men. One of the participants was very outgoing and funny, and he got the group rolling by answering "diapers" to every question. Before long, each group had a great list of things to talk about. Another benefit was that we could see what kinds of things were likely to come up as shared concerns and make some adjustments to the home study/preparation process. We then shared each list with the larger group. My field instructor and I led this part, but we regularly asked members of the men's group or women's group to elaborate or explain certain responses. The men tended to focus on financial worries and the effect of stress on their partners. The women talked about being disappointed if they weren't chosen right away, and whether they would be good parents. But most remarkable was the camaraderie that developed in that room—laughter that was conspicuously absent in the first meeting, and the conversations that continued into the break between and among couples and their new acquaintances.

The second part of the group centered on an adoptive parent and her child's birthmother talking together about their experience. Both had managed to negotiate several challenges in this new terrain of open adoption, honoring the commitments they made to each other on behalf of the little boy who was at that point four years old. In previous sessions, there had been few questions. But today, not only were there questions, but the good will toward our speakers was clear—the participants were respectful but friendly and very curious. How did that work? Who does the baby think you are? How do you explain it to people? How do you feel about it in your quiet times alone? Do you ever regret your decisions? The speakers debriefed with us later, when we asked them how they felt it went. The birthmother shared that she had considered not doing this again, as she sometimes felt pressure and some judgment about the situation. Both were now willing to continue serving as ambassadors for openness in adoption, and we felt encouraged about the changes. We were also encouraged by conversations we heard of participants exchanging phone numbers and e-mails. Two couples decided to go to lunch together following the meeting.

During my supervision, my field instructor asked me how I thought it went. I said I knew I needed a lot more experience, but the changing moment for me was at a point when I was facilitating questions between the speakers and the participants. The discussion had taken off, and participants were speaking to each other. The pace of the conversation was steady and had taken on a life of its own. I said I felt I could have walked away at that point and it would have been fine. We talked about what had happened in the prior session to make that possible.

As I reflected later that evening, I wrote in my practicum journal that in a great group, a good facilitator is like a conductor in a symphony. He or she isn't playing the instruments. The musicians have that talent. They know what they need to know to be able to play the music. They just need someone to help establish the tempo, to draw out the woodwinds, and to keep the horns from drowning the others out. Eventually the conductor could step out and the performance could continue. Like the conductor, a good facilitator can set the tone for the group; help decide goals and purposes; encourage members; and challenge them to work harder, work together, and support each other. Eventually the talent of the group may carry them over the difficulties presented in what we call the "working phase" of the group, and the attentive facilitator can identify when the group needs someone to step in and provide direction.

This is the part I call the magic—when a participant says something that sparks a thought or response from another, and that leads to something else, setting off a chain reaction of some kind that could never happen without the synergy of the group. I use this metaphor with my students to describe what it feels like both for participants and facilitators or group leaders when group work works.

I was a reluctant convert, but I'm set on convincing even the most resistant social worker about the power of group work. It is the essence of what we do and where we come from as a profession. It is not appropriate for every client, for every issue, but it is extremely effective for many. It is a strategy that belongs in every skilled social worker's repertoire. And most of all, it's great fun.

Think About It

1.   In what ways can tone or climate affect the outcome of a group?

2. What kind of client characteristics might prevent one from functioning successfully in a group?

3. In social work, we talk about the importance of the "use of self." Why is it important to have insight about one's own personality, skills, and attitudes in preparing to work with clients?

Additional Reading

Brooks, D., Allen, J., & Barth, R. (2002). Adoption services use, helpfulness, and need: A comparison of public and private agency and independent adoptive families. *Children and Youth Services Review, 24* (4), 213–238.

Gross, H. E. (1993). Open adoption: A research-based literature review and new data. *Child Welfare: Journal of Policy, Practice, and Program, 72* (3), 269-284.

Siegel, D. H. (1993). Open adoption of infants: Adoptive parents' perceptions of advantages and disadvantages. *Social Work, 38* (1), 15-23.

Chapter 9
Keeping the Hope Alive: Family Nurturing Camp™

IIIIIIIIIIIIIIIIIIIIIIIIIIIIIIIIIIIIIIIIIIIIIIIIIIIIIIIIIIIIIIIIIIIIIIIIIIIIIIIIIIIIIIIIIIIIIIIIIIIIIIIIIIIIIIIIIIIIIIIIII

by Lucille Geiser Tyler, MSW

A depressed mother who could not get out of a chair earlier in the week walks tentatively with her three children toward the dining hall. Another mom—a recovering substance abuser—greets her five children, all of whom are in foster care. A "blended family" with six children gathered from three different homes joins them. They join several other families to spend the weekend at Family Nurturing Camp™.

It all started with a phone call. A social worker from the community, knowing my background in working with children and adolescents, asked if I could develop a respite weekend for teenagers. I responded that I would, but only if we would also include the entire family. As a former child welfare worker, I firmly believe that the best chance of helping the children is by empowering the family to meet their needs. I established a collaboration among child welfare, juvenile justice, mental health, and camp professionals to offer our first Family Nurturing Camp™.

Fast forward: It is late Friday afternoon and my car is packed. I think I've covered all the details—family referrals, staff, camp coordination, family craft supplies, parent group materials, clothes, and gas in the car. I begin the hour and a half drive to the camp to greet the staff—professionals, paraprofessionals, and social work students who have assembled from all over the state to provide a multiple family group intervention for at-risk families. I need to leave the concerns of my full-time faculty position behind and focus instead on the families for this weekend. Even though I've already worked a demanding week, I am strangely energized and excited to reconnect each month with this team of professionals and to greet a new group of families.

I arrive at camp, and a whirl of activity begins—staff meetings, families' arrival and assignment to their sleeping arrangements, and gathering in the dining hall for a family meal. Along with the camp director, I welcome the families, ask staff to introduce themselves, and ask one family member from each family to introduce the family to the larger group. Each person, each family, gets a rousing "we are glad you are here" round of applause. I then start the group participation show to share an overview of the weekend. I ask for a young volunteer who will become our model. The young person selected comes forward and stands on a chair (spotted by a staff member modeling safety). I ask the group to participate by answering my brief questions and by responding with cheers, stomps, clapping, or arm waving whenever they hear me use the word "fun." I proceed, holding up various items—ball, paint, magic marker, fork, helmet, ropes, CD, DVD—asking for the group to identify the item, commenting how this represents an activity (games, crafts, group time, meals, high and low ropes course, dance, movie night) we'll participate in during the weekend. The room becomes electrified, and the "fun" begins.

Group time is next, with each age group finding its own space and following with its own curriculum. The first session is always about beginning the process of forming a close, safe, and supportive group; clarifying the expectations and rules of the weekend; and sharing hopes and fears. As the session ends, excited participants come together for a family night hike before lights out. All staff and all family members gather and walk as a community in the dark down the lane. Folks are both excited and a bit scared; there are few lights on this 260-acre waterfront camp, with big people and little people all taking care of one another. We are now bonded in mutual support.

After breakfast on Saturday morning, the staff takes family and group pictures. While waiting their turn, family members and camp staff are leading fun games, including jump rope, sidewalk chalk, and ball games. After family portraits are completed, it is group time again, and all age groups assemble and proceed to their areas.

Along with overall camp coordination, I am responsible for running the four sessions of the parent group. Responses from a parent group early in offering this program affirmed the power of bringing people together, by structuring a process to create both physical and emotional safety, and allowing the mutual support, growth, and healing to emerge. Each session of the parent group starts with sentence completions, with the expectation that each member will take a turn "filling in the blanks" of the offered sentences. This segment is followed by a parenting lesson utilizing multiple modalities, a self awareness component, and then ending with a group hug. As an example, the open ended sentences for the second session held on Saturday morning are: *Name one person who has hurt you, why they have hurt you, and what you would like to say to that person?*

The participants each respond in turn. The first one, a mother, says, "The person who has hurt me is the man who shot and killed my son in a drive-by shooting." The next, a father who has come with his two little girls, offers, "The girls' mother, who chose drugs over being with her children." He then continues, "I could have said the drug dealer who killed her because she was about to be a state's witness in a trial." The next father, who has joined us with his four children, bravely relays the story of his wife's substance abuse and his efforts to help her and stay together as a family. However, the person who has hurt him is his wife who, like the mother in the previous family, chose drugs over family. The next woman speaks of her need to leave her husband because of domestic violence. Now, as a single parent of two teenage boys, she struggles to find positive male role models for her sons.

The next mom describes how her extended family has hurt her by not supporting her. Her children have been placed in foster care as a result of her substance abuse. Now she is in recovery, and her family will not help her, because she has come out as gay and they do not accept her or her partner. This mom finds that hard for herself, but especially painful because the family also has rejected her children. Another victim of domestic violence responds next, relating to the mother who spoke earlier about needing positive male role models for her children. After many years of abuse, the next mom left and took her children to live with her parents. This decision threw her into a depression and she had difficulty being a mother. Months later, her husband committed suicide and, in his note, blamed the mother. The mother was then hospitalized for depression, and her children were placed in foster care. She is now out of the hospital, living with her parents, and working on having the children returned to her. Her 10-year-old son, also suffering with depression, is in a therapeutic group home.

There are no words to describe what happens in these moments. The "all in the same boat" phenomenon does not do it justice. We take a break and walk to the waterfront. On the way, various pairs share stories and messages of hope. We return to our group and focus on the lesson of the importance of praise and encouragement as a primary parenting technique. We watch a short video and practice within our circle. The activity is to ask the person next to you what he or she would like to be acknowledged for, and the participant praises the person for that. The interactions are so genuine, so heartfelt, that it brings tears to my eyes even now. I quietly think how grateful I am to be in the presence of such extraordinary, resilient people. We end our second group with a group hug.

The other age groups have the same topic about praise, but present it in different ways. The adolescents combine talking with an activity of praise basketball. Both youth and teenagers spend some time on the low elements of a team building challenge course. The "littles" play games, using song and art to approach this subject. The collective good will shows at meal time. There are more pleases and thank yous, more helpful interactions, and such a positive energy in the room. I smile.

After lunch is family craft time. A favorite is building a flower box. Volunteers have cut the wood and prepared the kits to ensure success. Each family is given a kit, and as a large group, they are given the assembly instructions, along with the expectation that every member of the family will participate. A facilitator is assigned to each family to hover, to assist as necessary, and to encourage positive interactions and full family participation. I hover close to one mother and her children. The mom does an admirable job of organizing her children around the task. Each family member takes a turn to hammer one nail. There is much intensity during Mom's turn. From the morning parents' session, I have a sense of where the anger is coming from. I whisper in her ear, "I know who you are pounding," and together we share a quiet laugh. Together, the family fills the planter with dirt and plants flowers. All are proud of the family making something beautiful together.

The rest of the afternoon is filled with age-appropriate activities and more group time. Both the parent and adolescent groups have another structured session focusing on self awareness and strengths. Meanwhile, the youth proceed to the high ropes elements of the challenge course. Parents and adolescents will join them there. The high and low ropes challenge course activities facilitate a process through "challenge by choice" for individuals to push past their comfort zones (physically, emotionally, intellectually, and spiritually) into their personal growth zone in a supportive and safe environment. I, along with other staff members, am on the ground coaching both parents and children in genuine encouragement. More than one individual has proclaimed upon completing the 35-foot climb, in essence, "If I can do that, I can do anything!" I find this experience especially meaningful for parents in substance abuse recovery.

The focus of the evening is about having fun as a family. The meal is followed by a family craft, decorating a picture frame for the family's portrait, singing around the campfire, making s'mores, and ending with a full camp dance. Our informal D.J. selects songs that all age groups can enjoy together, as well as a few like "We Are Family" that carry a message. After breakfast on Sunday morning, all participants return to group for an ending process. Lunch and an uplifting family celebration ceremony follow. I note what a privilege it has been to have witnessed firsthand the growth, healing, and laughter throughout the weekend.

How can a mere weekend make a difference in the lives of families facing such challenges? The feedback from both the participants and the referring professionals has been overwhelmingly positive. As one parent described in a thank-you letter, "It was one of the most rewarding experiences of my life. We were able to talk freely and openly about our fears and desires, our hopes and dreams. We learned there is hope. When there is hope, there is a desire to be better."

The depressed mom sits next to her daughter on the hay ride, singing, "If you're happy and you know it clap your hands." The recovering mom and her five children build and plant a beautiful flower box to be placed in their new home when the children are returned from foster care. The "blended family" comes together to cheer each member on as they face the challenge of the vertical wall to the ropes course. All leave with family photos, family crafts, family lessons learned, and family hope affirmed.

Think About It

1. Comment on the observation that "structure creates safety."

2. Can you think of other populations who might benefit from being brought together in a residential group experience?

3. In what ways might an experience such as Family Nurturing Camp™ help "keep hope alive" for the participants?

Additional Reading

Tyler, L. (2005). *Family Nurturing Camp™.* Family Development Resources, Park City, Utah.

Resources

The Nurturing Parenting Programs: *www.nurturing-parenting.com*

These programs are recognized by the Substance Abuse and Mental Health Services Administration (SAMHSA), the National Registry for Evidence-based Parenting Programs (NREPP), the Office of Juvenile Justice and Delinquency Prevention (OJJPD), and a number of state and local agencies as proven programs for the prevention and treatment of child abuse and neglect.

Chapter 10

Don't Count Me Out: Short- and Long-Term Outcomes With Groups With Disabilities

||||||||||||||||||||||||||||||||||||||||||||||||||||||||||||||||||||||||||||||||||||||||||||||||||||||||||||||||||||||||||

by Emma Giordano Quartaro, DSW, ACSW, LCSW

As I prepared a lecture/discussion for my social work students about the power of client/patient/member groups, I found myself recalling the groups with whom I have worked over the years. These ranged from natural friendship groups of all ages and cultures with a wide range of activities and norms to formed and formal groups with homogeneous memberships and very focused missions and agendas. Each group flashed by quickly, but one image lingered in my mind as the most profound group experience of my professional lifetime: an intensive two weeks in a summer vacation experience for adolescents who were orthopedically handicapped, as we referred to persons with disabilities then. This experience was called the Teen Trek.

The Teen Trek was designed by an agency far ahead of its time with fearless and compassionate leadership who provided service and advocacy for persons with disabilities. No one claimed individual ownership of the idea, but the staff and the board supported the unusual attempt to try to provide a low- to no-cost vacation for adolescents who otherwise could neither afford nor were considered capable by most onlookers of sustaining such an excursion. Many of the adolescents' disabilities were considered very severe, including dwarfism, spina bifida, missing and incomplete limbs, and other skeletal abnormalities. Some were independently ambulatory; others needed braces, a wheelchair, a walker, or some combination of these assistive devices. I was one of four counselors and one supervisor on the first Teen Trek who, as we got to know each other, came to call ourselves "the original motley group." Although physically challenged, most of the members were very bright and some very gifted. All went to special schools or to special education classes in regular schools. Most people, except the teens themselves and the agency, thought what we planned could not be done.

Eating out and sleeping accommodations in motels and hotels were arranged in advance. Nevertheless, our hosts often were not delighted with us when we showed up. In many ways, we were not "pretty," and access both physical and interpersonal was often more difficult than anticipated. Some group members needed assistance with meals, which at times relegated us to the isolation of a back dining room. But we managed to manage, even to thrive joyfully, as the bus traveled to New England vacation and sightseeing sites such as the New London Submarine Base, Cape Cod, Monticello, Campobello Island, and FDR's home. There, we were greeted by Eleanor Roosevelt, who demonstrated her disability by hesitating several times to adjust her hearing aid. Most group members were familiar with her husband's disability and the fact that he spent a great part of his adult life in a wheelchair consequent to the polio epidemic and before the effective Salk vaccine. Mrs. Roosevelt's hearing problem was a surprise.

After we visited other "hot" and "not-so-hot" tourist attractions, the Teen Trek culminated in a 3-day camp-out in the Maine woods. We had to manage for ourselves in a rustic lodge with individual, double, and quadruple occupancy rooms. We did almost everything people might want and need to do in the woods, including all maintenance (now called Activities of Daily Living, or ADL), outdoor and indoor games when it rained, an expedition on a trail into the woods, and an evening campfire on the last night replete with sing-alongs and marshmallows. It was in this unlikely setting for persons with disabilities that I learned more about the power of groups and the yearning to be accepted than I had before and have since.

One sunny afternoon, the more mobile kids decided to play softball. They formed two teams excluding those with dwarfism or "little ones," explaining that they could not play because they could not help either team of more capable members to win—and the game was about winning, after all. The ensuing debate was heated and sometimes very "raw." The original teams finally agreed to permit one very short but hardy young man, John, to play, but only as a pinch-hitter and with an assigned runner for him when and if he came up to bat.

As it happened, when they allowed John to pinch-hit, he connected with the ball squarely and strongly—not a home run, but close. The howl of cheers at the hit turned to awed silence as John threw himself on the ground, made a ball of his body, and rolled himself safely to first base. The designated runner stood open-mouthed and dumbfounded, as did we all.

I often wonder what became of John and the other members of the Teen Trek and whether they recalled the experience with the same fondness and gratitude as I still do today. Every once in a while, we social workers have the rare gift of learning about the long-term outcomes of our short-term experiences with clients/patients/members. Although I kept in touch with our staff and our supervisor over the years, and still do today, I made no attempt to find out how our clients/patients/members had fared over time. That's the function of research, which we should build into our professional agendas whenever we can. At that time, I didn't know enough to push to be included in that pursuit, but I would do it in some way today. At the very least, I would have asked how the agency planned to evaluate the effectiveness of the unusual intervention for our clients/patients/members. We knew how the professional staff were to be evaluated, but that was insufficient and, in retrospect, short-sighted and strangely self-absorbed. It is no wonder so little published research emanates from direct practice.

Academicians are not the sole arbiters nor generators of good research. Evidence-based best practice can be very real, and we all share responsibility for its advancement, especially those of us who do it every day. So be it!

Think About It

1. How are groups of persons with disabilities the same and/or different from groups with "normal" members?

2. List and define the universal processes of groups. One formulation in the literature suggests four: morale, activity, interaction, and norm formation. There are others. Which group process do you consider the most powerful, and why?

3. "Having fun" is often the avowed purpose of groups. Why is helping groups "have fun" an important professional function?

4. The demands for the protection of client/patient/member confidentiality sometimes render the long-term outcomes of group experiences inaccessible to professionals. Why and how can this dilemma be acknowledged and incorporated into best practice?

Additional Reading

ADA National Network. (2009). *ADA – Findings, purpose, and history.* Available: http.//adaanniversary.org/2009/ap02_nada_findings_history/ap02_ada_findings_history 09-natl.html.

Association for the Advancement of Social Work With Groups. (2008). *Standards for social work practice with groups.* Available: http://www.aaswg.org/node/377.

Garland, C. D., & Galinsky, M. J. (2008). *Groups.* In Mizrahi, T. & Davis, L.E. *Encyclopedia of Social Work,* 2nd ed. (pp 2:287-298). Washington, DC and New York: NASW Press and Oxford University Press.

Goldberg, J. (2008, May).The unforgiven. *The Atlantic.* Available: http://www.theatlantic.com/magazine/archive/2008/05/unforgiven/6776/.

Paraquad. (n.d.). *Words with dignity* (online). Available: http://www.paraquad.org.

Reamer, F. G. (2006). *Social work values and ethics* (3rd ed.). New York: Columbia University Press.

Chapter 11
The Job Club Support Group: Multiple Disabilities

IIIIIIIIIIIIIIIIIIIIIIIIIIIIIIIIIIIIIIIIIIIIIIIIIIIIIIIIIIIIIIIIIIIIIIIIIIIIIIIIIIIIIIIIIIIIIIII

by Johanna Slivinske, MSW, LSW

I did not realize when I began this job that I would learn as much from my clients as they would learn from me. In my official capacity as a social worker for individuals with disabilities, I enjoy the opportunity to lead a weekly "job club support group" for people seeking employment outside of the sheltered workshop. On this particular Thursday, I eagerly await facilitating our group and the opportunity to interact with and motivate a diverse and resilient group of people. The group composition is quite varied, including adult men and women, some who are blind, some who are physically disabled, and some who are cognitively disabled. This composition is unique and contributes to uncovering various obstacles, as well as discovering hidden strengths and compassion of various members.

As a social worker employed in a sheltered workshop for individuals with disabilities, I encounter numerous joys and hurdles on a daily basis. Throughout this narrative, I have written about ideas, issues, and concerns of group members and of myself. The names of specific group members have been changed and specific characteristics of members altered to protect the privacy and confidentiality of individuals.

In my role as facilitator of the "job club support group," I should mention that the group composition is chosen for me by my supervisors. Heterogeneity of membership definitely is an issue. As I prepare for group, I recall last week's meeting when Jacob expressed the desire to belong to a group only for members who are blind or physically disabled. He said he felt more comfortable with those members, as he had more in common with them. I agreed that it might be beneficial to facilitate two groups, one for those with physical impairments and another for those with mental impairments, to better provide for peoples' individualized needs. However, I do not have the authority to make this decision in my current position. I wonder if he will become very upset when I tell him that I am not able to run two separate groups. The thought of this conversation makes me feel uncomfortable.

As I prepare for today's group, I reflect on our progress thus far. I realize that most of the group members work together in the sheltered workshop and some have attended school together in the past. They have a shared history with one another. Because of this familiarity, there was less anxiety and tension in the forming stage of the group than typically would occur. Most members who are blind were able to recognize each others' voices prior to entering the group.

I realize, however, that in most groups in which there are blind or visually impaired members, it would be advisable to have individual members verbally identify themselves by name at the beginning of each session until voice recognition has occurred. I read that it is also customary for the group leader to ask members with physical disabilities or visual impairments if any assistance is needed. The article mentioned that as the group leader, you may find that it helps to verbally identify yourself by name and position held, and when appropriate, to lightly touch individuals' arms to indicate your presence (Patterson, McKenzie, & Jenkins, 1995).

Today is a particularly hot Thursday afternoon, and the workshop environment feels extremely stifling, so the group members welcome the opportunity to enter the air conditioned rehabilitation group room. I have gathered my materials needed for the group throughout the week, including a list of current job opportunities that may interest members, information about adaptive equipment, and ideas regarding potential training opportunities. I feel confident and prepared.

On this particular day, we begin group by discussing members' job search progress. I pose the question, "How are you feeling about your job search?" Members' reactions are as varied as the composition of this particular group. Some members are excited, and others express feelings of sadness and dejection. Jacob is a man who progressively lost his vision over a number of years as a result of a genetic disorder. Today, he is feeling rather depressed about this and its impact on his job search. He mentions to the group, "I feel so down. If I could see, everything would be easier." The group members, many of whom are blind themselves, agree with him.

They allow him to continue expressing his feelings of grief and loss. He then emotionally blurts out, "Who would ever want to hire me? I'm blind." Sherry empathizes with him, and shares that she "knows what he is going through." I sense that this makes Jacob feel less alone in his personal struggles and adjustment to his disability. I respond to their feelings with supportive listening, but after a while, I feel the need to use the techniques of gentle confrontation and reality testing. I remind them both that they are intelligent, caring human beings with wonderful potential, talents, and assets that could be applied in the work setting. Other group members agree and support my position. Jack, who is developmentally disabled, tells Jacob that he is "the smartest person" he knows, and I see Jacob crack a slight smile. I mention that I will help to ease the stress of the hiring process by talking with potential employers about the strengths Jacob can bring to the job.

In last week's group, we discussed the importance of technology. We mentioned how advances in technology have opened many doors for those with physical and mental challenges. I also explained that as accessibility of Web sites, computers, personal devices, and mechanical and electronic devices become more mainstream, this increases opportunities for employment and independence for those with disabilities. During this educational segment of group, I focused on the importance of receiving training in how to fully utilize these technological devices, adaptations and accommodations. I stressed how this remains essential toward creating independent, self-sufficient, prosperous, and successful individuals living with physical or mental impairments.

I want to follow up on this previous discussion now, so I ask Jacob if he is continuing his training on the software program Job Access With Speech (JAWS). This is a screen reading program that enables people who are blind to hear the screen read aloud from their computers. He says he is meeting with his instructor weekly, and is making progress. Group members applaud him for this. Sherry says that since he is able to make progress, maybe she can, too. I affirm her readiness to be trained on JAWS, and we discuss that we will make arrangements for her to receive private tutoring, as well.

The topic then shifts as Karen, a group member with a mild developmental disability, mentions that she is afraid. I ask her why. She says she is afraid of getting a job outside of the workshop, because she likes it here. "What if I can't remember what I am supposed to do?" she asks. I remind her that we will send a job coach with her for three weeks until she feels comfortable with the job. Also, I tell her that we can make a special card for her to take to work, with pictures of the steps she needs to complete when she is filling the salad bar at a local restaurant, as this is the job she desires. I also mention that I have been talking with the manager of a nearby restaurant, and he is considering allowing her to "shadow" someone on the job, and then possibly hiring her. This excites her, and other members chime in that they "think she can do it" with a bit of help and support.

Last week, as part of our group session, we discussed "out of the box thinking" when attempting to find ways and methods for accommodating persons with diverse disabilities regarding their job search and when seeking nontraditional ways of accomplishing a work-related task. I mentioned the importance of keeping an open mind, always seeking new ideas and alternative approaches or ways of performing work-related tasks. We talked about the importance of this unique type of thinking and its relevance to group members when developing their résumés. I explained that it may be necessary to rely strongly on transferable skills learned in the community, and not necessarily on past work history. For example, we talked about the experiences of Sherry, who is blind and has a limited work history, and how in her given situation it may be necessary to build on skills such as organization, creativity, budgeting, responsibility, and volunteering at her daughter's school—in other words, skills that were learned in the capacity of child rearing, household management, or elsewhere. Creativity and innovation are qualities that definitely serve as assets for a social worker serving in this capacity.

As I realize that our time is running short, I decide to follow up on last week's discussion about accommodations. I ask the group in general, "What types of accommodations do you think you will need to help you perform the kind of work that you want to obtain?" The group brainstorms, and the mood shifts to a more positive, almost jovial tone. Group members animatedly pitch suggestions, such as creating a memory book for those who are cognitively impaired, using adaptive computer software, or asking an employer for a flexible schedule so they can take the bus to and from work independently. I can feel their confidence levels lift, as they feel better able to describe to an employer how they can perform the duties necessary in a specific employment setting. I realize that this is a sign that they are hopeful that they may one day be hired at the job of their dreams. This feeling of hope, mutual support, and joy brings us to the conclusion of our group session, as I see we have run out of time. We look forward to meeting again next week.

As I begin to exit the room, I hear Jacob call out that he wants to talk to me privately. He mentions that he still would feel more comfortable if the group could be split into two separate groups, those who are mentally disabled and those who are physically disabled. I acknowledge his concern and concede that there are very real differences and needs between the two diverse populations. However, I also tell him that I do not have the authority to conduct two separate groups, but that I will continue to address his concern with my supervisors and at our team meeting. I can see from his frowning face that he is disappointed, but he also thanks me for trying. I thank him for his understanding of the situation, and I'm happy he is not overly upset.

As I ponder our conversation, I plan my suggestions for the next team meeting. When the time feels right, I will recommend that group members be more alike than different for this particular type of group. I feel that their individual needs could be better addressed by composing one group of individuals with physical impairments and visual impairments and another distinct group for those with mental impairments such as head injuries or developmental disabilities. This would allow for individuals to relate better to one another's difficulties and strengths, based on similarities of challenges as well as levels of cognitive functioning.

As I reflect on past group sessions, I am encouraged by the progress we are making and the challenges we continue to overcome. Although the major formal task dimension of the group is to find employment outside of the sheltered workshop environment, additional themes and concerns of the group are emerging. The issues we have dealt with include overlying manifestations of depression, feelings of incompetence, low self-esteem, social support concerns, transportation issues, discrimination, and self-doubt. I am glad that today's group ended on such a positive and hopeful note.

Later in the day, I collaborate with the state bureau of vocational rehabilitation to ensure that funding is available to provide Sherry with individualized training on JAWS, as we discussed earlier in group. I am optimistic that this will promote her technological, personal, and professional development. State organizations and bureaus, as well as private philanthropic organizations such as Rotary and Lions clubs, hold potential to contribute financially toward specialized adaptive technological equipment for those in need who show promise of success in their personal and professional endeavors. In my experiences leading groups with this special population, technology continues to remain fundamental in promoting independence and prosperity of those with physical and mental challenges (Slivinske & Slivinske, 2005/2006).

As I recollect the events of the day, I conclude that despite obstacles, group process was actually quite positive and functional in many regards today. If I could foresee the future, I would predict that a few group members eventually would reach their goals of finding permanent employment outside of the sheltered workshop environment. I recall reading that developing hopefulness can be positive in both the product and process dimensions of groups, and it is a quality that members often seek to gain when entering into a therapeutic group setting (Cramer, 2011). Perhaps of even more importance than finding a job, I would project that many members will acquire a sense of hope that despite the hardships they have endured, they too can potentially find employment if they remain optimistic and diligent in their search efforts.

Think About It

1. Discuss some issues that may arise when leading a job search support group for individuals with disabilities. As a facilitator, what types of statements might you make to encourage group members?

2. In forming a job search group for people who have disabilities, is it appropriate to combine people who have cognitive disabilities with those who are blind or physically disabled in the same group? What are the pros and cons of either type of group composition?

3. What strengths do you possess that could positively contribute toward your leading a group for people with various disabilities? In your self-assessment, what areas of your personality might conflict with your ability to run a group for individuals with diverse disabilities?

4. How do you project that running a group for individuals with disabilities might affect you, both personally and professionally?

Additional Reading

DePoy, E., & Gilson, S. F. (2011). *Studying disability: Multiple theories and responses.* Thousand Oaks, CA: Sage.

Dickson, M. B. (1994). *Working effectively with people who are blind or visually impaired.* Ithaca, NY: ILR Program on Employment and Disability, Cornell University.

Goodley, D. (2011). *Disability studies: An interdisciplinary introduction.* London: Sage.

Mackelprang, R. W., & Salsgiver, R. O. (2009). *Disability: A diversity model approach in human service practice* (2nd ed.). Chicago: Lyceum Books.

Sargent, L. D., & Sue-Chan, C. (2001). Does diversity affect group efficacy? The intervening role of cohesion and task independence. *Small Group Research, 32* (4), 426-450.

Shapiro, J. P. (1993). *No pity: People with disabilities forging a new civil rights movement.* New York: Times Books.

Slivinske, J., & Slivinske, L. (2011). *Storytelling and other activities for children in therapy.* Hoboken, NJ: Wiley.

Zastrow, C. H. (2009). *Social work with groups: A comprehensive workbook* (7th ed.). Belmont, CA: Brooks/Cole.

References

Cramer, E. P. (2011). *Small groups.* In E. D. Hutchison (Ed.), *Dimensions of human behavior: Person and environment* (4th ed.) (pp. 355-383). Thousand Oaks, CA: Sage.

Patterson, J. B., McKenzie, B., & Jenkins, J. (1995). Creating accessible groups for individuals with disabilities. *The Journal for Specialists in Group Work, 20* (2): 76-82.

Slivinske, L., & Slivinske, J. (2005/2006). Technology in long-term care: A pilot study. *International Journal of Technology, Knowledge, and Society, 1* (4), 83-92.

Chapter 12
Refugees in a Community Health Clinic

||||||||||||||||||||||||||||||||||||||||||||||||||||||||||||||||||||||||||||||||||||||||||||||||||||||||||||||||||

by Nicole Dubus, MSW, LICSW, Ph.D.

C ommunity health centers offer challenges and opportunities unlike those in many other settings. A community health center receives federal funds to provide accessible health services for a community. Community health centers are on the front lines of delivering health services and behavioral health care to diverse populations who are at risk of not receiving adequate care as a result of cultural and economic barriers. Each community health center is unique, because it defines itself by the needs of the community. This particular health center is based in an urban environment that has a large population of southeast Asian immigrants and refugees.

The health center provides culturally relevant health care for individuals and families, offering western medical services, as well as acupuncture, nutrition counseling, and behavioral health counseling. The providers are either bilingual in English and Khmer, or they have a bilingual Cambodian interpreter with them throughout the client's visit.

Most of the clients are Cambodians who fled Cambodia in the early 1980s after the end of the brutal genocidal reign of the Khmer Rouge. After a number of years in a United Nations sponsored refugee camp in Thailand, the refugees were assigned countries in which to relocate. Being a refugee is a different experience from being an immigrant who chose to relocate to a new country. Whereas immigrants may have hopes of building a better life in the new country they chose, refugees have to rebuild a life torn apart by war and displacement in the country assigned to them.

Cambodian refugees often suffer from post-traumatic stress disorder from their experiences during the Khmer Rouge. Those who escaped Cambodia and came to this country in the early 1980s are now in their forties, fifties, and older. They came as young adults and have raised their children in this country. And now, as their children reach the age they were when they arrived, new feelings arise. After thirty years of working in factories, they find they cannot work as fast, stand as long, or endure the stressors of younger, seemingly impatient supervisors. Their nightmares return and are vivid. They worry about their children, about their families in Cambodia, about their own health, and about what their lives will be like as their children adopt western beliefs of moving out on their own—separate from their parents. These worries, the increase in nightmares, the dizziness that strikes when they are overwhelmed with feelings, and the insomnia bring them into the doctor's office.

Most in this community avoid doctors, especially western trained doctors. They might seek a friend who coins them (rubbing the side of a coin on the skin until a bruise appears) or gives them a tincture to drink, but they don't often think of medical doctors as a source of care. Yet, these new symptoms bring them to the clinic. The doctor, who after examining the client realizes these symptoms are emotionally based, refers the client for behavioral health services. Because the center is physically small, the doctors' offices and the behavioral health services share the same hall. The doctors and counselors often talk and share concerns regarding specific clients. This allows the care to be continuous, culturally appropriate, and enhancing of both the physical and emotional needs of the client.

The center has ongoing weekly support groups for Cambodian women who have symptoms of post-traumatic stress disorder. They have been referred to this group by their behavioral health counselor or their primary care clinician. Most of them also have a chronic medical condition such as diabetes or high blood pressure, or are at risk for heart related disorders. All the women are in their mid-forties to late sixties. It is an open group, which means the new women can join at any time. Some of the women have been coming for two years, and some are very new.

The group is co-facilitated by a western trained licensed social worker and a bilingual Cambodian interpreter. The co-facilitation is done as a team; not as a clinician with an interpreter, but as two specialists, one specialized in western skills and knowledge of clinical social work, and the other specialized in the Khmer culture, and the refugee experience. This model strives to be both clinically effective and culturally relevant.

As the clinical social worker, I have a fascinating and role. I am an English speaker and cannot speak or interpret My co-facilitator is fluent in both languages and yet foreign to the concepts I feel are my primary language: feelings, group dynamics, and therapeutic interventions. How do I, as a western trained English speaking social worker, make the group feel safe and help the individual members?

I was scared my first day in the group. Although the eight women present welcomed me with smiles and waves, I felt ill-equipped to offer them more than a quiet smile back. They talked among themselves and with my co-facilitator. I sat and watched and wondered what I was doing there. Then I realized that watching was easy. What I mean is that watching is one of the things I do as a social worker. I watch facial expressions and body language, and I listen for pauses and feel for shifts in the energy of the room. I hadn't realized until then how much I relied on these forms of communication. I felt a renewed confidence. I looked around me, and although the language was indecipherable to me, I understood so much more about their interactions and moods than I ever could have predicted. Depression, sadness, joy, and worry looked the same to me whether the person spoke a language I knew or not. I settled into my seat. I felt my body relax. I watched my co-facilitator and noticed when she leaned forward, when she responded to a member, when her face lit up by a shared experience with the members, and when she was more still waiting for a moment to speak.

As the weeks went on, I felt clearer in my role. I learned the rhythm of the group. I watched and listened for the pauses to know when and how to intervene. My relationship with my co-facilitator deepened, and I became more aware of her role, not only as interpreter but as the cultural liaison for me with the members, and for the members with me. She taught me the Cambodian culture while also teaching the members about western culture. I counted on her to tell me if an intervention I wanted to execute would be effective.

There are challenges when co-facilitating. There are many interventions that I would have performed had I been able to speak the language, know the culture, and be a source of comfort that comes from knowing that the person helping you has also survived a similar journey. In working with clients who don't share my language, I realize how much I use specific words, most often drawn from the words used by the clients, as the medium for the intervention. In my own practice, I listen to their words. I feel for the silences and the moments of opening. My words are carefully chosen. There is poetry to that type of work.

...ot know how my words are interpreted into
...how the concepts are translated. I often ask
...group if it would work if we talked about, for
...em. "No," my co-facilitator will say, "we don't have
...elf-esteem." Okay, I offer, how about talking about
...don't have that concept." Okay, how about bound-
...e talk about how to set boundaries with her children?
"... ... Not only do we not understand this concept, but you
cann... ...sk her to bring this up to her daughter." Okay, I say, then
let's ask her how she can feel less scared when her daughter gets
angry about her traditional cooking.

Another challenge is that the co-facilitator is also a survivor
of the same violence and terror that members of the group experienced in Cambodia. As our mutual trust develops, I learn how
to read her, when to move the discussion away from reliving the
torture of the past, and when to check in with her after the group.
My role is not only as a co-facilitator, but also as her mentor and
emotional ally. Members often describe the torture they experienced or witnessed. This can be an important aspect of the healing.
This is also a painful re-living for the co-facilitator. I have to balance the member's need to share with protecting my co-facilitator
from re-triggering trauma. This challenge brings many questions
to the forefront: *What is in the best interest of the member? Of the
co-facilitator? What is the objective of the group? How much, if any,
of the group should be about the traumatic past versus the present-
day needs of learning to develop social support, managing health
concerns, and expressing feelings regarding families?*

Unlike group work in private counseling centers, group work in
community health centers entails helping group members outside
of the group, as well. Members in this group often need me to fill
out applications for other services, coordinate their medical care
with the clinicians at the center, and connect them with specialists outside of the center. A member might hand me a letter after
group, in essence saying, "Will you fix this for me?" I read the letter, make the calls necessary, and fill out any paperwork involved.
Often these letters are related to citizenship issues or continuation
of their food stamps or transitional assistance. Sometimes the letters are from immigration and law firms in regard to trying to get
a grown child a visa to come to the United States. Many of these
families were torn apart during the re-settlement, separated from
each other, and then relocated to different countries. Some of the
women in this group are still waiting to see their children again,
thirty years after resettling.

Working in a community health center is work at the juncture of medical social work and behavioral health care in poor, multi-need, ethnically diverse communities. To live a day in the life of a social worker in this setting is to work with individuals, families, and in groups bridging the medical needs of the client with the experiences, feelings, and needs of the client and the client's community. While the primary care clinician prescribes medications for the client's diabetes, the social worker learns why diet changes and medication compliance are difficult for the client. The social worker finds ways to help the client understand his or her medical diagnosis, develop culturally relevant action plans with the client, connect the client to community resources, work with family members to enhance the client's care, and be proactive in ensuring federal funds and state and local support for the community health center and its clients. Working in a community health center as a group social worker requires interest in the medical field; an openness to other cultures' understanding of health, illness, and treatments; case managing skills; and willingness to be a learner with every new ethnic group encountered.

Think About It

1. How might past traumatic events affect current medical conditions?

2. How might current and proposed immigration policies affect the ability of a community health center to provide care to community members?

3. The social worker in the group is Caucasian and is mono-lingual in English. How might this affect the clients' experiences of her?

4. How do the different characteristics of each facilitator affect the dynamics in the group? In what ways might they have a negative impact on the group? Are there ways these different characteristics of the facilitators create a positive impact on the group? If so, how?

Additional Reading

Amodeo, M., Peou, S., Grigg-Saito, D., Berke, H., Pin-Riebe, S., & Jones, L. (2004). Providing culturally specific substance abuse services in refugee and immigrant communities: Lessons from a

Cambodian treatment and demonstration project. *Journal of Social Work Practice in the Addictions, 4* (3), 23-46.

Auxier, A., Farley, T., & Seifert, K. (2011). Establishing an integrated care practice in a community health center. *Professional Psychology, Research & Practice, 42* (5), 391-397.

Tucker, S. (2011). Psychotherapy groups for traumatized refugees and asylum seekers. *Group Analysis, 44* (1), 68-82.

Warner, D. C. (2012). Access to health services for immigrants in the USA: From the Great Society to the 2010 Health Reform Act and after. *Ethnic & Racial Studies, 35* (1), 40-55.

Resources

National Association of Community Health Centers: *http://www. nachc.org/default.cfm*

Chapter 13
Red Flags and Common Themes in an Addictions Group

IllIllIllIllIllIllIllIllIllIllIllIllIllIllIllIllIllIllIllIllIllIllIllIllIllIllIllIllIllIllIllIllIllIll

by Golnaz Agahi, MPH, LCSW

As a social worker, I have the opportunity to work in both macro and micro settings. I am fortunate to be able to use my macro skills to plan, develop, and evaluate behavioral health programs during the week, while also enjoying the opportunity to use my clinical skills to facilitate patient support groups on weekends. I work as a per diem licensed clinical social worker at an addiction medicine outpatient clinic, facilitating groups on Saturdays. These one-hour support groups are open-ended, mixed gender (open to both males and females) for individuals over the age of 18. The average number of people per group varies from five to 15.

My goal as a facilitator is to use cognitive behavioral therapy to provide positive reinforcement and to model appropriate interactions by role playing and/or highlighting positive interactions among group members, all with respect to individual and group boundaries. I never pre-select topics for discussion, instead allowing the group to initiate the discussion by having a member raise an issue that he or she desires support for from the group. The groups enable the clients to witness other members' recovery, and thereby help develop interpersonal skills.

For me, a typical Saturday morning starts at 9 a.m. with 30 minutes for preparation for my group meeting. I start with the room, making sure that the chairs are in a circle so all members will be facing each other. I also place a box of tissue in the middle of the circle. I then return to the lobby and greet patients as they enter. I find it a good practice to greet the patients in the lobby, because it helps to personalize their visit to the clinic and gives that extra personal touch, reinforcing that they are not a number but a person that I care about. I call them by name and engage in small conversations while waiting to start the meeting. Group starts at 9:30 with my own introduction as the licensed clinical social worker facilitating the group. I then review group rules, including no eating or drinking, no talking over each other, respecting all individuals in the group, and the limits of confidentiality. This introduction is then followed by asking each participant to check in by answering the following six questions (which I have also written on the board):

1. What is your first name?

2. How are you feeling?

3. What is your drug of choice?

4. How many days/months/years have you been sober?

5. Do you attend 12-Step meetings?

6. What is your recovery goal for the day?

While we go around the room for the individual check-in, I make sure that each person keeps his/her check-in limited to answering the six questions listed above and does not diverge into sharing life stories. So when Sam, who appears overwhelmed, starts talking about his near relapse experience the previous night, I redirect him by asking him to focus on answering the six questions, reminding everyone that they will have time later during the session to share in more detail. The only time that I write during the session is at this initial check-in stage, so I can use the notes for calling on individuals who I believe may present with red flags.

What are red flags that I am concerned about? At check-in, I pay close attention to how the person is feeling. I don't allow anyone to check in with feelings such as "okay," "good," or "fine." When Julie checks in and says, "I am okay, fine today," I ask her to identify true emotions so she can process these emotions and identify thoughts associated with them. When she looks at me blankly, I refer her to the emotion poster (drawing of faces that reflect various emotions) that is posted on the wall. She looks at the poster and says, "This is hard, 'cause I don't know what I'm feeling. No one ever asked me that before." I reassure her that it is normal for us not to be able to identify our true feelings, because for many years we have masked our feelings with alcohol or other drugs. And so she looks at the poster again and starts crying and says, "I am overwhelmed." Another client passes her the box of tissue, and I thank her for being honest. "It is okay to be overwhelmed," I tell her, "and we want to hear more after we have everyone check in."

We continue to check in, and I document if any other client reports feelings of "overwhelmed, sad, depressed, angry, pissed off, agitated, frustrated," or other similar feelings. I make sure that these individuals have a chance to address their feelings in the safety of the group environment.

Another red flag is the number of days sober. When participants report less than 30 days of sobriety, I want to make sure that they engage the appropriate support systems available and utilize healthy coping tools to help them maintain their sobriety. So when John reports, "I have two days clean, and all I can think about is using again," I make a note of this and make sure I give John a chance to share later in the group.

After we make our rounds and everyone has checked in based on the six items listed above, I ask the group if anyone would like to start by sharing good things, bad things, happy, or sad moments. Most of the time, I have a volunteer who will jump start the group by sharing about his or her experience in the prior week, or by raising an issue to the group and asking for their guidance. Occasionally, when I ask the question about who wants to start, I get avoidance, with faces looking down and shunning eye contact. When this happens, I play the "game of silence," and inevitably someone in the group who doesn't feel comfortable with silence takes a deep breath and says, "I can't take this. I'll start." In turn, I thank the member and proceed to listen to his or her story. If no one volunteers to jump start the group, I will turn to a client who has presented with multiple red flags during check-in and ask if he or she would like to share with the group.

Today after check-in, Julie starts the group off by sharing that she is trying to get sober for herself and her adult children, but she feels that she has done too much damage to the relationship and can never make up for the lost time with her children. "I'm a failure and have lost everything. I hate myself," she continues. I stop her and say, "That is 'stinking thinking,'" and ask her to identify the negative thought patterns. I engage other group members to assist Julie in identifying healthy coping skills and more positive thinking to support her recovery. After Julie has shared, I ask other group members if Julie's situation resonates with any of them and if they would like to share their feelings or experiences.

As a facilitator, I work through my initial notes to make sure I allow other clients with red flag issues to also have a chance to share. So, of course, I will make time to go back to John, who indicated at check-in that he is having a hard time staying sober. I ask John to identify potential high risk situations that may cause him to relapse. He looks around and says, "Well, I have been listening to the group yesterday and today, and I have learned that hanging with family or friends who are still using is a trigger, and the presence of drug paraphernalia (such as needles, bongs, or bottles) in the house or carrying the phone number for my drug dealer is not a good idea. So I am going to go home and get rid of the bottles and tell my friends I am trying to sober up, so not to call me. Maybe I will even delete their numbers." The group claps for John and assures him he is on the right track. Danny also adds, "And John, when you feel like using, I want you to call me. I don't care what time of the day or night it is. I will stay with you on the phone until the craving subsides." I thank Danny for his offer and remind people that an important part of recovery is having a healthy support system.

At times, group facilitation requires me to be assertive, as well as nurturing. So when Tracy continuously interrupts other clients and wants to dominate the group's conversation by trying to direct all group issues to be about her, I tell her, "Sounds like you have a lot to share, and I thank you for what you have shared up to this point, but at this time I would like to have someone else in the group to have an opportunity to respond or share about his or her experience."

Additionally, I have to strike a balance to engage individuals who are withdrawn and not engaged in the group process. So I turn toward Sally, who has yet to share, and say, "I haven't heard from you yet, and I would like to know what you think or what has been your experience." Sally tearfully looks down and says, "I don't want to talk." In response, I state, "That is okay, and whenever you are ready to share, we are here to listen."

At this point, I look at the time and I see we have only five minutes left in group, so I need to start the wrap-up. I like to end my groups by encouraging and supporting positive behaviors, so I ask everyone in the group to share one healthy activity he or she will engage in today to support self care and "thrive." Even Sally smiles and says, "I like Jesse's idea of going for a 15-minute walk today to get out of the house and get some fresh air." I then thank the group for coming today and wish them a safe and healthy weekend.

Each Saturday that I facilitate groups, I hear and witness these common themes:

- *Avoid isolation:* I hear from those new to the group and to recovery how much they appreciate hearing stories from other people in recovery. They don't feel that they are in this "disease" alone and that others in the room understand the emotional rollercoaster that they are on.

- *The group is a resource:* The group can be a great source of information. For example group members who attend 12-Step meetings can share their experiences and inform other members about the local 12-Step meetings available, as well as share information on how to find a sponsor.

- *Positive support:* When a person new to recovery hears about someone who has remained sober for more than 10 years, it gives hope to the new person. Group members also become accountable to each other and often look forward to the next meeting as an opportunity to see each other and share accomplishments in recovery.

- *Coping skills:* Participants learn the coping skills to stay sober from the facilitator and each other. I call these coping skills the "tool box." During each session, we learn about new tools that can be added.

- *Confronting:* The group also creates an opportunity for me as facilitator, as well as peers, to address and process an individual's ambivalence, as well as negative andd/or risky behaviors regarding substance abuse, in a safe setting.

Every group that I facilitate presents not only an opportunity for the group to use each other as a support system, but also an opportunity for me to learn. I have the opportunity to view firsthand their resiliency and the power of support systems in one's life.

Think About It

1. How do you think support groups can benefit an individuals in recovery?

2. What are some characteristics of a good facilitator?

3. What are red flags that you want to identify with people in recovery?

Additional Reading

Brabender, V., Smolar, A. I., & Fallon, A. E. (2004). *Ethical, legal and group management issues*. In V. Brabender, A. I. Smolar, & A. E. Fallon, *Essentials of group therapy* (pp. 183-204). Hoboken, NJ: Wiley.

Enhancing motivation for change in substance abuse treatment, Number 35 in the Treatment Improvement Protocol (TIP) Series published by the Center for Substance Abuse Treatment (CSAT), Substance Abuse and Mental Health Services Administration. DHHS Publication No. (SMA) 01-3602 Printed 2001

Shulman, L. (2009). *The skills of helping individuals, families, groups and communities* (6th ed.) Pacific Grove, CA: Thomson Brooks/Cole.

Substance abuse treatment: Group therapy, Number 41 in the Treatment Improvement Protocol (TIP) series published by the Center for Substance Abuse Treatment (CSAT), Substance Abuse and Mental Health Services Administration (SAMHSA). HHS Publication No. (SMA) 09-4024. Printed 2005.

Chapter 14
Group Therapy for Social Phobias and Panic Attacks

IIIIIIIIIIIIIIIIIIIIIIIIIIIIIIIIIIIIIIIIIIIIIIIIIIIIIIIIIIIIIIIIIIIIIIIIIIIIIIIIIIIIIIIIIIIIIIIIIIIIIIIIIIIIIIIIIIIIIIIIIIIIIIIIIIIIII

by Denise M. Ellis, Ph.D., MSW

N ot long after receiving my MSW, I obtained a position as a psychiatric social worker in the outpatient department of psychiatry of a hospital in a northern Manhattan suburb. My clients were dealing with mental and medical health issues. My previous group experience consisted mainly of co-facilitating a group during a graduate internship, and my theoretical knowledge was obtained in generalist practice courses that covered group work processes.

I became very interested in the issue of phobias after working on an individual basis with a number of clients, both male and female, who had this mental health condition. I became aware of the way the panic attacks severely restricted their lives on a daily basis. I believed that group therapy would be an effective and efficient type of intervention.

The group consisted of six females and one male, who ranged in age from 25 to 60. Members of the group included Lisa, a 29-year-old single mother of a 9-year-old son; Melissa, a 32-year-old single mother of an 8-year-old daughter and 10-year-old son; Susan, 48, a married mother of a 25-year-old daughter, who lives at home; Joanne, 60, a mother of a 30-year-old son and grandmother of a 2-year-old grandson; Joseph, 30, a single male living "temporarily" with a brother; Inelda, 27, a single woman with no children; and Chantel, 30, a single mother of a 12-year-old son and 10-year-old daughter.

Most had completed high school or had a GED equivalent. No cognitive deficits were evident. Two members had some college credits, but had dropped out. The reason given by both had to do with uncontrolled panic attacks. Several were receiving some form of public assistance or disability income, which was often supplemented by some periodic form of financial support from relatives. Others were employed in part-time, unskilled jobs. Alcohol abuse was common among them as an apparent form of self medication. To this day, Joanne, the grandmother, was the one who made a major impression on me. I will discuss my reasons toward the end of this chapter.

I used a cognitive behavior group therapy approach. In addition to holding traditional meetings at the hospital, the group was primarily structured to provide members with exposure to anxiety-producing situations. My overall goals for the group were to assist members with identifying the triggers that occur prior to a panic attack occurring, developing the skills needed to cope with an attack, learning from and modeling constructive behavior of other members, and developing the ability to increase levels of functioning and independence.

All members were diagnosed with several types of phobias that were accompanied by panic attacks. Their experiences severely restricted their ability to function independently. The types of fears the group worked on included fear of being alone, traveling alone, and speaking to strangers in a public setting, for example to ask for help or directions. The group session occurred on Monday morning at 10:00 a.m. My intervention strategy included taking clients out of the building and going on a short train ride.

Each client was required to sign a permission form, basically releasing the hospital from any and all liability in the event that a group member became ill, injured, or died during a trip off the premises. It's very important to make sure that you, your clients, and your agency are protected from any potential liability issues. When unsure, it's always best to ask for advice and direction from someone at your agency who can help you consider any possible legal ramifications. The most ethical decision or course of action isn't always the easiest.

The group met at 10:00 a.m. in a meeting room in the outpatient department of psychiatry. The time was selected because it was after rush hour and we could expect less crowding at our destination. Members reviewed the past week's experiences and determined that they were ready to attempt a ride on a train. I checked to make sure that there were not any pressing issues that would necessitate that the group session take place at the hospital. Once I ascertained that there were no obstacles to prevent us from going into the community, we formulated a strategy for continuing our session. Members self selected into pairs and functioned as a support system for one another. I personally accompanied the most anxious member of the group.

We walked a few short blocks to the elevated train stop. One member in each pair was responsible for purchasing tokens from the station agent for the pair. This responsibility shifted to the other person for the return trip. What, to me, seemed like a short wait for the train, members of the group described as seeming like an eternity. I watched them closely, looking for any signs of panic. Finally, we could see and hear the train approaching. As I watched the train come closer, I knew intellectually and professionally that it was possible that some members of the group might not be willing, or able, to board the train. I admit, however, that I would have been disappointed had we failed. At that point, I had to use my energy to control my body language—to not signal any expression of concern or nervousness. Members looked to me for encouragement, and I decided if it was the last thing I did, they would only see confidence and encouragement, not disappointment. The group had an agreement that if any one member felt unable to board the train, none of us would do so. In spite of their anxiety, all members signaled their willingness to get on the train. Once we boarded, I was calmed and relieved.

The group pairs included: Lisa and Inelda, Melissa and Susan, and Robert and Chantel. When each pair felt ready, they would move to different train cars, and stand or sit, depending on their comfort level. I moved from car to car and either joined them or, at a minimum, maintained eye contact from another car. I was quite pleasantly surprised when Joanne, the group member who I had paired with, signaled that it would be okay for me to leave her for a few minutes and check on others in the next car. I then moved to the next car, stayed a few minutes, and returned to her. She signaled she was okay.

On this particular day, Robert had a panic attack. Chantel was a great support to him. I had been watching from the next car and immediately went to be of assistance, if needed. The others suspected things weren't going well with Robert in that car. Somehow, they all found the strength to go to his aid. As the therapist, it was heartening to me to see members put their own fears second to come to the aid of one of their own.

The group got off the train several stops later. They decided they wanted to take the train back instead of taking several taxis. We did so, and they indicated they wanted to try it again at our next session.

In hindsight, I'm sure passengers were wondering what we were doing and why we were moving from car to car. However, at the time, I was so focused on my group that I paid little attention to other passengers. It was amazing to me how others in the group would come to the assistance of one and help him survive the experience, and not jump off the train. I believe they cued off me and picked up on my sheer will, enthusiasm, and belief in their capacity to change and achieve their goals.

Factors to Consider

I would suggest that anyone attempting to replicate this experience consider the following points. It was very helpful to have supportive supervisors and colleagues. No one I was working with at the time had any experience running this type of group. However, the encouragement, suggestions, and resources made the process run smoothly. I'm not saying you should not move forward without support, but rather, be aware that it's easier to have it than not. Additionally, a supervisor typically has organizational experience at your facility getting projects accomplished and might be aware of the pitfalls that lie ahead. It is also helpful to have some confidence in one's ability to undertake new projects. Read and familiarize yourself with as much as possible before beginning any type of group. There are many resources available, electronically and in book and journal format.

What I Learned From the Experience

It's important not to make decisions based on fear. Some of my best experiences came from following my instincts and taking chances. Additionally, it's helpful to have supportive colleagues.

Overall, it was extremely gratifying when members felt comfortable enough to move to a train car by themselves. I will never forget how proud I was of each of the group members when they trusted themselves, and each other, enough to take the chance. I'm sure my elation paled in comparison to the sense of accomplishment they each experienced from achieving their goals. To people not plagued by panic attacks and phobias, going one train stop might seem like a minor accomplishment, but for someone who had never been on a train, didn't think they would ever be able to board one, or hadn't been on one in years, these were major accomplishments. They were very proud of themselves. They described feeling elevated in the eyes of each other, and particularly their children and family members. Ultimately, I believe people are capable of achieving amazing things when they receive support, encouragement, and the skills needed to achieve their goals.

Post Script: Joanne, the elder in our group that I previously identified as having made the decision to remain alone in the train car, made several substantial changes in her life. She made a decision to stop drinking and smoking after achieving her triumph over years of struggle with phobias and panic attacks. She said she wanted to become a positive role model for her son, who was actively abusing alcohol, and her grandson who was a toddler. She succeeded. Tragically, about six months after becoming fully sober, she discovered that she had an inoperable cancer. I regularly visited her on the oncology unit at the hospital where I worked. What I continue to be struck by is how she always had something positive to say, no matter her circumstances. I had had extremely limited experience with death. After all her sacrifice, it seemed so unfair and still does to this day. She has become a role model for me of how to handle adversity with dignity and grace. Life is not always fair. Until the day she died she reminded me how grateful she was that she was able to achieve her goals. She hoped that her sacrifices and achievements would motivate her son to also overcome his addictions. It did.

Think About It

1. What role might a social worker's supportive attitude have in influencing client change?

2. Why is it important to be knowledgeable about an issue prior to working with clients?

3. What are some ways clients might affect social workers?

Additional Reading

Heimburg, R., & Becker, R. (2002). *Cognitive-behavioral group therapy for social phobia: Basic mechanisms and clinical strategies.* New

York: Guilford Press.

National Institute of Mental Health. *Treatment of anxiety disorders.* http://www.nimh.nih.gov/health/publications/anxiety-disorders/ treatment-of-anxiety-disorders.shtml.

Yalom, I., & Leszcz, M. (2005). *Theory and practice of group psychotherapy* (5th Ed.). New York: Basic Books.

Chapter 15

Overcoming the Secret of Shy Bladder in a Group Weekend Workshop

||||||||||||||||||||||||||||||||||||||||||||||||||||||||||||||||||||||||||||||||||||||||||||||||||||||||||||||||||||||||||||||||||||||||||||||||

by Steven Soifer, Ph.D., MSW

Imagine going through life with a secret. You have difficulty urinating in the presence of others, either in public bathrooms or in your own home. This embarrassing secret limits your daily activities. Still, you have hope that you can someday overcome it.

I have been working with people who have paruresis since about 1996. Having suffered from this anxiety disorder myself since the age of eleven, once I found effective treatment, I decided to dedicate myself to helping others with the problem. I co-founded the International Paruresis Association (IPA—http://www.paruresis.org), the Shy Bladder Center (SBC—http://www.shybladder.org), and the American Restroom Association (ARA—http://www.americanrestroom.org).

Beyond a doubt, I have found that the most effective form of treatment for this problem is cognitive-behavioral therapy, which helps 80-90 percent of people with this issue. I used this protocol to treat myself, adopting the methods that my colleague, Dr. Joseph Himle, developed to treat individuals with paruresis in the early 1990s. Even though individual treatment is effective, another colleague and I, Carl Robbins (the other co-founder of the IPA), decided to try treating paruresis in a weekend workshop format very early in the game.

I am getting ready to do a weekend workshop in an American city. As always, I am looking forward to hearing people's stories, which are both familiar and different at the same time. There are 12 people awaiting me at 7 p.m., looking quite anxious. This time,

"Joe" talks about the time he was bullied in the bathroom in public school. "Mary" speaks about the time she was a kid trying to use the bathroom at home, and her brothers barged in teasing her. After we finish our stories, people are already less anxious, some having told a "secret" never shared with anyone before—even spouses, significant others, or best friends. Unbelievable, I tell myself. Imagine being married 25 years and hiding this little "fact" from your beloved. And someone never taking a vacation or having kids because of this little "secret" phobia. What a nightmare!

Saturday morning, people come prepared to "fluid load" and practice, many for the first time. To begin, I share information on the origins of paruresis, its mechanism (as we best understand it today), and typical symptoms people can experience. Paruresis, better known as shy bladder syndrome, afflicts about 7 percent of the U.S. population. Classified as a social phobia (DSM-IV-TR, 300.23), the major symptom is the fear of not being able to void in the presence of other people. It is a continuum disorder, so one person may suffer from an occasional bout that hardly interferes with his or her life, and others may become housebound because they believe that the only safe bathroom is in their own home. Paruresis afflicts men, women, and children in equal numbers. Interestingly though, probably because of the design of public restrooms, the ratio of males to females coming in for treatment is about 9:1.

Next, I explain how the graduated exposure work will go for the weekend. The whole time, people are drinking fluids (instead of the typical dehydration people with paruresis will often do in group settings), so they will be ready to practice with their peers. At 10:15, people start their first practice session. These 45-minute sessions are done in pairs or groups of three, at least for the first few practice rounds. The idea is to have people practice peeing with others around in a safe environment. The "clients" are in charge of how close someone is to them. For the men, the ultimate goal is to be able to pee with someone standing behind them in the hotel room bathroom, thus simulating the experience of being in a public bathroom with a line-up behind you. For the women, the goal is simpler: to be able to go with someone outside the hotel bathroom door, perhaps talking to her to simulate the experience of someone bothering you to use the stall in a public bathroom situation.

People gather after the first practice session, and you can feel a little excitement in the room. We debrief the session, and "Tom" explains how he couldn't believe he was peeing in a hotel bathroom with someone else in the room. People share similar experiences, except "John," who had difficulties. I'm going to have to work with him next round.

Throughout the morning and afternoon, we continue this routine—practice, debriefing, sharing with others. By the end of the day, there is some electricity in the room. People are tired, some aching physically (having drunk more water, in some cases, than ever before), but there is a lot of happiness with their personal progress. Many in the group choose to go to dinner together with people who were strangers the night before and who now feel like "best buddies." Some, for the first time, are going out with a newly found sense of freedom. There are a lot of "happy campers" around the dinner table. People are so relaxed compared to the anxiety experienced last night.

Sunday morning at 9:00, we gather again. The mood is significantly different than it was just 24 hours before. We do a check-in, and everyone but "Tom" is palpably excited. He, unfortunately, is not doing well. He made a little progress yesterday, especially when I worked with him, but his anxiety is just too high to do this work, and he is not presently on medications.

People are ready for the next phase of practice, which requires them to go out to "semi-public" bathrooms, that is, isolated hotel public bathrooms, and practice there with a group of people from the workshop. Once again, people simulate the scenes that transpire in public restroom situations, and people get used to, through graduated exposure exercises, peeing near or next to others in these situations. Again, the safety of the group makes a big difference in people being able to do things they haven't in 5, 10, 20, or even 30 years within the course of a weekend. This is often an exhilarating experience, as people report in the debriefing later that morning. Harry exclaims, "I was able to pee next to someone at a urinal for the first time in decades!"

After an exciting lunch, the third and final stage of workshop practice begins. People are ready to practice peeing in public restroom situations in real life. This weekend, we are practicing at the largest regional mall in the area. Having fluid loaded, and together in groups, people go into these public restrooms with the safety of their "pee-buddies" and practice going with strangers present. Participants watch me stand at a urinal not peeing for 15 minutes—and complaining about it—to see that nothing bad happens and that one can practice "not peeing in public"—that is, standing at a urinal and not peeing just to experience being in that situation and exposing himself to the feared situation. For "Jim," this is very therapeutic, and he feels it will be an important step in his recovery.

After the last practice session, we reconvene to do a group wrap-up and also a written evaluation of the workshop. For the most part, people seem to be transformed—from anxious, worried, and even frightened individuals on Friday, not knowing what to expect during the course of the weekend, to very happy people who experience a weight being lifted from their shoulders. The expression I use is to say that "the albatross is lifted from the neck." People reflect that they have made positive gains, have a set of practice tools to use when they go home, and can continue their progress on their own or in one of the many IPA support groups across the globe.

In conclusion, group work has turned out to be a great way to treat paruresis, or shy bladder. The healing power of the workshops is truly amazing to witness. After each workshop, I am literally amazed at the transformation most people have undergone during the course of the weekend. These transformational stories have sustained my work in this area throughout the years, and I expect to be conducting IPA workshops for many more years to come.

Think About It

1. What is the importance of telling others your "secret" in relationship to recovery?

2. What added "therapeutic" effect is there in working on an issue like shy bladder in a group setting versus counseling one-on-one?

3. What educational efforts can be made to inform people about stigmatized issues like paruresis?

Additional Reading

McCullough, C. (2000). *Free2P: A self-help guide for men with paruresis.* Baltimore, MD.: IPA.

Olmert, C. (2008). *Bathrooms make me nervous: A guidebook for women with urination anxiety (shy bladder).* Walnut Creek, CA: CJOB Publications.

Soifer, S., Zgourides, G., Himle, J., & Pickering, N. (2001). *Shy bladder syndrome: Your step-by-step guide to overcoming paruresis.* Oakland, CA: New Harbinger Publications.

Typaldos, S. (2004). *The secret phobia: Stories from the private lives of paruretics, written by people with "shy bladder syndrome."* Huntington Beach, CA: Haven Harbor.

Chapter 16
Graduation Day

||||||||||||||||||||||||||||||||||||||||||||||||||||||||

by Marge Shirilla, MSW, LCSW

Sandy looked around the group with tears running down her cheeks, a tremulous smile on her face. "I've learned so much about myself...and I couldn't have done it without all of you!" Seated in a circle, the group members smiled at Sandy. Each member, including me and our small clinical team, took our turn telling Sandy about her growth, expressing confidence in her ability to continue her healing process, and saying good-bye to her. This psychotherapy group was the core of the partial hospitalization program, where I served as the lead clinician and program clinical coordinator. And today, after weeks of intensive therapeutic work that took place almost exclusively in group therapy, Sandy was graduating.

Five weeks earlier, I was in my office following our program's daily psychotherapy group when my phone rang. It was the admissions social worker at the not-for-profit psychiatric hospital where I'd worked for my first two years of professional practice, requesting that I come to the office to meet and assess a potential patient for the partial hospitalization program. This was a common request in my job, and sometimes I could be called to admissions several times a day.

Entering the room, I saw Sandy, curled up in a chair and crying. Her roommate looked at me with a worried expression. Sandy, who was 24 years old, had been in outpatient treatment with a psychiatrist and a therapist for six months. According to her roommate, Sandy had recently experienced a painful breakup with her boyfriend of three years, after she learned that he had been cheating on her. Sandy's roommate had taken her to the hospital after Sandy was unable to get out of bed for days, refused to contact her therapist, and told her roommate, "I can't take it anymore. I want to die!"

The intake assessment revealed that Sandy had survived years of childhood sexual abuse at the hands of her uncle and two cousins. Sandy reported that she had been diagnosed with Major Depressive Disorder, Post Traumatic Stress Disorder, and Borderline Personality Disorder by her outpatient psychiatrist. During her initial interview, Sandy said, "I can't promise I won't try to hurt myself," and while I spoke to her, Sandy confirmed her suicidal ideation and, sobbing, added a plan: "When I get home, I'm going to take every pill in our apartment!" In consultation with our medical director, it was determined that Sandy would spend the night in our in-patient unit; once stabilized, she would step-down to the partial hospitalization program. Sandy agreed to the plan. Once she was admitted and gave me permission to do so, I notified her outpatient psychiatrist and therapist of her condition and treatment plan. It was agreed that Sandy would return to her doctor and therapist when her treatment in partial hospitalization was complete.

Sandy's history was typical for members of the psychotherapy group in our program, which had approximately 15 to 18 members at any given time. The program had a rolling admissions policy, meaning new patients could join the group at any time. A typical day in the program for patients included attending a psychotherapy group, a psychoeducation group, recreational and art therapy groups, and medication management with the attending psychiatrist. A family therapy group was held once a week.

My typical day in this job was always very busy and never boring! In the clinical aspects of my job, I facilitated the psychotherapy group, supervised my psych tech (who facilitated the psychoeducation group), consulted with the recreational therapist and the art therapist, and performed conjoint therapy with two of our program psychiatrists. Once a week, I facilitated the family therapy group. I also consulted with the in-patient social worker when a patient appeared to be appropriate for the partial program, and I met with the patients prior to their discharge, so they would see a friendly face the next morning when they returned for treatment. Finally, I was on call for the program five nights a week. Many nights, the pager never went off, but some nights, it seemed like it would never stop! Some patient calls occurred when a stressful event shook their confidence in their ability to practice newly learned skills. At times, the calls took a more serious turn, such as a call from an upset, younger patient with a history of cutting, who had a razor in her hand and wasn't sure she could keep herself from using it. Strong clinical skills, as well as patience and determination, are very important for this type of work.

Documentation always follows clinical work, so I would spend part of my afternoons charting group notes, creating treatment plans in conjunction with my patients, performing treatment reviews, and writing family therapy notes. Discharge planning always began at admission, so part of my day could include phone calls to community resources such as EAPs, the health department, housing officials, or community mental health and substance abuse programs.

The heart and soul of this work for me was always the daily morning psychotherapy group. The composition of the group could alter throughout the week, with newcomers joining and "old-timers" graduating. Group always began with a brief "check-in" with each member, including the member using a feeling word to identify how he or she was feeling that day. Many of our group members entered the program with little experience at acknowledging their feelings, let alone identifying them (with the exception of anger), particularly if they were trauma survivors or had abused substances. Nancy, a relative newcomer, once put it succinctly when she said, "Nobody cared how I felt when they were abusing me, so I stopped caring, too." Our work together began with that statement.

The dynamics within the group changed as the composition changed. One newcomer, Jackie, entered the group with an "attitude," defying staff and being sarcastic with other group members in an effort to protect her vulnerabilities. Annie, another newcomer, attempted to be invisible by curling up in her chair and refusing eye contact for several days. Invariably, other group members would gently (and sometimes not so gently!) confront and encourage the new members by sharing their own stories and challenging individuals to try something new.

Being a group facilitator is not unlike conducting an orchestra. Each person (musician) must be attended to and encouraged to participate without dominating the group, the group eventually creates its own synergy (music), and, as the conductor, the facilitator must guide the group with the goal of each member attaining an optimal degree of healing and growth. Some days, that "music" was downright out of tune, but most days, the group reached at least some degree of harmony.

As the facilitator, one of my most important roles was modeling appropriate behavior and demonstrating good social skills. Because so many of my group members came from abusive childhood homes or abusive relationships or had a co-occurring substance abuse diagnosis, most members did not have effective skills to help them achieve their needs and goals. By watching how I interacted with individuals, many members learned how to adopt new behaviors to help them negotiate thorny relationships within and outside of the group. As the group members practiced their new skills and began to gain confidence, their support of their fellow group members grew. As that support grew, the group would become more and more positive about their ability to recover. Over time, I began to notice that once this new energy and positivity appeared, it wouldn't be long before several members would be ready to graduate from the program. The power engendered by the group process was astonishing!

Graduation from the program was created after my psych tech learned that so many of our group members had rarely celebrated birthdays or special milestones such as school graduations. So, when a member was ready to leave the program, we always held a "graduation group." Each group member told the person who was graduating how he/she had grown and what the experience of being in group together had meant to them. The graduating person responded to each member, sometimes in happy tears, like Sandy, and sometimes with great joy. The group culminated with a cake (always the graduate's favorite flavor) and lots of well-wishes and hugs. These groups were incredibly special to me and the entire team.

When I graduated from my master's degree program, I asked my mentors for some help figuring out where to work. I knew I wanted to work with adults in psychiatric social work. Each one recommended working in a psychiatric hospital, and one said, "Work there because you'll see everything!" They were right. But what they didn't tell me was how much my patients would teach me or how working as a group facilitator would present opportunities to continually stretch and grow my clinical skills. They didn't mention that working with groups could be so professionally gratifying. I believe that becoming skilled at facilitating group therapy can be one of the most powerful tools a social worker can possess.

Think About It

1. Identify the personal and professional skills necessary to practice in a partial hospitalization group therapy program. What personal and professional characteristics do you need to have

to work in an intensive mental health environment?

2. What aspects of group therapy appeal to you?

Additional Reading

Chen, M. W., & Rybak, C.J. (2004). *Group leadership skills: Interpersonal process in group counseling and therapy.* Belmont, CA: Cengage.

Sweig, T. L. (2000) Women healing women: Time-limited psychoeducational group therapy for childhood sexual abuse survivors. *Art therapy: Journal of the American Art Therapy Association, 17* (4), 255-64.

Toseland, R. W., & Rivas, R.F. (2012). *An introduction to group work practice.* Boston, MA: Pearson.

Chapter 17
Shattering Stereotypes:
A Group for "Mature Women"

‖‖‖

by Elaine S. Rinfrette, Ph.D., LCSW-R

I began my social work career in an outpatient mental health treatment setting, as this was what I knew I wanted to do when I started graduate school. My program had an excellent group work faculty, so I felt I had been well-trained to lead groups. At my first job, I did not have the opportunity to run groups, so I was excited when I moved to a community mental health center where group work was a big part of the agency. I learned a lot there and was lucky to have supervision from one of the group work professors from my graduate program who did consultation for the agency. After two years there, I moved to another state, where I was to do the majority of my clinical work.

My typical day as an agency clinical social worker consisted of taking calls from clients seeking services, conducting assessment interviews, making diagnoses, developing treatment plans with clients, and providing treatment. Additionally, I attended daily intake meetings where the clinical staff met as a group to review and assign clients seeking services. I participated in weekly supervision, met with the physician regarding clients needing medication evaluations, and attended a variety of other meetings. My first year at this agency was in the chemical dependency treatment program, as I wanted to be better versed in the treatment of addictions, a common complicating factor for mental health clients. The majority of the work in this program was group oriented, so my group skills improved quickly. After a year, I moved to the mental health program and became the supervisor of the site, so part of my time was spent providing individual and group supervision for clinical staff and students, overseeing the daily activities of the office, and of course, paperwork. This resulted in a lot of group experience— some with my coworkers in professional work groups and some with clients in treatment groups.

The influence of managed care on reimbursement put pressure on social workers to consider using groups to see more clients. Getting enough "units of service" became the mantra we learned to live by. This meant seeing a specific number of clients every week. It was important to meet the 100% minimum number of clients required weekly, and it was highly encouraged that we see more than the minimum. This was a lot of stress when added to the many other daily responsibilities.

I had group work experience with mandated clients in the chemical dependency treatment program, but group work in the mental health clinic was different. I had to "convince" clients that a group was an appropriate and helpful modality, as many felt it to be a step down from individual sessions. I was already working with a group composed of clients who had serious and persistent mental health problems. The focus with this group was on building relationships, improving social skills, developing meaningful daily activities, and finding productive ways to spend leisure time.

The group I hoped to start next was labeled the "mature women's group." This was an unusual group, as most of the agency's clients were younger in age, but I plowed ahead and asked for referrals from other staff and put up a notice in the waiting room that a group was being formed for "mature women."

As always when starting a group, I was worried that I would not get enough members. I had tried to start groups in the past with varied success. It often seemed that by the time I got enough referrals and did the intake interviews, some of the clients I had initially interviewed had changed their minds about being willing to be in a group or had dropped out of treatment. This was frustrating. It was a lot of work to recruit, interview, and manage the clients who were waiting to start the group only to have it fall apart. Sometimes I wondered if it was worth the effort. Yet I persevered, as the agency wanted more groups, and I really wanted to work with a group that had a different focus from the one I was already running.

Eventually, it happened. It took several weeks of work, but the group finally came together with seven women. After a few weeks, I got two additional members. Nine women. Hurray! So this was my first experience with an entire group of clients who were much older than me. These women were retired and ranged in age from 65 to 77. Some were twice my age! I had worked with three of the women in individual treatment, so I felt I had some allies in the room who knew I was sensitive to their needs regardless of our age differences. I hoped I could prove this to the other women. I knew the stages of group development, and I had a good grasp of the theories of human development. I had several years of individual and group therapy experience. I was good to go—at least I hoped so!

This was a group of women from a generation that was taught to put themselves last, make the best of things, keep silent about their problems with others, and put on a happy face. They were supposed to be living happily with their retired husbands while also helping their grown children and taking pride in their grand-children. They had so many rules to live by, so many expectations to meet, so much to keep hidden. Just coming to the agency was a huge step for them. What would these women need from the group?

So we began our journey together. I had come to truly appreci-ate that the process of working with clients had an impact on my life as much as it did theirs. I worked hard to be alert on several levels. I listened to what the group members were saying and how they said it, and I paid attention to their body language. I remembered their history and tried to understand how that affected their current concerns, feelings, self-concepts, and behavior. I was alert to how this all played out in their interactions in group with one another and with me. On another level, I paid attention to myself. How did what these women were talking about make me feel? How did they tap into my own experiences? How did they make me think about my own mother and other significant older women in my life? How did all of this affect my responses to them? I also tried hard to be alert for opportunities to comment and interpret, ask questions, provide support, and create safety. I had been taught to be quiet as much as possible with a group once it became established and to let the group process do the work, so I had to overcome my anxiety about "doing nothing" and let the group develop.

The group met on a weekly basis and went well for five or six weeks. The women shared their frustrations with their lives, their husbands, and their children. They talked about their depression and anxiety. They spoke of loss, as some had lost spouses and others had lost other family members.

Then it happened. One of the women spoke about how she had been in a foster home as a child more than 60 years earlier. Her father had abandoned the family, and her mother had put her and her brother in the care of the state. They were separated, and she went to a family with an older son. She was twelve when the son raped her. He did this on numerous occasions until she was returned to her mother. She had never told anyone about what had happened to her. She told the group, "I want to talk about this before I die. It has caused problems for me all my life." The group was quiet for a minute or two. I asked how the members were feeling about this revelation, and they began to talk about what it was like when they were girls, how these things happened but could not be talked about. Revealing abuse would ruin the family's reputation as they would have a "damaged" daughter whose chances for marriage were tarnished. The group gently asked her about what had happened and how it had affected her life.

In the meantime, I was reeling. This was not what I expected from a group of "mature" women. I expected to hear about the trials of aging; the loss of husbands, family, and friends; the difficulties of transitioning from a work life to a retired life; problems with health; what I thought would be the "typical" aging problems. I was shocked—but the biggest shock was yet to come. Over the next few weeks, more and more of these women began to reveal their secrets. They, too, had experienced sexual abuse as girls or young women. By the time it was all out in the open, more than half of the women had revealed a sexual abuse history. One had a history of domestic violence, one was experiencing intermittent domestic violence, and one had an adult child killed in a horrible auto accident. Their "shame" was out in the light, and I had a group I had not expected to have. I had a group of trauma survivors.

Fortunately, trauma was something I understood. I had worked with many trauma survivors in individual treatment, both in the mental health setting and in the chemical dependency clinic. I was comfortable with this topic and knew that avoiding the issue was the worst thing to do when trying to recover from the impact of traumatic experiences. So the group and I renegotiated our treatment contract. We began to deal with trauma and recovery. I would sometimes feel astonished that I was sitting with these older women talking about trauma. I had put trauma survivors in a slot in my head. They were supposed to be in their twenties, maybe thirties, but certainly not sixties and seventies. I was just plain dumbstruck by this new realization.

The group progressed. Many tears, lots of anger, enormous amounts of shame, painful regrets, and a myriad of other emotions were addressed. Sometimes these came freely, and sometimes they were wrapped in confusion and histories of self-destructive behaviors. Sometimes they came as a surprise to the abused women themselves. The group learned about trauma and its impact on their lives. They began to understand the need to face the pain, and they slowly began the process of recovery, building trust again on a level they had lost many years before. During the weeks we met, my heart ached with their pain, marveled at their courage, and rejoiced in their progress. I could not believe how lucky I was to have this group! Never had I expected this "mature women's" group to be such an incredible experience. It taught me so much and shook my unrecognized stereotype about older women to its foundation.

Once again, I realized why I loved social work. No matter how much I put into my work, I always get more back from it. From my experience with this group, I knew myself better and learned something that I could use in my work with other clients. I was touched by the courage of my clients, and I understood that there was hope for their lives to get better regardless of their age.

Think About It

1. What will help social workers remember to explore trauma histories with older adults?

2. What will help social workers remember that all clients are capable of growth regardless of their age?

3. Are there any risks of exploring trauma issues with older adults?

Additional Reading

Averill, P. M., & Beck, J. G. (2000). Posttraumatic stress disorder in older adults: A conceptual review. *Journal of Anxiety Disorders, 14,* 133-156.

Gagnon, M., & Hersen, M. (2000). Unresolved childhood sexual abuse and older adults: Late-life vulnerabilities. *Journal of Clinical Geropsychology, 6,* 187-198.

Gellis, Z. D. (2006). *Mental health and emotional disorders among older adults.* In B. Berkman (Ed.), *Oxford Handbook of Social Work in Health and Aging* (pp. 129-139). New York: Oxford University Press.

van Zelst, W. H., DeBeurs, E., Beekman, A. T. F., Deeg, D. J. H., & Van Dyck, R. (2003). Prevalence and risk factors of posttraumatic stress disorder in older adults. *Psychotherapy and Psychosomatics, 72,* 333-342.

Resources

Council on Social Work Education: *http://www.cswe.org/18949.aspx?catGroupId=6&CFVTopics=77*

CSWE Gero-Ed Center: National Center for Gerontological Social Work Education: *http://www.cswe.org/CentersInitiatives/GeroEd-Center.aspx*

David Baldwin's Trauma Information Pages: *http://www.trauma-pages.com/*

National Center for Post-traumatic Stress Disorder: *http://www.ptsd.va.gov/*

National Institute on Aging: *http://www.nia.nih.gov/*

NIMH PTSD: *http://www.nimh.nih.gov/health/topics/post-traumatic-stress-disorder-ptsd/index.shtml*

Chapter 18
Talking the Talk and Walking the Walk With the Sexuality and Gender Identity Group

IIIIIIIIIIIIIIIIIIIIIIIIIIIIIIIIIIIIIIIIIIIIIIIIIIIIIIIIIIIIIIIIIIIIIIIIIIIIIIIIIIIIIIIIIIIIIIIIIIIIII

by Elizabeth P. Cramer, Ph.D., LCSW, ACSW

I buzz the intercom of the building that houses the women's residential substance abuse treatment program, and a "runner" lets me in. I'm a bit sticky and warm, as it is an unusually hot day in May and I don't have air conditioning in my car. I'm told that the women and my co-facilitator Jody are already upstairs in one of the lounges. As I walk into the lounge, I immediately notice two things: it feels cooler in the room than in my car, and the group is large in number today.

I smile at the group members and remark that I hope the air conditioning is on, because the drive over was stifling. For many of these women, a car itself is a luxury that they can't afford, much less one with AC. There are no seats left in the room, and one of the group members politely gives me her seat and goes to get another chair.

The agency runs a 90-day program. Because I co-facilitate this group every two to three weeks, there are changes in the group composition each time I come. Therefore, I start off by introducing myself: "My name is Liz. I'm a lesbian. I'm not in recovery, but I have worked with many women who are. I've been facilitating this group for about a year."

I then ask my co-facilitator, who began leading the group with me about a month ago, to introduce herself. She tells the women her name, that she is in recovery, and that she is a counselor at the facility. What she says next comes as a great surprise to me. "I'm a lesbian," she declares. I'm looking at her so intently that I forget to check the reactions of the group members. Jody and I had a long discussion before she joined me in facilitating the group. She told me that she's a lesbian, but she seemed to feel strongly about not telling the group. She feared any potential boundary problems with the gay clients, and homophobia or distrust of her from the straight ones. She's also fairly closeted among the staff. Homophobic remarks and jokes are not uncommon among the staff at this facility. I throw her a supportive smile, but I don't think she is looking.

Then, the women introduce themselves using first names only. Occasionally, a woman will slip into AA/NA mode and say, "I'm Tonya, and I'm an addict." Today, I notice that there are several "repeaters" (women who've come to the group before) and several newcomers. I briefly describe the purpose of the group and the confidentiality rule: "This is a group to talk about sexual orientation, whether you are lesbian, bisexual, or just questioning your sexuality. What we say in this room stays here. We don't share someone's story with others outside of the group. This is an open group, and you can discuss what you want freely."

The first few moments of the group can be awkward. I remind members about a wonderful video we saw in the last session called *All God's Children* (Mosbacher, Reid, & Rhue, 1996). For the benefit of those who weren't at that last session, I summarize the topic of the video—the experiences of lesbian, gay, and bisexual African Americans, including their families, church, and community. Since the majority of group members are African American, the movie speaks to their experience. There was quite a bit of discussion last session that was sparked from the video, one topic being whether we are "born gay" or choose to be gay. I decide to raise that issue again.

"So, are we born gay, or do we make a decision or choice to be gay?" Silence for 10 seconds (always seems like an eternity). One of the group members says, "Alicia, start us off." Alicia is an African American woman, perhaps in her thirties, who isn't shy about talking and who often is very insightful. She relays her story of having same-sex attractions at a young age, having boyfriends, and getting married to please parents and friends, and "discovering" her lesbian identity while in her unhappy marriage. This is a story I've heard before from many other women. She adds a piece to her story, that after she told her husband about her feelings for women, he raped her. She shares some of the details. I feel deep sorrow for her. I say how awful that must have been.

Group members begin to talk about sex and sexuality and specifically why some women will give pleasure to other women but will not permit themselves to receive pleasure from their partners. These women are sometimes referred to as "stone butches" (Feinberg, 1993). Overt discussion of sexual acts and sexuality often occurs in the group. It is one of the only times in the treatment program that the women are "permitted" to discuss sex so freely.

I suggest to the group that for some women, the desire to give but not receive pleasure may be related to control, but for others, it could relate to feelings of vulnerability and safety. I see nods in the room and my co-facilitator picks up on my comment and discusses intimacy in general. For some women in recovery, intimacy can be a dangerous trigger. Jody shares with the group that she was in a serious relationship for six years. When that ended, she had difficulty breaking away from the relationship and the feelings that surrounded the relationship.

In the midst of this discussion about sex and sexuality, one group member stops in mid-sentence, and then remarks about how surprised she was when Jody disclosed her sexual orientation at the beginning of group. I make an encouraging comment, "Wow, Jody, you told the group you were a lesbian!" Some of the women say they figured she was a lesbian. The group member asks Jody why she decided to tell them about her sexual orientation. Jody explains that she is comfortable with her sexual orientation and has been employed in jobs where her sexual orientation was not a problem at all. Since coming to work at this facility, she believes she has been forced "back into the closet" by the homophobic comments of some of the staff. She decided that she wanted to tell the group that she is a lesbian.

The group members seem to react well. I make a mental note to check in with Jody after the group to see how she felt about the disclosure and to discuss any apprehensions she may have now that "the word is out." (We hope that the women will keep the confidentiality regarding what the facilitators disclose, but we also recognize the gossip and innuendo that happens in residential settings.)

The women continue to discuss giving and receiving pleasure. Marie is new to the group. As she is speaking, I wonder if she is on medication and/or if she has an intellectual disability. Earlier in the session, she shared with the group that she feels good about her sexual orientation. At this point of the discussion, she says,"Women know how to touch." A group member inquires whether Marie means touch intimately. Marie says, "Women know how to touch your body and your mind and heart." I am moved by what Marie says. Alicia chimes in, "I want a woman to touch my mind. I want her to touch my mind before she touches anything else."

One group member, Sheila, raises the issue of parenting when one is in a same-sex partnership. Sheila comments that she doesn't think it would be right for kids to see two women lying in bed together. Alicia suggests to Sheila that she may have some negative feelings about her sexual orientation and might not be entirely comfortable with it. Internalized homophobia occurs when a gay/lesbian/bisexual/questioning person internalizes society's negative stereotypes, images, and attitudes about gays (Pharr, 1988). It happens to the best of us—even those of us who say we are very comfortable with who we are. Some of the mothers in the group talk about how they have handled their disclosure of their sexual orientation with their children.

I notice that there is a wedge of women in the room to my left who haven't spoken at all. I point this out and ask them if they would like to talk. When the group is small, usually everyone says something, but when there is a big group like today, everyone does not speak. Olivia speaks up and says that she came to the group today to try to learn more about gays. She herself has not had a sexual experience with a woman, but she did consider it while she was incarcerated.

The issue of "prison socialization" or "situational homosexuality" has arisen in past group sessions. Some of the group members have served jail time, and some of those women say they were "turned out" while in jail. There are women who were turned out in jail who say they had feelings of same-sex attraction prior to incarceration; others will say they had no feelings of same-sex attraction before serving jail time. The former group will often claim that lesbian is their "true" sexual orientation, whereas the latter group often identify as heterosexual, but curious or lonely.

When the topic of situational homosexuality comes up, I often describe the continuum of sexuality (Kinsey, 1953) and that most of us fall somewhere in the middle of exclusively heterosexual and exclusively homosexual. Sexual orientation is more fluid, rather than rigid or fixed (Rust, 1993). Women can go back and forth along the continuum. Being with a woman who says she is a lesbian does not mean that the woman will not ever leave you for a man one day. Furthermore, being with a bisexual woman does not guarantee that you will be left for a man.

I also tend to bring up the issue of engaging in sex with a woman when one has been using drugs. This is an activity in which some of the women say they would not have engaged if they were not high. The reasons why they would not be intimate with women except while high includes lack of same-sex attraction, belief that homosexuality is wrong, and internalized homophobia. The latter reason is often the tricky one, because these are the women who may have same-sex attractions, but feel very bad about this. Therefore, the only way they will act on those attractions is by getting high first. This may be the case with Barb. She says that she can't "perform" with a woman unless she gets drunk first. In fact, she doesn't know what if feels like to have sex with a woman without getting drunk first. Sheila says the same thing. She gets high to be able to perform sexually. She fears that if she doesn't use before being intimate, then she will not perform very well. I offer a perspective from a non-user about what it is like to be intimate with someone who is drunk or high—it feels like the person isn't really there. I gently ask whether she could, in fact, perform better when she is not high. She avoids the question at the moment, but later circles back to it and acknowledges that she probably could perform better when she isn't high, but is afraid that she won't.

It is getting toward the end of group and I suspect some of the women want a smoke break soon. I notice non-verbals that tell me that it is time to end the group. The women leave the room. Some days, I get hugs on the way out from some of the women. Jody approaches me and says, "Good group." I share my concerns about the number of women who did not speak during group today. She says she thinks it is because of the size of the group.

On the way out of the facility, I ask Jody how she felt about disclosing her sexual orientation. She says she is glad she did it, and she will see what comes of it as she interacts with the residents. We plan to hold group again in two weeks. We talk about potential topics and settle on the issue of relationships. This has been an important discussion topic in the past.

On the way back to my office, snapshots of the women and their stories play through my mind. They are portraits of courage and resilience. There are many parallels to the experience of being gay and the experience of having addiction (Cramer, 2003). The pervasiveness of shame is one of them. The judgment of others is another. For both, acceptance of oneself is key to growth and healing. I am privileged to walk along the path of the journeys of these women—if only for a short while.

Think About It

1. What are some parallel process issues for people who are lesbian, bisexual, or transgendered and who are experiencing an addiction?

2. How comfortable would you be with overt discussion of sex and sexuality within a group context?

3. What are some ways in which co-facilitators can assist each other in processing self disclosures and their impact within groups?

References

Cramer, E. P. (2003). *Making connections: Parallel process in lesbian and bisexual women's recovery from addiction and healing from homophobia.* In J.S. Whitman & C.J. Boyd (Eds). *The therapist's notebook for lesbian, gay, and bisexual clients: Homework, handouts, and activities for use in psychotherapy* (pp. 256-261). Binghamton, NY: The Haworth Press Clinical Practice Press.

Feinberg, L. (1993). *Stone butch blues.* Ithaca, NY: Firebrand Books.

Kinsey, A. C. (1953). *Sexual behavior in the human female.* Philadelphia: Saunders.

Mosbacher, D., Reid, F., & Rhue, S. (1996). *All god's children.* Videorecording]. (Available from Woman Vision, 3145 Geary Blvd., Box 421, San Francisco, California, 94118, 415-273-1145).

Pharr, S. (1988). *Homophobia: A weapon of sexism.* Inverness, CA: Chardon Press.

Rust, P. C. (1993). "Coming out" in the age of social constructionism: Sexual identity formation among lesbian and bisexual women. *Gender and Society, 7* (1), 50-77.

Additional Reading

Alcoholics Anonymous. (1989). *AA and the gay/lesbian alcoholic.* Available at: http://www.aa.org/catalog.cfm?origpage=159&product=54

Morrow, D.F., & Messinger, L. (2006). *Sexual orientation and gender expression in social work practice: Working with gay, lesbian, bisexual, and transgender people.* New York: Columbia University Press.

U.S. Department of Health and Human Services, Substance Abuse and Mental Health Services Administration. (2009). *A provider's introduction to substance abuse treatment for lesbian, gay, bisexual, and transgender individuals.* Rockville, MD: Author. Available at: http://kap.samhsa.gov/products/manuals/pdfs/lgbt.pdf.

Resources

National Association of Lesbian and Gay Bisexual and Transgender Addiction Professionals: *http://www.nalgap.org/*

PRIDE Institute: *http://pride-institute.com/*

Chapter 19
Fight Club: A Support Group for LGBT College Students

IIIIIIIIIIIIIIIIIIIIIIIIIIIIIIIIIIIIIIIIIIIIIIIIIIIIIIIIIIIIIIIIIIIIIIIIIIIIIIIIIIIIIIIIIIIIIIIIIIIIIIIIIIIIIIIIIIIIIIIIIIIIIII

by Andy Dunlap, Ph.D., LCSW

Aquiet chime sounded as another e-mail appeared in my inbox. The subject line read "Fight Club," and I had to chuckle. The students last year had really taken this tongue-in-cheek joke to heart. Scanning through the e-mail, I saw that the message was from a student who was returning for her fourth year of college and was excited to come to "Fight Club" to meet the newest LGBT students. Merissa's message brought the total to eight confirmed returning students. Seven first-year students had contacted me and asked for information about the support group. There was no way of knowing how many of them might show up. I made a mental note to order an extra pizza as I straightened up my office for my first client of the day.

Working in the counseling center of a small private college suited me very well. A wide variety of problems from high functioning young adults made for engaging therapy sessions. This day was no different. My calendar showed that there were three clients in the morning: a young man struggling with anxiety, a homesick first-year student, and a young woman struggling with an eating disorder. No lunch meetings were scheduled today, which was a relief. My afternoon schedule consisted of three clients in the afternoon: a young man with a new diagnosis of depression, a young woman whose mother had recently passed away, and social skills training for a young man with Asperger's. After that, a short break was scheduled before Thursday night's LGBT Support Group.

Checking my e-mail between sessions, I found a message with the subject line "Hi." This seemed to come from an anonymous e-mail address. Normally, I wouldn't open unsolicited messages such as this, but I had a feeling it was about tonight's support group. It turned out to be a message from a first-year student named Mike. Mike wrote that he had seen the flier posted for the support group and he wanted more information about it. The flier only stated that there was a confidential support group for Gay, Lesbian, Bisexual, and Transgender students and provided my contact information. If anyone wanted to find out when and where the group met, they had to talk to me first.

This arrangement was a bit cumbersome, but it was an effective way to both screen group participants and to help participants feel that they could attend the meeting without anyone knowing what they were up to. On a small college campus, this was crucial to the success of a group like this.

Mike wrote that he was gay, but that he had never come out to anyone. He wondered what the group was all about, who came to the group, and if he could join. I quickly shot off an e-mail to him letting him know that the support group was a confidential place for LGBT students to talk about coming out issues and to just generally relax. I told him that some participants said they liked the group because it was the one place where they didn't have to pretend to be straight. I also told him that the time and location was confidential, and that we were meeting tonight at 6:30 in the counseling center group room. I signed off by inviting him to join us and letting him know that there would be pizza.

On some college campuses, the counseling center might not be the best place for an LGBT support group. Some students might find stigma attached to mental health care to be a barrier to group participation. Others might feel that the historical wrongs done by a misguided mental health system toward LGBT folks might also be a barrier. Groups choosing to meet in otherwise well-meaning religious spaces might also find that there is a similar barrier for some students.

In my case, the counseling center enjoyed a carefully cultivated and unusually positive reputation among the student body as a safe and welcoming place for all. Additionally, the building itself was in a remote, yet accessible, corner of campus. The counseling center was not used in the evenings, so the students generally enjoyed the privacy that this provided.

I hoped Mike would come to the meeting. New members often brought a lot of new energy to the group. Having new faces around also helped upper class folk realize how far they had come since their first year of college.

As my day of individual sessions wound down, I found myself looking forward to the group, even getting a little excited about it. Last year, there was a core group of weekly students who attended, and there were a few who came off and on. There was a high degree of group cohesion, which meant lots of laughter and lots of tears. More often than not, I found myself leaving those meetings feeling very proud of the support that the students had been able to provide to each other. I wondered if this year would be the same.

Around 5:30, when my colleagues in the counseling center had all gone home for the day, I began to make my preparations for the group. I pulled all the extra chairs from around the building into the group room. I was able to tightly pack fifteen chairs into the cozy space. Last year, our top number of attendees was fifteen, so I was reasonably sure that this would be enough. I ordered the pizzas for the secret meeting, remembering to get an extra one, just in case. I scheduled the delivery for a half hour into the meeting. That way, I could go downstairs and pay for the pizzas without disturbing the meeting and also preserve everyone's privacy.

I printed out new copies of the group guidelines and privacy agreement forms. The guidelines provided an outline of the group and its purpose:

This group meets on a weekly basis, always in the same place and at the same time. Group members are free to attend as many or as few meetings as they would like. The purpose of this group is to provide a safe environment for discussion and support around lesbian, gay, bisexual and transgender issues.

The guidelines also outlined the few rules of the group:

All group members agree to protect the confidentiality of the group by keeping all group discussions within the group. Nothing that another person says in the group should be repeated outside of the group.

Attendance of the group is confidential. If you see another group member outside of the group, it is best to not acknowledge knowing them, unless a prearranged agreement has been made. People that you are with may become curious and begin asking questions like "Where do you know her from?"

All group members agree to work to promote a safe space for discussion of lesbian, gay, bisexual, and transgender issues. This means (but is not limited to) listening when other members are speaking, using "I statements" to talk about thoughts and feelings, and respecting difference of opinions.

No discussion is "off limits," the group members decide what issues we will discuss during any given meeting. However, discussion of people not in attendance of a meeting can quickly become unproductive gossip and should be avoided by group members.

Last but not least, I unlocked the front door and put up a sign reading "Group Meeting Upstairs."

I then went and sat in the group room to compose my thoughts. I realized I was a bit nervous to see who would show up and how the group dynamics would be this year. It didn't take long before my first guests arrived. Three upper class students who had participated last year came early to help set up. I interpreted this as them wanting a little extra time with me before the group, but I didn't call them on it. Instead, I just enjoyed catching up with them and hearing about their summers. Soon we could all hear the downstairs door open and close. We listened to the careful tread of nervous feet on the stairs, and then our newest member arrived. She was excited to make some new friends and quickly began chatting with the older members. I facilitated introductions and passed out information sheets and agreement forms for confidentiality.

Soon, group members were arriving in small groups and on their own. For about five minutes, there was a steady flow of fresh and familiar faces, lots of chatting, and nervous smiles. I was glad to see that Mike, the young man who had e-mailed earlier in the day, had come. Before I knew it, the room was full to capacity! Several students sat on the floor, and a few even sat on the table. There were 23 students. This was a new record!

"Well," I began. "We certainly have a lot of folks here tonight. Welcome everyone to the first meeting of the LGBT Support Group. I'm glad you all could make it tonight." I went on to introduce myself and describe my role in the group as host and facilitator. I outed myself and shared that I was a social worker and counselor at the college. The body language around the room told me that everyone was settling in to the meeting. Next, I asked "Would any of our seasoned members care to explain the rules of the group for our new members?"

Stan, a returning junior, raised his hand immediately. "First rule of Fight Club...you don't talk about Fight Club." The group dissolved in peals of laughter. Pillows were thrown at Stan, and he was the target of several good natured thumps on the arm and head. "Hey," he squirmed, "and no hitting!"

We all laughed. "No hitting indeed," I echoed. Several members then went on to discuss the rules of the group outlined in the handout. I added just a few comments for emphasis, but was happy that the group members had taken such ownership for the group. New members listened carefully, and older members chimed in when they felt the need.

"And our meetings always begin with a check-in," Gina finished the explanations. "Would you like to start?" I invited her. Gina led by example and provided the two necessary components of the check-in. She shared how she was doing that evening and shared a topic that she wanted to "put on the table" for discussion.

In this fashion, we went around the room accumulating a moderate list of items for discussion. The check-in helped me to gauge how everyone was doing and to begin to tune in to any potential problems between group members. It was also the structure that made up the group. It was a ritual of beginning for each group session.

Part way through the check-in, the pizza arrived. This was a brief interruption as group members went on talking as they ate their pizza. I was very glad I had ordered the extra pizza!

Once the check-in was done, the group settled on the topics they wanted to discuss. These included changing the name of the group; discussing which teachers were out at the school; talking about social events coming up; and discussing parents who were having trouble understanding their child's sexuality. That evening, like most, was a rather wide ranging discussion. But, as always, the imparting of information was a secondary function of the group. Members benefited from a sense of mutuality. New members benefited from the experience of the older students, and the older students benefited by becoming guides for the newcomers.

Ninety minutes later, when the time was up, the students grumbled and complained that they wanted more time. I stuck to my guns and called the meeting to a close. I invited them all back the next week and was gratified to see them drifting off in small groups back toward campus. No singletons leaving tonight. Good.

I locked the door, took down my sign, cleaned up the pizza, and returned all the chairs to their rightful places. As I turned out the lights and locked up the building I reflected on the success of the group that night. I had a feeling that "Fight Club" was going to go very well this year...although I would need a larger room!

Think About It

1. What are the universal needs of young adults? What are some specific needs of LGBT young adults?

2. What are the therapeutic aspects of a support group like this?

3. This social worker chooses to reveal his sexual orientation to this group of clients. Would you make this kind of disclosure to a group like this?

4. What barriers might young adults find that keep them from participating in this kind of group? What has this social worker done to dismantle those barriers? What would you do?

Additional Reading

DeBord, K. A., & Perez, R. M. (2000). *Group counseling theory and practice with lesbian, gay, and bisexual clients.* In R. M. Perez, K. A. DeBord, & K. J. Bieschke (Eds.), *Handbook of counseling and psychotherapy with lesbian, gay, bisexual, and transgender clients* (pp. 183-206). Washington, DC: American Psychological Association.

Kulkin, H. S. (2006). Factors enhancing adaptive coping and mental health in lesbian youth: A review of the literature. *Journal of Homosexuality, 50* (4), 97-111.

Ryan, C., Diaz, R. M., & Sanchez, J. (2009). Family rejection as a predictor of negative health outcomes in white and latino lesbian, gay, and bisexual young adults. *Pediatrics, 123* (1), 346-352.

Savin-Williams, R. C. (2005). *The new gay teenager.* Cambridge, MA: Harvard University Press.

Yalom, I. D. (1995). *The theory and practice of group psychotherapy* (4th ed.). New York: Basic Books.

Chapter 20
In the Company of Others: How Groups of Social Work Students Helped Me Become a Better Social Worker

by Christopher M. Sims, MSW, LCSW

To call it sobbing wouldn't be right. But it was crying that spoke to an intensely personal pain and conveyed a real sense of hurt and powerlessness. As the young woman's story ended, other students told her how they could relate. Their own tearful stories tumbled out, about the death of clients, about working with parents who continue to abuse their kids, about a client they cared for more than they thought they would—about those collective experiences when we, practitioners of social work, throw our hearts into the too often painful predicaments of client life.

I don't think I was ever asked about teaching a field class for MSW students. Instead, my mentor (and Jedi master of all things social work), who had been supervising me, suggested I might do a good job. My immediate response was disbelief: "Who did she mistake me for?" It was my experience that people who led such groups knew what they were talking about. If she thought I was one of those people, she was sorely mistaken.

I thought about me leading a group of eager social work students through their field experiences. I thought of their expectant faces looking to me as if I had something to offer. This was accompanied by something akin to terror. I was certain that in taking the role, I would finally be exposed for the unknowing fraud I secretly knew myself to be.

Still, through my work with incredible social workers, clients, and having received superb supervision, I had learned that feelings of not knowing what to say or how to react or how to handle certain situations in this work are normal. It had taken me several years to acknowledge this "not knowing," and resultant sense of fear, into my personal experience of professional practice. (I admit that these same fears continue to badger me almost every day in sometimes small, sometimes big ways.) The desire to share this truth with budding professionals outweighed the risks of presenting myself as a sub-par professional or under-qualified instructor. I wanted to let these early practitioners know that their experiences were okay—even the experiences that left them, at times, feeling hurt.

Despite months of recurrent nightmares and panic about accepting the role, the first day of my field group arrived as scheduled. Second year MSW students began to fill the room, until twelve or so were sitting in a circle. My rapidly rising panic worsened as they opened notebooks and computers, as if I was going to tell them something worthy of writing down!

My first words to that initial group of promising MSWs were this: "Put your notebooks and computers away—this is not going to be that kind of class."

As I think of those words now, I'm not sure if they were more inspired by my desire to run a process focused group, or if they got me off the hook of having to tell them something worth recording. However, those familiar feelings of being "found out" were tempered by my belief in what I was trying to accomplish. I felt that by offering an environment where we were able to talk about what it's like to practice real-life social work and all that came with it, we as a group could move beyond the pretense and insecurities that don't serve practitioners, the clients, or the profession in any helpful way.

As we started, I discussed my own experiences as a social worker in the field and how they hurt, or provoked feelings of incompetence, or inspired me, or made me feel I was practicing in the exact right field, or made me absolutely certain I had chosen the wrong field. I told them that I feel all those things, sometimes in the same day. I let them know that my intention was to set up these field class groups to provide a place to talk about what it's like to be a social worker, balancing the needs of the client, the needs of the agency, and the needs of self (a juggling act that I have come to recognize as an extreme challenge for even the most seasoned and competent of those in the profession).

It took time. Many of the first sessions included a lot of phrases from group members, like "everything is going great," or "I feel so lucky because I don't have any problems." But slowly, our group participants began to trust one another in incremental ways. This was evidenced most often through humor—a student sharing a time that she had performed disastrously on a paperwork task or another who had become comically frightened as he conducted his first clinical session.

I credit some of these opening episodes of trust to sharing my own experiences and modeling how they had challenged me professionally and personally. Others seemed to find familiarity in the stories of my own practice and were supported by the group as they timidly shared their similar experiences in the field.

Eventually, some brave souls began to discuss their own challenges in practice with the group on their own, in earnest and with deep sincerity. In these stories they admitted to places of vulnerability and times they felt professionally or personally inadequate.

I always admired the courage of these first participants. In my experience, it often feels particularly important to seem like we are capable and competent to not just do good work, but able to do the kind of work that would set us apart as exemplary. These first heroes of our groups would present a case or experience and admit they had come to a place of not knowing and professional and/or personal uncertainty. These courageous acts of sharing fly in the face of fears that promote feelings of insecurity and incompetence and threaten to suggest a persona of someone who clearly does not belong. But the group protected these pioneers by thanking them for their stories, or better, relating their own similar experiences.

Early in our group process, these first tentative steps of admitting to self and others how taxing and challenging this work really is, generated group responses that offered simple and concrete solutions and advice. Fears of hearing stories of abuse, concerns of working with a client who faces dangerous challenge, or the powerlessness to change clients the way that the students thought they should be changed were likely answered with pragmatic tips for how to manipulate the involved systems in an effort to simply "fix" the issue presented. Although at times this was appropriate—when related to safety and confidentiality, for instance—at other times, it seemed to me that such advice giving was more about the insecurities or fears of the person giving the advice than what was actually being presented.

Eventually, as trust was fortified through the sharing of our experiences, those stories of pain and powerlessness seemed to be received by students more with recognition than with efforts of resolution. More and more often, those not quite sobbing stories were reciprocated by similar experiences from others in class. The result of this developing membership was the acknowledgment and reverence for the human part of our work that exists outside of a classroom, government agency, or any outcome measures. What was revealed over and over is just how hard this work is. With each discussion, everyone in the group knew this work more intimately, because we all could recognize the feelings and aspects of each incident of every story shared. Often they were feelings we in the group had assumed were unique to us in our practice.

Not every class was able to get to these tender and honest places. And as I write, I think about those classes in particular, and feel sorry that we somehow missed out. I find myself thinking, "I wish I could have...," but to think like that devalues the influence and needs of the other members of the group. That puts my own ambitions ahead of the group, and that wouldn't be fair to any of us who contributed to the whole. No matter how much I would have liked to create an environment that included lots of honest dialogue on a consistent basis, there were groups that just wouldn't, or couldn't, let that happen. Instead of focusing on those initial feelings of regret that the group had not developed in the way I had hoped, I work to believe that the students in the group got what they needed.

No matter the processes or depth of these groups, I cared about each member. All of them. After all, they were choosing to dedicate themselves to a profession that demands heroic effort and self-sacrifice other professions could not imagine. At the end of each academic year when our classes ended, I had this urge to keep working with my groups. I had the recurrent thought that I should give the members my home number. That way, they could call me in case they needed me to normalize or validate their experience. But those feelings say more about me than them.

Thinking back, I have such a deep appreciation for those "not quite sobbing" stories and for those who responded "me, too." Not only were those gifts to each group member, including me, but it also reminded us all of just how hard this work is and the sublime feelings that are often a part of it. Even more, it reminded me of the fact that it is an honor to do this work. I am certain that the human experiences shared in those groups will remain some of the true treasures of my practice.

Think About It

1.   What specific group aspects would be required for you to participate in honest conversations related to the challenging aspects of social work practice?

2. What might be the benefits and/or detriments to discussing aspects of our professional experience in a group instead of one-on-one?

Additional Reading

Grobman, L. M. (2012). *Days in the lives of social workers: 58 professionals tell "real-life" stories from social work practice.* Harrisburg, PA: White Hat Communications.

Peck, S. M. (2003). *The road less traveled, 25th anniversary edition: A new psychology of love, traditional values and spiritual growth.* New York: Touchstone.

Pipher, M. (2005). *Letters to a young therapist.* New York: Basic Books.

Chapter 21

An Intergenerational Group Experience for Social Work Students

IIIIIIIIIIIIIIIIIIIIIIIIIIIIIIIIIIIIIIIIIIIIIIIIIIIIIIIIIIIIIIIIIIIIIIIIIIIIIIIIIIIIIIIIIIIIIIIIIIIIIIIIIIIIIIIIIIIIIIIIIIIIIIIIIIIIIIIIIIIIIIIIIIIIIIII

by Rochelle E. Rottenberg, MSW, LISW

For the past 12 years, I have taught an elective course for BSW and MSW students called "Working with Older Adults and their Families" at St. Catherine University and the University of St. Thomas. The course involves both experiential learning and lectures by speakers from the community who are currently involved in direct gerontological practice. The major take-away lessons from the course relate to changing our attitudes about aging. This is accomplished in a variety of ways, such as asking students to describe what an 80-year-old person is like and then asking them what they will be like at 80, or asking students to bring in birthday cards and then helping them realize how ageist most of them are. The students have to journal after each class, and these journals provide an opportunity for them to make sense out of each new idea they hear or read about and any new experiences or reactions they have in class. Several journals are read aloud each week, so the writers' classmates will recognize how what the writers said the week before in class may have influenced them or, perhaps, how each of them picks up on different ideas or concepts. By sharing these "directive" personal journals every week, the students begin to feel connected to one another regarding their learning experience and the exploration of topics on aging.

The course syllabus defines directive journaling as follows:

The purpose of each assignment is to integrate the readings, class discussion, and speaker's and students' personal and professional experience. After each class, students will incorporate the topic at hand; their reading assignments; points made in class by other

149

students, teacher, and guest speakers; films; etc. with their own reactions and thoughts about what was said or not said. What were students' further questions? We will spend the first half hour of class on our journals every week. They will be collected weekly and reviewed with regard to class themes and concerns. Students should be prepared to share their journal writings with the class.

The most meaningful and influential component of the class is the "Mentoring Project." The purpose of this assignment is to introduce students to a unique older person with whom they will share life experiences. Each student is matched with an older adult mentor (expert in aging), and he or she is expected to meet with the mentor twice during the semester and include him or her in the student's journal writing. A community round-table discussion near the end of the semester includes the mentors, who are invited to join the class. As the discussion date approaches, the class decides on the topics for discussion.

I have long-time contacts at Little Brothers, Friends of the Elderly, and the Jewish Community Center's Adult program, so I can recruit older adult mentors for each of my students (15 this year). The older adults ranged in age from 65 to 85; some of them have chosen to participate since the inception of this course in 2000. During the 2011 academic year, several of the mentors were older adults of color, and there was a mix in terms of socio-economic status and educational background. The majority of this student cohort were Caucasian, but several students were of Asian ethnicity, and one student was Brazilian.

The round-table intergenerational discussion occurs in the tenth week of class. This allows for students to have the time and opportunity to meet with their mentors, as well as to feel comfortable with their peers in the class. I ask the students whether they want to select their mentors based on gender or age. Usually, they just want to pick a name from "a hat," and this year the matches were arbitrary. We usually come up with a list of questions that could be asked of their mentors such as: *What helps you through difficult times? What is one of your favorite memories? Have you ever experienced discrimination? What is life like for you now? What would you like to change about your life or the world?* Having selected the questions and discussing them in class helps the students feel less anxious about the first meeting with their mentors. However, the students rarely do use these questions, and what I have been told time and again, this year being no exception, is that when students and mentors first meet, it feels like they have known each other for a while and that they just talk, get to know one another, and realize after two hours that the time has flown by. These intergenerational connections are powerful, and they never feel like a classroom assignment.

The Pre-Group Planning Stage

Like any good group worker, I spend time planning our one-session intergenerational discussion. I keep in mind that the beginnings, middles, and endings all have to be included in a two-hour class period. The easiest part to plan for is the food. The students and I supply all the food, dividing the meal into appetizers, main dishes, and desserts (like the beginnings, middles, and endings). Someone has to bring drinks and someone else breads. We talk about our agenda for the day, as our one session is really a psychoeducational group. We decide to follow some of what was done in the past, such as having each person introduce his or her partner and tell one or two interesting facts or stories about the partner. This offers structure and a way to put people at ease. The students then decide the topics that they want to discuss. This year's topics were:

- What motivates and inspires you?
- What changes in technology have had the most impact on your life?
- What do the mentors appreciate about the students' generation, and how does it compare to their generation?
- What advice would the mentors give social workers working with older adults?

Our agenda will be typed and copied for each student and mentor, and we decide to put a flower at each place where the mentors will sit.

The Day of the Single-Session Round Table Discussion Group

I come early that day to do the set-up, and several students arrive early to help. We have tables pushed together with seating for 30. I bring tablecloths, flowers to put at each mentor's place, and extra flowers for the table to help soften the classroom environment. There is an agenda at each person's place, so they will know what topics will be discussed. As class time draws near, students arrive with their mentors, and the others wait anxiously by the entrance for them to arrive. Students add to the buffet dinner as they come in, and the tables are overflowing with homemade and store-bought foods. We are finally ready to start with our introductions. Unfortunately, two mentors don't show up—one has forgotten, and the other could not locate the building (lessons learned).

I start by thanking everyone and making a statement about what it means to be a mentor and the importance of having different generations come together to share points of view in an intergenerational dialogue. The introductions somehow turn out to validate each other (mutual aid), so that people begin joking and laughing. The ice has been broken, and the rest of the conversation flows easily. We talk about each of the topics agreed upon earlier and share experiences, stories, and jokes. Our purpose has been established, and we have a rich and meaningful conversation with enough structure, but also with enough flexibility, to allow for individual stories and responses.

I do some summarizing of common themes, and for the ending, I employ the ritual of a large cord of ribbon that goes all around the room with each person holding onto a section of it. Then I ask everyone what they will take away from this mentoring project, and I walk around the room as people acknowledge making a new friend, having hope for the future, and so forth. I cut a piece of the ribbon off, and each mentor or mentee ties it on the partner's wrist—a symbolic gesture. We were all one entity for a short time, and as we go our separate ways, we take a piece of the experience with us.

The students write about the experience in their journals. The following are a few examples:

> *It felt like both generations walked away with a special experience, because everyone got the chance to talk and explain their perspective. I really heard what the older adults said about how I could be the most effective social worker when working with the elderly. I recall certain advice like "listen with a third ear," "treat others with respect and dignity," "do not give up even if a person gives you a hard time," and "take time to hear a person's story." What wonderful advice.*

> *Besides just sharing wisdom, life experiences, and lessons, there was a lot of sharing cultures. I am certain that the word used most often throughout the night was "inspire." I am confident that all students felt inspired by their mentors and by hearing from the other mentors in the room.*

The project allows us to create a sense of community with our fellow students and older adult mentors. Relationships are built, and bonds are strengthened between the young and old. In this process we create a greater sense of community with each other and with those around us.

Overall, I felt privileged to sit in the presence of so much wisdom and to hear these individuals' stories and experiences. Pipher (1999) writes that much valuable learning comes from our elders if we take the time to receive it, and this experience taught me that this is very true. I will never forget it, and I plan to take more time to ask my own grandparents about their lives, so that I may learn from them, as well.

In conclusion, this was a wonderful group experience in terms of validating and appreciating one another and learning what each generation can offer to the other if only people have the opportunity to spend some time together. It also speaks to any good group opportunity, as Helen Northen says in her book *Social Work With Groups:*

We are all parts of dynamic interacting systems of people who influence and are influenced by each other.

Think About It

1. If you are a practicing social worker or a social work student in field placement, how could you add an intergenerational component to the work that you are already doing?

2. What other topics would you want to discuss during an intergenerational dialogue?

3. How could social work students have more exposure to older adults in their undergraduate and graduate studies?

4. How can we better utilize our aging population?

Additional reading

Erikson, E. H., Erikson, J. M., & Kivnick, H. (1986). *Vital involvement in old age.* New York: W.W. Norton.

Kivnick, H. Q., Stoffel, S., & Hanlon, D. (2003). Eloise's tale: Vital involvement, occupation, and story. *Generations, 27* (3), 39-43.

Kurland, R., & Salmon, R. (1998). *Teaching a methods course in social work with groups.* Alexandria, VA: Council on Social Work Education.

Pipher, M. (1999). *Another country, navigating the emotional terrain of our elders.* New York: Riverhead Books.

Chapter 22

Group Work in a Homeless Shelter

IIIIIIIIIIIIIIIIIIIIIIIIIIIIIIIIIIIIIIIIIIIIIIIIIIIIIIIIIIIIIIIIIIIIIIIIIIIIIIIIIIIIIIIIIIIIIIIIIIIIIIIIIIIIIIIIIIIIIIIIIIIIIIIIIII

by Mitchell Rosenwald, Ph.D., LCSW

I have always wanted to "do something" about the issue of homelessness, and like many of us, I was only aware of homeless people based on what we see in the media or what we see when a homeless person approaches us asking for money. In the past year and a half or so, I decided to volunteer at a local homeless shelter in South Florida and facilitate a weekly group there. Because I have a flexible schedule as a social work faculty member, I am able to facilitate this group on Wednesdays for approximately an hour. This also keeps me updated on practice, which is important for me and for my students.

Let me describe how I became connected to the shelter in the first place. I did not know anyone who worked at any homeless shelters, so I called the county information line to see if they could use volunteers at homeless shelters. This did not prove to be too useful, as I ended up in a maze of bureaucracy. Initially, I actually gave up trying to help, but randomly, I happened to meet the volunteer coordinator of the homeless shelter at a social function. Shortly thereafter, I was volunteering and soon providing group facilitation. (Please note that if I had to reach out again—and this is my advice to others—I would have directly shown up at the homeless shelter in person and asked to speak to the volunteer coordinator.) I spoke to the social worker in charge of providing mental health services, including group services. He said I could facilitate a group if I wanted and gave me a lot of leeway in how to conduct it.

I thought about what was the best type of group to facilitate. I certainly thought support would be the most valuable, because those touched by homelessness often have little support. A person who is homeless may not have much family support. They certainly do not have much, if any, money, and their self-esteem "takes a dive," because to be homeless in America is the opposite of the American dream of success, in which everyone can provide a home for themselves. Therefore, I thought support was an important function for the group, and knowing the importance of mutual aid in groups, I knew that the group would help support each other and provide its members with resources. As the group began, I also applied a therapy function to the group. Specifically, I draw on aspects of narrative therapy, in which members share how they see their "old" lives and how they envision the "new" lives they want to lead. After all, I typically mention that few people, when they are children, think they will be homeless as adults.

Now let me describe the composition and then how the group is run. Once I arrive, one of the staff members typically has between two and 15 people waiting for the group. The number varies based on the census of new members and how many have attended other groups that week. The people, who are all adults, vary in gender, race, age, sexual orientation, nationality, education, and physical/ mental health status. The group is required for people when they first attend the shelter. (Shelter residents typically stay for about two and half months, and they need to attend a certain number of groups to earn privileges that take them to the next "level," which allows them to leave the shelter to attend job interviews.) However, I sometimes share with group members that while the rules "require" their attendance, this attendance fundamentally is voluntary, because no one is forcing them to stay in the shelter. In this way, I am trying to empower the group members to realize that they have chosen to come to a shelter and, therefore, agree to the requirements of staying. This is said in the context that they know a number of people who decide not to come to the shelter (their nods affirm this statement), and so this statement hopefully resonates with members. Finally, because members might come and go—they might attend different groups the following week or they might violate a rule (such as using alcohol or other drugs) that requires them to leave the shelter—I approach each group as a single session group. That is, each time I facilitate the group, although a few faces might be familiar, the group is largely new.

I begin the session by describing the purpose of the group—to identify what brought the group members to homelessness as well as to identify how they can successfully leave homelessness. After getting a collective buy-in from members, which is verbal contracting, I state the ground rules of mutual respect and confidentiality (and its limits). Then I facilitate a "round robin" segment in which members check in by sharing their name, how long they have been at the shelter, and what brings them to the shelter. The reasons certainly vary, but members have shared any combination of the recession, medical issues, mental health issues, incarceration, substance abuse, domestic violence, and family issues among the reasons associated with their losing a place to stay (and often losing their incomes, as well).

It is in the main work of this group (and keep in mind that I need to approach this as a single session group) that I try to facilitate not only mutual aid but apply narrative therapy concepts in which members can identify their "old" life stories or narratives that led them to becoming homeless, as well as their "new" life stories that they are attempting to live, or would like to live, in which their lives are more stable. I encourage members to ask questions, make observations, and even share drawings (of their stories) with each other. In fact, I observe that the mutual aid is often the catalyst that helps members feel more confident in the new stories they would like to live. For example, someone who states her drug addiction was the cause of her homelessness tries to envision a new story of how sobriety is the key to more stability in her life. Or, as another example, a member who has been laid off because of a medical disability and has low self-esteem might have a goal to feel pride in himself.

I have been heartened by facilitating the group. Still, it is not without its challenges. For example, I wish I could have a closed group for 10 weeks, so I could really get in-depth and help members over time. Also, when individuals leave the group (and the shelter for that matter), I am unsure how they are doing and how their long-term success is. This is an important question for research. Finally, although I prefer to be very non-authoritarian in a group setting, I find that I need to be more structured than is my ideal style. This is because the group is a single session group, and I need to quickly provide structure as well as components of narrative therapy.

What has also been confirmed for me is that homeless people are just that—people, who typically are in need of great support, and who need reminders of their dignity, which has often been trampled on and cast aside. And while their personal responsibility varies for why they are homeless, there are also structural factors and, therefore, policy implications for why they are homeless. For example, a few members of the group have had major health issues and have had to wait for a very long time for their Social Security Disability benefits to start. As such, they have not had the income to afford housing, and they end up homeless. Additionally, we are all familiar with the Great Recession that began several years ago—this macro problem has had direct responsibility for some people losing their homes and needing the shelter's services.

In conclusion, I hope this narrative of my work with a group for homeless individuals gives you not only information but a perspective that helps you understand more about people who are homeless, their dignity, and the role of group work in helping them. If you have the time, consider facilitating a group for this population. It does not take much time per week, but the time you do provide helps remind people that they are indeed worthy of their humanity as human beings, rather than common stereotypes full of stigma. You can inspire people by facilitating group work with this population, and that is one of the best rewards of all.

Think About It

1. How might group work help people who are experiencing homelessness?

2. If you were the facilitator of this group, would you want to follow up with individuals who are homeless once they left the shelter? How would you do this?

3. View the two Web sites provided under Resources. What are the important factors to consider when working with the homeless population?

Additional Readings/Resources

Cohen, M. B. & Mullender, A. (2006). The personal in the political: Exploring the group work continuum from individual to social change goals. *Social Work With Groups, 28* (1/2), 187-204.

Plasse, B. R. (2002). A stress reduction and self-care group for homeless and addicted women: Meditation, relaxation and cognitive methods. *Social Work With Groups, 24* (3), 117-133.

Racine, G., & Sevigny, O. (2001). Changing the rules: A board game lets homeless women tell their stories. *Social Work With Groups, 23* (4), 25-38.

Resources

National Alliance to End Homelessness: *http://www.endhomeless-ness.org/*

National Coalition for the Homeless: *http://www.nationalhomeless.org/*

Chapter 23

The Power of Men's Stories: Facilitating Men's Changes in Domestic Abuse

IIIIIIIIIIIIIIIIIIIIIIIIIIIIIIIIIIIIIIIIIIIIIIIIIIIIIIIIIIIIIIIIIIIIIIIIIIIIIIIIIIIIIIIIIIIIIIIIIIIIIIIIIIIIIIIIIIIIIIIIIIIIIIIIIIIII

by Michael G. Chovanec, Ph.D., LICSW

At our weekly group session, comprised of men who have been working on examining their abusive behavior, I ask for volunteers in the group to see who would like to present one of their completed tasks. John reluctantly agrees. John has been in the group for over a month. He was initially court-ordered into the program after an argument with his girlfriend escalated to him "reaching" for her neck. She became frightened and called the police. Of all the group members, he is most unhappy about being in the group. Acknowledging that he should not have grabbed his girlfriend's neck, and admitting to feeling bad about what he did, he states he wants to move on and doesn't think he needs the group. He claims, "I'll never do that again." His anger is easy to read and he has a glare when he gets upset in group that keeps people at a distance. But to his credit, this is the first task he has volunteered to present.

John: Yes, I guess I can go. I have the control plan. (He passes out copies of his task to the other group members, including the facilitator.)

Facilitator: Why don't you give us an example of getting to the high end of your anger scale.

John: Well, I found out that my girlfriend had stolen my mother's charge card. I just happened to see a billing notice from the credit card company that listed a large amount of women's lingerie charged to my mother's account.

Facilitator: Can you tell us your emotional cues?

161

John: I felt betrayed.

Facilitator: What else? (I pass a feeling chart to him for his review.)

John: (Gives me the "glare.") I don't know. I feel bad enough about the incident. Why do I have to explore every gory detail? I don't even know these guys (in the group) or you.

Another group member: Yeah, but we are all in the same boat.

Facilitator: I encourage men to identify a variety of feelings. Having you identify and track feelings triggered by a given incident can help make it less likely you will act on those feelings in the future.

John: What degrees do you have anyway? Why should I believe you?

Facilitator: (Finding myself reacting to his questions) I have a bachelor's, master's, and a Ph.D. in social work, but the number of degrees won't help you trust me.

John: I feel you are just trying to put words in my mouth.

Another veteran group member jumps in: I hear him asking you, not telling you how you feel.

John: Okay, (taking the feeling chart) I was feeling hurt, betrayed, and full of rage. How dare she do that to my mother!

Facilitator: Good job. Now I've got a better understanding of what was going on for you at that time.

This drama plays out regularly as men who are abusive struggle to take responsibility for their actions and make efforts to change. And to think I stumbled on this vocation more than twenty years ago, when I volunteered to fill in for a co-worker who had started a domestic abuse group and then left the agency! Although I had no experience with this client population starting out, my courage, curiosity, and persistence—along with past experience in working with groups and families—has helped.

I facilitate an 18-week psychoeducational open-ended domestic abuse group for up to ten men. Most of the men are court-ordered. The presenting problem that men enter the program with is that they have lost control of their anger with their partners, their children, and/or others. I facilitate a discussion with the men on educational materials presented in the first half of a two-hour group, examining cues that trigger one's anger, assertiveness and empathy skills, communication skills that aid in problem solving, and gender power differences. In the second half of group sessions, the men demonstrate these skills through a series of required tasks they present in group.

The previous example with John represents the kind of challenge men often present when they enter a program. Facilitators need to be able to respond rather than react to the anger men initially present in group. As a facilitator, I needed to find a way to respond to John's glare that did not duplicate the abuse he experienced growing up. This takes an ability to separate out the abusive acts from who these men are as individuals. John's glare was not a personal attack. It was a way to protect himself. I admired his loyalty to his mother and his effort to make a better life for himself. However, for me to "see" these strengths and respond without reacting, I needed a supportive learning environment.

I have been fortunate to have a collection of co-workers, supervisors, and family who have provided support over the years. The context of my work environment aids in my learning. I have transitioned from working full time in a mental health setting to associate professor at a local university, as I continue to facilitate the group. My teaching and scholarship allow me to examine my work from a variety of perspectives and share my learning with my students.

Interestingly, John's anger—once he began trusting me—was channeled into his efforts to change, and he became an active group member. The challenge and mutual aid group members provided John were keys to the changes he made. They listened to his story and directly challenged him to change, as in the example above, as well as indirectly by discussing changes they were attempting to make.

When the men returned from break, we finished up John's task, which flowed much more easily after he took the risk to share more of his feelings. The next person up for a group task was Bob. Bob is a soft spoken man in his 30s who has been in the group for the past two months. He is attentive in the group discussions but remains relatively quiet. He had been a fighter throughout his earlier life and mentioned how he had grown tired of the struggle and wanted to change, now that he was raising a family. Bob shared that he had gotten into an argument with his younger brother at home when he was 20 years old. The argument escalated quickly, with Bob shooting a gun and the bullet barely missing his brother. Bob was charged with assault with a deadly weapon and sentenced to five years in prison. Bob expressed how bad he felt about the incident, yet he had never discussed the incident with his brother. His brother was the first to see him when he was released from prison, and they now spend a lot of time together. Yet, Bob thinks about the shooting incident and is fearful about bringing this topic up with his brother. He decides he wants to use this issue for his role-play exercise in group.

During this exercise, the group member chooses a potential conflict in his life he would like to resolve. In the past, men have chosen a variety of situations for the role-play, including conflict with ex-partners, bosses, and family members. Group members are split into two groups, one helping the group member carry out his part of the role-play and the other group helping me to offer ideas on what challenging things the other person might say. My goal as facilitator is to provide a challenging partner who tests the group member's ability to regulate himself without getting verbally abusive. In this case, Bob was anticipating his brother being upset with him, and the challenge was about how he could bring up something he had much shame about.

Facilitator: So, how do you want to set up the conversation with your brother?

Bob: I will go over to his house. He is usually in the garage working on his car.

Facilitator: Okay, let's start the role-play there.

Bob: Jim, there is something I have been thinking a lot about lately, and I would like to talk to you about it.

Facilitator (playing Jim): What's up?

Bob: Well, lately I have been thinking a lot about the shooting incident that got me in prison. I keep thinking about how I almost killed you.

Facilitator (playing Jim): No big deal. Bob, why don't you hand me that tool over there. (Trying to intentionally avoid the conversation.)

Bob (getting quiet): Okay.

Group member (offering a suggestion): Bob, tell him it is a big deal to you.

Bob: But it was a big deal to me. I haven't stopped thinking about it since it happened. I would play it over and over in my head while I was in jail. I can't believe how stupid I was. I just wanted you to know how sorry I am about what I did.

Facilitator (Breaking out of role-play): Great job, Bob. You came across very clear and didn't allow your brother to re-direct the conversation. Do any group members have any reactions or comments about the role-play?

The group members were very supportive of Bob and what he was trying to do. Most of the group members thought his brother would be relieved that Bob had brought up the shooting incident and predicted he would be receptive to Bob's effort to discuss it. I asked how confident he was that he could carry out the conversation with his brother on a one to ten scale. He said eight. The group and I wished him luck, and we ended the session.

Bob came back to the group a week later looking lighter and relieved. He reported back that he had been successful, and that he felt a huge weight had been lifted off his shoulders. His brother was receptive to his apology, mentioning how he also had felt bad about the incident and how this one argument 10 years earlier had led to Bob being taken away from the family and how much he missed him while he was away. He said he had forgiven him a long time ago, although he had never shared this with Bob before.

This example articulates the power of shame in clients' lives. Shame is an internal process of feeling bad that prevents one from learning or seeking help from others. The group provides an opportunity for men to gain the courage, with the help of other group members, to face their shame and strengthen their relationships with those significant in their lives. Both men in the above case examples felt shame about their earlier actions. John's shame made it difficult for him to discuss his thoughts and feelings around the abusive incident. Bob carried his shame for 10 years and now had the courage to face his shame in group. A group facilitator working in domestic abuse needs to be sensitive to the shame men bring with them to group. This includes the shame of actions they have committed, as well as shame attached to the label of "abusive" man.

Over the years, I have experienced strong reactions from others when they find out I facilitate a domestic abuse group. They usually either tell me about a friend of theirs who has been abusive to a partner or they ask how I can work with "those" people. My response is that I enjoy the challenge of working with "those people" and try to remember that they were all babies once—and that with support and respectful challenge, they can make changes. I have been honored to be witness to these men's efforts to change, observing the support and challenge group members provide each other. Men telling their stories of efforts to change are powerful ways of engaging other group members in the change process. These stories also tap my passion as I continue to learn how to assist these men in their life journeys.

Think About It

1. How does mutual aid affect men's efforts to change?
2. How might shame present itself in domestic abuse group work?
3. What facilitator characteristics are useful in conducting groups with abusive men?

Resources

Adams, D. (2003). Treatment programs for batterers. *Clinics in Family Practice, 5* (1), pp. 159-176.

Chovanec, M. (2009). *Work with men in domestic abuse treatment* (Chapter 12). In *Strategies for Work with Involuntary Clients* (2nd Ed.). New York: Columbia University Press.

Stefanakis, H. (2008). Caring and compassion when working with offenders of crime and violence. *Violence and Victims, 23* (5), 652-661.

Chapter 24

A Focus on Relational Needs: Supporting Group Work Goals With Mandated Clients

IIIIIIIIIIIIIIIIIIIIIIIIIIIIIIIIIIIIIIIIIIIIIIIIIIIIIIIIIIIIIIIIIIIIIIIIIIIIIIIIIIIIIIIIIIIIIIIIIIIIIIIIIIIIIIIIIIIIIIIII

by Tom Caplan, MSW

As director and supervisor of the McGill Domestic Violence Clinic, I am required to fill in for one of my interns or facilitators from time to time. I also run one of the men's treatment groups during the summer months or between terms. I have been involved with the McGill Domestic Violence Clinic for more than 25 years. This clinic is a state-of-the-art facility for service provision and student training. It provides counseling on issues related to all forms of violence in intimate relationships and the effect such violence has on families and their social networks. Since 1975, the clinic has trained graduate students from the disciplines of social work, counseling, and psychology, providing them with expertise in individual, couple, family, and group therapy using the most up-to-date intervention strategies. The clinic offers treatment to men who perpetrate the abuse, as well as support for the women survivors. Group work is the central focus of the clinic, and graduate student interns do clinical work with men, women, and when appropriate, their partners or families. Even though this recollection occurred a long time ago, I vividly remember it to this day.

About 20 years ago, in my early days at the McGill Domestic Violence Clinic, I stepped in to facilitate a men's group when one of my students, who was supposed to have run the group that day, was unable to do so. Supervision is done in a team and all sessions are videotaped and reviewed during the supervision meetings. As a result, I was already acquainted with most of the men and with their presenting issues. At that time, I was becoming interested in the notion of what I considered to be "universal themes"— themes that seemed to be in common with group members as a whole, or as a cluster within the group. In my clinical experience, thus far, generalizing these themes to the group had proven to be a method that was useful in helping clients to form links with each other and increase the potential for discussion and self-disclosure during the group's "working phase." These themes were simply put and included concepts such as *feeling criticized, getting closer, ability to trust,* and *taking responsibility.* These were themes that were often expressed in the narratives of various members of these groups and could be easily understood by those in attendance, whether or not they were specifically relevant to all participants. In other words, even if a client did not have specific issues with trusting others, he could still understand conceptually someone who did.

In the previous week, my group work intern had had some difficulty in keeping the group members focused on the task at hand. Much of the group was spent with "system bashing" or "yes buts." As I walked down the hall to the group room feeling some-what apprehensive as to what extent I would be challenged this week, I remember thinking: "Time to make the donuts" ("here we go again"). On this day, I felt an exceptional pressure to keep the group "on track," as well as demonstrate to my students what good group work is all about.

I began the group with my usual injunction: "Please sign in by telling the group how things have been going for you since we last met with regard to the problem that brings you here." Matt, one of the more confident group members, began by saying that his wife was more encouraged now that he was coming to the group, even though she still seemed quite distant. I responded that it seemed positive that he felt he was gaining his partner's trust, but that there seemed to be a great deal more work to be done to help her to come closer. Petrov, the next in turn, continued by saying, "It's really annoying to always be walking on eggshells. Any wrong move and I'm back here again." We continued around the circle until we arrived at Etienne, who was one of the last group members to take his turn. Etienne stated that his wife never listened to him because "everything I do is either wrong or stupid." He wondered if it was worth even trying to reconcile at this point. I intervened by saying, "It's a bit scary to think that you can never get your wife's atten-tion, and when you do, it doesn't measure up." Etienne responded, "That's really not what I need...to feel like an 'idiot' all the time.... I need to feel like I count...like I'm needed."

After the sign-in was completed, I began the group discussion with an invitation to discuss some of the themes that had come up during the sign-in. I suggested that some members were feeling inadequate in the eyes of their partners, and others were feeling distrustful of, or invisible in, their relationships. An animated discussion ensued for quite some time when Lloyd suggested that his partner was all he had ever needed in a relationship—that before he "lost it," she was extremely supportive and caring. At this point, Etienne broke in exclaiming that all he ever got from his wife was ridicule and criticism, that Lloyd "was lucky to get what he needs but [he] never gets what he needs from his wife." At this point, I started to wonder why everyone was so "needy" and what was causing this neediness. With that, Fred, a client who often acted like "co-therapist" of the group, responded, "I suppose what you 'need' is to always have it your way!" At this point I prepared an intervention, expecting Etienne to "blow." Surprisingly, Etienne, looking down at the floor, responded in an almost inaudible and sad tone, saying, "All I want from her is to validate me—to feel that I can do something right. When we first got together, I felt that she looked up to me. As soon as Sara was born, I couldn't even put a diaper on her properly."

The group became silent. This was surprising. It seemed that we had all expected an angry reaction and were silenced by its absence. I used this opportunity to regain my composure and consider how to make an intervention that would connect group members to each other based on what had just been said. I hesitantly interjected: "Not being able to measure up is a bit scary to be sure, and I guess it's hard to focus on your responsibility in all this for fear of being punished." Fortunately, this seemed to energize the group. It was as if they were afraid to intrude on Etienne's thoughts and had needed permission to discuss what he had said. Jonah was the first to speak, and he began by concurring that both his wife and his boss set very high standards—that he often felt that he also "could do nothing right." Petrov added to the discussion by admitting that he had often struggled with living up to his girlfriend's "high standards," and Justin disclosed that "sometimes I have to give up trying to win my point and let my wife to do it her way."

This was a defining moment in my social work group work career. It was at this point that it suddenly became clear to me that the dysfunctional behaviors these men were displaying were attempts at getting specific needs met within the context of their relationships, and that the themes actually represented what they needed from their intimate partners. If they were able to acquire these needs more functionally, then their behaviors should change for the better. Another revelation was the fact that it seemed as though when the group worker focused on a client's needs (what he wanted from his partner) rather than on his behavior (which could predict more discomfort or shame), the participants became less defensive. The group worker's task was, therefore, to identify the various group members' needs from their narratives and generalize these to the group. The challenge for the group members was, through the mutual aid and group work process, to collaboratively look for ways in getting these needs met productively. As well, the dramatic difference in affect that Etienne portrayed (sadness vs. anger) in expressing to the group what he "needed" from his wife allowed group members to more readily "hear" what was concerning Etienne—a more useful emotion for communicating relational needs.

This was an incredible learning experience for me—a veritable epiphany. Later that week, I took my list of "universal themes" that had been used in teaching my students group and client process based interventions, to see if I could match these themes to specific client relational needs. For example, I considered that feeling marginalized or invisible in one's relationship was a need for respect, that not being able to trust was a need for loyalty, feeling inadequate or criticized was a need for competence, and so on. It also appeared evident that, even though all emotions had validity, some emotional states were more productive in relational problem-solving than others, and helping clients to access these more productive states was an adjunct to the group work facilitation challenge. Overall, defining the themes as client-specific relational needs seemed to clarify why less productive emotional states existed in clients who came into the clinic, why they were not getting what they wanted relationally from their partners, and why they were employing strategies that were only further frustrating their attempts to acquire these needs.

Think About It

1. How do you see relational needs being helpful with non-mandated clients?

2. Could you use this concept with adolescents or latency-aged children?

3. What other strategies could you integrate into this concept to further establish a mutual aid relationship?

Additional Reading

Caplan, T. (2008). *After the fall: Using the needs ABC model with couples affected by domestic violence.* In J. Hamel (Ed.), *Intimate partner and family abuse: A casebook of gender inclusive therapy* (pp. 45-58). New York: Springer Publishing Company.

Caplan, T. (2008). *Needs-ABC: A needs acquisition and behavior change model for group work and other psychotherapies.* London: Whiting & Birch.

Caplan, T. (2009). *Needs acquisition and behavior change approach.* In Gitterman, A., & Salmon, R. (Eds.). *Encyclopedia of social work with groups.* New York: Routledge, pp. 89-94.

Chapter 25
Uplifting Fathers and Strengthening Families

llllllllllllllllllllllllllllllllllllllllllllllllllllllllllllllllllllllll

by Charles C. Daniels, Jr., MSW

As a child, I witnessed my mother's struggles as a single parent as my father moved in and out of my life. Data suggest that 80% of single-parent homes are headed by women. This means that, although many women are remaining in their children's lives, many fathers are not. If we can identify the problems that are preventing them from being in their children's lives, we can find ways to help them work through those problems and remain engaged.

One day I thought about the things my father was going through that prevented him from remaining active in my life. Then I said to myself, "What if someone had been there to help him?" It might have made a tremendous difference. The goal of my work and life purpose is to provide low-income fathers with a place where they can receive support, guidance, and encouragement around fatherhood in a group setting. It doesn't take a lot of money to be a good father—what matters most is their presence.

My groups are held weekly at a community health center in Massachusetts. I facilitate these groups and provide fathers with the tools to deal with various levels of oppression, systemic and individual. The groups are not based on a specific curriculum or time frame. It is simply an open supportive group for fathers in shelters, half-way houses, re-entry programs, and the community to receive guidance around presenting issues relating to poverty, lack of resources, having a criminal record, and child support. We provide psychoeducational support and task oriented activities that are geared toward empowering fathers.

It is Wednesday night, and Isaiah Sr., a committed participant, attended the group today. He was with his girlfriend and son Isaiah Jr. It was nice seeing them on this day. The group began at its normal time. Isaiah Sr. was eager to tell the group about his experience this past week. He sat in his chair and stared each member in the face. He was a little disappointed, but he was also happy that he was able to be at the group. Isaiah Sr. explained:

> *I was recently arrested downtown. They tried to charge me with selling drugs in a school zone. I was already on probation, and this could have put me away from my family for some time. I mean, who would take care of my son if I am in jail?*

Isaiah said his arrest was featured on the local news station. Some of the fathers in the group said they had heard about it. "The news said a couple were arrested downtown for selling drugs and neglecting their child," one said. Neglect—I couldn't believe this word was being used to describe Isaiah. From my time working with him, it was evident that Isaiah would do anything he could for his son. After sharing his story with the group, Isaiah walked his girlfriend to the bus stop so she could get back to the shelter before curfew. Then he returned to the group.

Upon Isaiah's return, the group took a sudden turn. At first, we were discussing the systemic inequities that one faces in the jail system: "It is all a game. My friend told me about it. He works in a prison. They bet to see who will come back or not," "They treat you like crap," "It is a big business set up to make money off of us." Many of the men have had varied experiences within the system. I asked the group, "Do you ever think about your family when you make decisions that can alter your life?"

One of the fathers said, "Well, for me, I didn't think about anyone. I was just focused on me. I was selfish. I didn't care about how my family felt. Now I have a better outlook."

This conversation was an eye opener for me. Before assuming the meaning of what I was hearing, I repeated what I thought was being said: "So, I am hearing that being selfish is when you don't think about how your decisions will affect others." The father confirmed my interpretation to be correct.

Without support, fathers can fall through the cracks. I was honored as I watched the group support one another and provide some insight to their colleagues through mutual aid and love. Many of them appeared to relate to the comment about being selfish and unable to think about those they could potentially hurt. One father said, "It is important that we think about our children and family before making decisions that can ultimately take us out of the picture temporarily or permanently." According to the group, thinking about those who care about us somehow serves as a buffer from engaging in harmful behaviors. After the meeting, Isaiah said he really appreciated the group; "They supported me. I felt like they understood what I was going through, they got it. I felt cared for." I walked him to the bus station and put some money on his card for transportation.

In the following session, the fathers pulled together as a team and wrote letters to the President of the United States. Erin entered the room first, Mario followed, and then Ryan and Timothy. Two new fathers entered afterwards, Eddie and Alan. Isaiah did not attend this group. We began the session with a check-in and weekly update. Mario started by saying that he had a good week: "Now that I am able to send my kids some money, I see my child's mother is not giving me any problems. I'm just happy that everything is getting better and I'm able to fulfill my fatherly duties." Mario smiled as he shared. It was Erin's turn. Erin talked about his struggle to find a job last week and how he managed to find employment: "After much hard work, I found a job and now I am looking for other sources of income." The group clapped and congratulated Erin on his achievements. After the congratulatory applaud, Erin said, "I spoke to my grandchild on the phone the other day." I asked Erin what his grandson said, and he replied, "He said 'Papa.'" He smiled in silence and signaled for the next person to go.

Ryan was next: "I called my daughter, and my granddaughter who is 19 picked up the phone. She called me 'Papa,' too, and that made me feel good. My daughter wasn't there when I spoke to her, but she called me back. She thanked me for calling and told me she missed me. She asked me did I miss her, too. I told her I did, every waking moment she is missed." Eddie and Alan said they were happy to be in a group that supported fathers. The group welcomed them with open arms.

Timothy was next in line. "I am happy I can be here, you know. I have my feelings back. I was down during the week, but Mario and Erin gave me some uplifting and encouragement." Timothy said he needed that and that he was thankful for his group members. It took a lot for him to share this with the group, but he was happy he did. When Timothy was finished, I asked Erin and Mario how it felt to hear Timothy thank them. Erin looked at Timothy and said, "That's what we are supposed to do—lift one another up with support and love." Mario said, "We are here for you Timothy." At this moment, I realized how important it was for me to remain attuned to what was happening in the group. I couldn't go on without acknowledging this moment between Erin, Mario, and Timothy. It felt good to know the group was bonding when they were not with me throughout the week.

Last year, I sent an invite to the President asking him to participate in a summit/resource fair that would be planned for fathers. His staff responded by saying they would contact me closer to the day of the event with a response. I thought about my work with the fathers and decided to send a follow-up invite. I asked the fathers if they would like to write a letter sharing their experiences as fathers in America. They responded unanimously. They all wanted to share their stories.

Afterwards, I asked, "How can one actively combat the problems they face without recognizing the systems that oppress them?" They shared their beliefs about the stipulations a criminal record has in the life of a father, "If you commit a crime, they take away all your rights. This in turn makes it hard for one to get a decent job, make a living for his family, and feel good about it when he can." They referenced Isaiah's situation as an example of what a father can go through when dealing with a system that appears not to support fathers. We spoke about the welfare system and how it required the father to be absent from the household in order for the mother to receive assistance. There are many systemic barriers that separate them from their families and make them feel less than the potential they possess. For the fathers sitting in this room, I observed firsthand how those systems affect them emotionally, mentally, and physically.

The group used the meeting time to write their letters. Some of the fathers needed help with spelling and sentence structure. The group worked together to make sure everyone had adequate assistance when needed. Many of the fathers chose to participate and write a letter despite feeling they would be judged if they couldn't write a complete sentence or spell a word correctly. They stepped outside of their comfort zones and wrote anyway. What these men did as a group on this day was remarkable. The President will hear their stories of struggle, resilience, and strength. We shared this moment together. I'll never forget it. They felt good about themselves when they submitted the letters, like they accomplished something great. They should be, because they did.

After submitting the letters, each one of them wanted a copy. I rushed to my office to photocopy their letters. The smiles on their faces were priceless. Towards the end of the group, Eddie said, "I accomplished something big." This was Eddie's first meeting. The members in the group patted him on the back and came together to form a group hug. I stared in admiration, taking in this moment one breath at a time. Even if the President does not respond to their stories, the fact that they were able to write a letter to the holder of the highest office in the land about their struggles as fathers speaks volumes about their character.

It has been transformational watching these fathers rise above their past experiences of struggle and degradation. It was clear that they did this for themselves and for fathers like Isaiah. Those we serve can effect change in the world and their communities by using their stories as vehicles to promote change. It should be our responsibility to help them bring those stories to life.

Think About It

1. What challenges might you need to consider when using group work as a form of advocacy?

2. How can group work be used to help fathers recognize their importance in their children's lives?

3. Check out the National Responsible Fatherhood Clearinghouse Web site and print out a resource to use in your work that could challenge the stereotype held against non-residing fathers.

Chapter 26

The Group Who Holds the Group: Supervision as a Critical Component in a Group With Infants Affected by Family Violence

‖‖

by Wendy Bunston, BSW, MaFT, GCertOrgDyn, GDipInfMH

After many years of developing and running a wide range of therapeutic group work interventions for children and families affected by mental health issues, I shifted my focus to working with infants, specifically those who had been affected by family violence. This has largely involved infants and their mothers, and more recently a new group work intervention for men who have participated in men's behavior change programs and their infants. This work is both challenging and confronting. The aim is to create a therapeutic space where the safety of the infant is paramount while exploring the complexity of the attachment between the infant and caregiver.

Within the infant/mother group, issues such as the mothers' own ambivalence toward their infants, their own aggression and that of their infants, the circumstances of the infant's conception, the violence within the couple relationship, and the feelings of the mother toward the father of the infants are considered. It is a therapeutic space in which we are enormously interested in and curious about the infants, their minds, and how they experience the world, their caregivers, and others. This work informed our more recent work with fathers who had been identified as perpetrators of violence within their families, who had committed to addressing their behaviors through treatment, and who were interested in creating different relational experiences with their infants. As with many of the mothers attending our groups, these fathers had largely experienced poor relational experiences within their own early childhood. Exploring their relationships with their own fathers and how this informed their perception of what a father should and could be, while in the presence of their infants, created many opportunities for emotional self revelations among these men.

But what of the facilitators running the groups? How does it feel to sit with men who have physically assaulted their partners and even their infants? What do you offer mothers who have been so beaten by their intimate relationships that they feel unworthy of their infant's love or may resent their infant's presence? They may blame their infant for keeping them stuck in an abusive relationship or, whenever they look at their infant's face, they may be reminded of the ex-partner, whom they now loath, fear, or even still love. Living with violence or any environmental or relational trauma requires a capacity to defend oneself against thinking about the enormity of what has happened or is happening. One can often need to react swiftly or shut down quickly in order to survive what is a crisis. In fact, much of the crisis driven nature of social work can lead us as social workers to move to more of a "doing role" rather than a "thinking role." That is why access to good supervision is so critical and, from my experience, no more so than dealing with the multiple dynamics present when working with groups.

My practice as a social worker has been predominantly in child and adolescent mental health. In my role as a facilitator, a supervisor, or a manager of others running groups, I have as a minimum had two facilitators and a maximum of four (particularly when training others in group work). Group work with infants (from 0 to 4 years old) and their caregivers is exacting work with much required of the facilitators in observing the infant in and of themselves, being attuned to the relationship between the infant and caregiver, being aware of the dynamics between all group members, and being a member of the group themselves. The facilitators hold the group together, both in mind and in spirit. They often represent, for the participants, figures of authority or custodians of some sort, and with that, the potential positive and negative experiences they associate with adults in charge (for both the mothers and their babies).

How the facilitators hold themselves individually and as a group can often depend on how they are held in supervision. In my role, I usually supervise a number of groups each week, but I am also a facilitator of at least one group and, thus, am part of a group that is also supervised. On this particular occasion, scheduling pressures resulted in a rather busy day each week, in which I was both a supervisee and a supervisor. This involved my participation in a facilitation team for an infant/father group, a process that took most of the day, as well as providing supervision for an infant/mother group last thing in the day.

My timetable during this particular day consisted of helping set up the room and organizing morning tea for our infant/father group, running the group for two hours with a male psychologist and a female psychology student, returning the room to its original state, writing up detailed process notes on what had occurred within the group with my colleagues, laying out the themes to address in the therapeutic newsletter we sent to the fathers in between each week of our group, and attending supervision. The day then ended with my providing supervision to a different team of workers, which consisted of two social workers and two maternal child health nurses running an infant/mother group.

I was conscious of the fact that my male colleague and I had very different styles of working as we came from different disciplines, had very different personalities, and were obviously different genders. In a group in which the issue of power differences between men and women is a very important part of the landscape of family violence, these differences could remain unspoken or they could be addressed overtly. In this particular group, three of the fathers' female partners (the infants' mothers) had been included in the group, and as such, we had a reasonably large number of participants with four fathers, three mothers, and five infants. The dynamic between the father and infant was of particular importance. However, so too was the dynamic between the couple and that between both parents and their infant. Here we had a direct parallel occurring with a male and female facilitator (figuratively speaking, the parents of the group) and then the less powerful facilitator, the student (the child).

Although there appeared to be some very positive shifts occurring within the group process, I was well aware that the male facilitator and I were experiencing some real power struggles. These were not solely related to the group, but included issues related to just who took on what roles within the group, how different our goals for the group were, and who did what in pre- and post-group tasks. The student seemed very aware of the need to remain neutral. It was week four of the group, halfway through an eight-week intervention, and I took a risk. I did not think it appropriate to enter into the finer details of some of the struggles we were experiencing, particularly in the presence of the student, but it did seem necessary to acknowledge in our supervision group, which included the facilitation team and our supervisor, that the issues we two as the main facilitators were experiencing may have been affecting our therapeutic work. With some degree of nervousness, I raised the issue first generally, so that my male colleague was aware of what I was flagging, and then—with his consent—we spoke. We did so without going into details about some of the more external tensions about what our facilitation team dynamic might be representing for the group, as well as what we might, as a facilitation team, be acting out for the group.

The reflections and discussion that ensued were managed effectively and sensitively by the supervisor. She was able to tease out our thinking safely and meaningfully around what "stereotypic" gender roles we were in some ways rigidly adhering to, just as the fathers and mothers in our group were. This rigidity in roles meant that we both missed out on experiencing and doing certain things, with one taking on the role of being "playful" in the group, while the other felt left to do "the hard talking stuff." This then limited how we felt in the group, as well as how the men, women, and infants in the room experienced us. Rather than expanding relational opportunities, it diminished them. This revelation allowed the third co-facilitator (the student) to voice anxiety about just how uncertain the student felt about fitting in within the group, something infants can also struggle with when parents are constricted by perceived rules and regulations about just what sort of parent they should be or what it means to be a male or a female.

Following this session, it was now the end of the day, and I moved from being supervised to being the supervisor. I needed to shift my head space somewhat, in order to hold a meta-perspective of what was possibly happening for the five infants and five mothers in this group, as well as what the four female workers were experiencing. It was week five for this group, and I was struck by the level of anxiety being expressed by the team. The staff member from my team was very experienced in running these groups. Her three co-facilitators were very experienced professionals who had run numerous infant groups before. However, they were first timers to running a therapeutic group specifically addressing family violence. In some ways, they appeared to have lost confidence, questioning themselves constantly about what to do when, and they were anxious to "do no harm" to these very vulnerable women and their infants.

Anxiety is something those who have lived with family violence know a great deal about. It assists with a doubting of self and naturally erodes trust in self as well as others. As the supervisor for this group, it seemed important for me to think about what was contributing to this "doubting of self," and to re-ground these very competent professionals in their confidence within self. As a supervisor, I had come to know these facilitators through a professional development session I had previously provided to them, and my sense of trust in them did not waver. The emotional holding I could provide to them through supervision was as integral to them as what they could provide to the mothers and infants in the group, as these mothers and infants grew to trust each other and themselves.

These two supervision scenarios cannot hope to fully capture the depth and rich value supervision provides to our work. I have selected examples that illustrate sessions that are not solely about our participants in groups, but also to explore what we as facilitators bring to the group process. Supervision provides a vital space within which to reflect upon our work as group work facilitators, to understand ourselves as part of rather than separate to the group process. Although not all agencies have the resources or commitment to providing supervision to those running therapeutic groups, it is worthwhile considering just how well we are placed to hold all the complex issues that arise when bringing together a disparate group of individuals (as we are not all the same). Working with groups can be complex, and just as we endeavor to create a supportive, healing, and productive space for our participants, so too do we benefit (and ultimately our clients) when given space to reflect, explore, and think about just what it is we are being asked to hold.

Think About It

1. What do you imagine are some of the issues that present themselves when working with other professionals in running groups?

2. How does your experience of supervision fit with the ideas and issues that present themselves in this chapter?

3. What components do you think are necessary in providing facilitators of groups with a positive and useful experience of receiving supervision?

4. What sort of experience do you think is required of a supervisor to provide good supervision to group work facilitators?

Additional Reading

Applegate, J. S. (1996). *The good enough social worker: Winnicott applied.* In J. Edward & J. Sanville (eds.) *Fostering healing and growth: A psychoanalytic social work approach* (pp. 77-96). Northvale, NJ: Jason Aronson.

Bunston, W. (2008). Baby lead the way: Mental health groupwork for infants, children and mothers affected by family violence, *Journal of Family Studies, Vol 14,* 2-1, pp 334-341.

Bunston W., Pavlidis, T, & Leyden, P. (2003). Putting the GRO into groupwork, *Australian Social Work, 56* (1) 40-49.

Kahn, E. M. (1979). The parallel process in social work treatment and supervision, *Social Casework: The Journal Of Contemporary Social Work, Nov:* 520-528

Chapter 27
Group Work With Male Adolescent Sex Offenders

||||||||||||||||||||||||||||||||||||||||||||||||||||||||||||||||||||||||||||||||||||||||||||||||||||||||||||||||||||

by Tuyen D. Nguyen, Ph.D.

A day in the life of a social worker who works with adolescent sex offenders in a group setting is both challenging and rewarding on many levels. As a group facilitator for male adolescent sex offenders for a county in a southwestern state, my job encompasses many aspects of these individuals' treatment process. This particular county has a counseling treatment program for adolescent sex offenders called I.P.O.P., which stands for In-Patient Offenders Program. This program has been run by the county for the past 11 years. Adolescents in the county who have been found to have molested other children are court-ordered to undergo this in-patient program for six months, in which they receive both individual and group counseling daily for their sexual offenses. There are 15 participants who live in a locked-down facility run by the county for the duration of their treatment.

My day starts at 8:00 a.m., when I am briefed by the ward's probation officers on any behavioral issues that have occurred the previous night. Usually there are no issues with the residents who have been at the facility for a while. However, there are times when residents have touched one another inappropriately, and that needs to be addressed immediately individually and with the parties involved. Once this is discussed and appropriate consequences explained, the involved residents then go to eat breakfast before school starts. Since the adolescents live at the facility, classes are held on the premises, so they won't fall behind in their studies while receiving counseling treatment. While residents are in class during the morning, I occasionally make unannounced visits to observe

185

them in a classroom setting, to determine how appropriately or inappropriately they interact with their teachers and other pupils. When residents consistently exhibit appropriate behaviors toward others, I reward them with points, which they can utilize to buy goods at the end of the week.

Every day at 10:00 a.m., group counseling takes place with all 15 residents. Group counseling is conducted by two group facilitators who are licensed clinicians. Between the two of us facilitators, we have more than 30 years of experience conducting groups with adolescent sex offenders. For the six-month period of group counseling treatment for I.P.O.P. clients, there is a curriculum that we facilitators follow. However, much process takes place in a group setting that is individualized to the topics under discussion. The group at this county's facility is an open group, because members enter the group when they are admitted and leave when their treatment is complete. Throughout the treatment process, I do witness great changes that the group members exhibit—initially from being sex offenders who show no empathy toward others to individuals who understand the pain that their victims have endured as a result of the abuse inflicted upon them. At these moments, my group co-facilitator and I feel rewarded for what we do on a daily basis with these adolescents in a group setting.

Group work takes two hours each week day. We normally begin the group each day by inviting group members to identify where they are emotionally on that day. Usually, the more experienced group members volunteer to go first, zoning in on their emotions accurately. For those few group members who have problems articulating what they feel on a particular day, for whatever reason, they can choose to wear t-shirts with emotional words that reflect their feelings for the time being, until their emotions change and/or they want to discuss what they are experiencing with the whole group. In the beginning phase of the group, when the members don't know one another, group facilitators often provide much structure to the group. However, after many weeks of working with one another in the group setting, group members do take initiative and less structure is needed. When difficult topics are discussed in the group, like accepting abuse that one has inflicted on others and abuse that has been inflicted on the residents by others, I sense resistance from the group members to a great extent. During these silent moments, my co-facilitator and I begin a dialogue between the two of us, to model appropriate ways for the group members to open up. Once our dialogue is complete, we usually leave the floor open for group members to start processing their thoughts, emotions, and experiences regarding the topic under discussion.

We have no doubt that the facilitators' degree of authenticity in their dialogue determines the extent that the group members will open up and share with the group.

Group work ends at 12:00 noon each week day. My co-facilitator and I usually eat lunch right after group and process what has taken place in group. We usually share our perspectives on each of the residents and their progress or lack thereof. We usually take a one-hour lunch and come back to the facility to write up our progress notes. This task takes my co-facilitator and me approximately one hour to complete. In our progress notes, we write about the residents' participation level in the group, mood/attitude, evidence of taking personal responsibility for their actions, and acceptance of constructive feedback from the group facilitators and/or other group members.

From 2:00 to 3:00 p.m., if any of the residents has to be in court, I usually have to be there, as well, to report to the judge how they have participated in the group over the past weeks. These are the times when I summarize our progress notes and present them in court on behalf of the residents. On days when there are no court appearances, I meet with the ward's probation officers to brief them on the residents' behavioral issues, so they are informed and understand the current pressing issues in order to interact with the residents more effectively.

From 4:00 to 5:00 p.m., I see residents for individual counseling. The residents who have exhibited the most behavioral issues or resistance during group are usually seen first. I begin the session by stating my observations of the residents' behavior in the group earlier in the day, and then allow them ample time to respond. Often, the topics discussed in group remind these adolescents of the traumas they have experienced in their families of origin, which makes them either overly reactive or withdrawn altogether in the group. I utilize the individual sessions to allow the residents to get to the root causes of their behavior and process their experiences in a way that they may have never done before with anyone else in their lives.

Career Path Reflections

Group work with male adolescent sex offenders has both positives and negatives. The greatest positive is that the group facilitator has an opportunity to make an ever-lasting impact on the adolescents who have sexually abused others in their lives. Perhaps the group treatment that these individuals receive will deter them from committing future offenses. If these adolescents don't receive the treatment they need, their continued abuse of other potential victims multiplies as they grow into adults. In other words, the group facilitator works every day for the betterment of society by reducing the number of horrendous sexual crimes committed by sex predators, through conducting groups with first-time offenders.

A huge negative is that the group facilitator may never know whether the male adolescent sex offender is successfully treated or will re-offend once released back into the community. Within a group setting, for instance, members share with the group how they have groomed their victims, and as a result, others may learn new grooming tactics that they may utilize with their future victims.

In my experience, effective group facilitators possess the following personal characteristics: authenticity, genuineness, consistency, ability to confront group members and provide constructive feedback, open-mindedness, empathy, and ability to communicate clearly within a group setting with diverse youth. In this career path, despite the clients' young age, they are keen in zoning in on the group facilitator's authenticity. They can tell whether the facilitator is an authentic person who exhibits consistent behavior, both in words and in actions. If the facilitator is empathic and communicates in a clear, respectful manner, these clients over time will open up in group with brutal honesty. When strong rapport exists between the group facilitator and the group members, and between the members themselves, productive sessions will take place. Because of the clients' developmental phase, the group facilitator still has an incredible opportunity to shape and mold these individuals to become compassionate citizens of society who are conscious of their actions.

I have worked with adult sex offenders in private practice previously, and no doubt, it's hard work, because I know that many may be just going through the motions to satisfy the judge's order. These individuals are hardcore sex predators who happened to get caught and are now suffering the consequences. Group therapy for these individuals may be just a game to play to get the judicial system off their backs. In comparing the male adolescent sex offenders and the adult sex offenders with whom I have worked, the former group gives me more hope with respect to successful treatment outcomes. Sex is a powerful drive and will be with each male adolescent sex offender until he draws his last breath. However, group counseling provides him with life-giving perspectives regarding his sexuality, as well as effective tools so that he can channel his sexual drive in a more acceptable fashion within the realm of a healthy intimate relationship.

Think About It

1. Would you work with the male adolescent sex offender population in a group setting? Why or why not?

2. In your opinion, what makes a person become a sex offender, and how can group counseling treatment help the person deal with his own perspectives regarding sexuality?

3. If you had an opportunity to facilitate either a male adolescent sex offender or an all male adult sex offender group, which would you choose? Provide a rationale for your choice.

Additional Reading

Burton, D. (2003). Male adolescents: Sexual victimization and subsequent sexual abuse. *Child and Adolescent Social Work Journal, 20* (4), 277–296.

Hunter, J. A., Figueredo, A. J., & Malamuth, N. M. (2009). Pathways into social and sexual deviance. *Journal of Family Violence,* doi:10.1007/s10896-009-9277-9.

Hunter, J. A., Figueredo, A. J., Malamuth, N. M., & Becker, J. V. (2003). Juvenile sex offenders: Toward the development of a typology. *Sexual Abuse: Journal of Research and Treatment, 15* (1), 27–48.

Ryan, G., Leversee, T., Lane, S. (2010). *Juvenile sexual offending: causes, consequences and correction* (3rd ed.). N.J: Wiley.

Veneziano, C., Veneziano, L., & LeGrand, S. (2000). The relationship between adolescent sex offender behaviors and victim characteristics with prior victimization. *Journal of Interpersonal Violence, 15* (4), 363–374.

Chapter 28
Crisis Oriented Group Work With Emergency Services Personnel

IIIIIIIIIIIIIIIIIIIIIIIIIIIIIIIIIIIIIIIIIIIIIIIIIIIIIIIIIIIIIIIIIIIIIIIIIIIIIIIIIIIIIIIIIIIIIIIIIIIIIIIIIIIIIIIIIIIIIIIII

by Ogden W. Rogers, Ph.D., LCSW, ACSW

When the phone rang, I looked over at my alarm clock: 2:15 a.m. A phone ringing at this hour means I knew this was going to be a long day. I coordinate Critical Incident Stress Management services for the Maryland Institute for Emergency Medical Services Systems and provide behavioral health consultation to the Baltimore City Fire-Police Medical Bureau.* I'm a clinical social worker in an adult psychiatric practice. My special interest is emergency services personnel and their families.

I mumbled "hello" into the receiver. I recognized Craig's voice, the shock-trauma syscom dispatcher. "Doc, wake up. Battalion 3 wants you at Carey and Mosher for a working fire that's gonna go three alarms...multiple fatalities and the Mayor is on the way."

"Okay, okay." I mumble back, waking all the way up and throwing on clothes. "I got it and I'm on the way." It's a hot summer night and the stoops are filled with people. It's a neighborhood filled with very poor people and nobody has air conditioning. Tonight has the added extra commotion of half of the block being on fire. I see on old woman in the distance. She is seated on her marble stoop wiping her brow with a washcloth. She is rocking back and forth slowly, worried, exhausted. I know she is softly singing a hymn. She is praying for the neighbors across the street.

In a large fire such as this, there are dozens of stories that emerge. I look around for a white helmet of the battalion chief. I

For purposes of confidentiality, names and identifying events have been "fictionalized" so as to protect living clients.

191

find him hunched over the bumper of a ladder truck jotting some things down on a clipboard and talking into a mike on his shoulder. There is more equipment approaching, and he is directing them to come in the south side of an alley and make an attack on the farthest house.

"I'm disengaging 30 Company and Truck 8. There was a problem getting water in the end house and the rescue went south. The guys were crawling all around and stepping all over sh– and each other. They almost bought it, it moved so fast. Probably arson. I almost lost a guy in the kitchen, and the floor collapsed. He's on the back step of Truck 8 with the EMTs. Five kids died and three adults. There was a boatload living in the first house. Maybe a dozen. Lotsa injuries.This thing has spread through three other connecting houses 'cause of old construction. The Mayor's over in the corner, and he's mugging all the cameras. Go look my guys over and we'll do a debrief tomorrow."

I take only enough time to nod affirmatively and reach out and grasp the Chief's shoulder. "Good luck. Call me if you need me. I'm gonna say 'Hi' to the guys."

I have always considered myself a generalist practitioner, and I prepare myself that a client can be a single individual, a small group, or even a large community such as a fire department. Tonight, my client will slide back and forth—one minute, a single firefighter sitting on the back step of a pumper; the next, an entire rescue company that found itself trapped on a stairwell. While tonight and today my work will be "clinical" or direct service, the fact I've been called out at all to attend in the street in the middle of the night is a product of many previous hours of meetings and presentations with "stakeholders" and "policy makers" that now have put into place "procedures and policy" that value putting a social worker onto the back of the fire line to meet with personnel in crisis. So, the clinical is policy. The policy gets personal. Now its 3 a.m. and I'll talk with the probie who almost got killed, and then quickly "defuse" the rest of the guys in the company.

I walk around the pumper and find the coffee wagon. There I find the rest of Truck 8 and 30 Company. They were first on the scene, and most of them look a little beat up and very sooty, but nobody's going to admit to anything that even smacks of vulnerability on the street. My "demobilization" group will take place right here with guys with their backs up against the coffee wagon. I get some grunts of respect and take some coarse humor. Some guys are a little pissed the chief has demobilized them. This is their 'hood, and they want to stay until the mop-up. I acknowledge the pissed, and I point out that life has SOP (standard operating procedures) that the chief has to follow. Everybody did their job. People died. You guys are all alive, and that's how this scene plays for now. I go through a small list of stress hygiene that they've all heard before, but it must be said. I tell them about the debriefing we'll have about 12 hours from now, before their shift is over.

I walk around the fire scene looking for anything that needs a little psychological first aid. The Red Cross has shown up and has started to work with some displaced families. The chaplain is on the scene and we compare some notes. The city medical examiner guys are comparing notes with some of the medic units. Some of the children's bodies were taken to nearby emergency rooms for "benefit of the doubt runs." There are some adult bodies still in some properties. The mayor is on the way out...he's been giving sound bites for the morning TV news and briefly shaking some hands. I put out my hand as he walks by, and he pumps it like he's campaigning. "Glad to see you. Thanks for helpin' out." I know he has no idea who I am.

I find the chief who is coordinating the mopping up. I give him the simplest of reports, give him an open door to anything else he might need, and ask him if he needs me for anything else.

"Naw. Thanks doc. You're good to go."

I have a clinic office a few blocks away. I will grab a shower and a nap before beginning the day. I have a few patients at some other sites downtown and "the wives' group" at noon. I need to reschedule some afternoon patients, as I will have to do a debriefing at 2:30 p.m.

The EMT's Wives' Support Group meets every other week. I co-lead it with a female social work colleague from a local community mental health agency. The group "moves" every other week, meeting one week in a small room at the Shock-Trauma Center, and alternately in a room at the Firefighter's Union Hall. This arrangement first came about because we couldn't get either room in either facility twice a month. It's come to pass that we could just start meeting in one place, but the group has grown accustomed to the alternation and has decided to keep it this way. The setting seems to support a tendency to alternate themes for the groups' focus. When we meet in the hospital, there's usually more discussion about health or mental health concerns, either those of the members themselves or their spouses. When we meet in the fire hall, the topics shift to the problems with the department, bosses, shift work, and labor related stresses. I think it's interesting how the external setting of the group seems to influence the content that arises.

I really didn't have a hand in developing the wives' group; they had really started themselves and came looking for me as a facilitator after they had already met a few times under the encouragement of a member, an emergency room nurse. They recognized in the first few meetings that they were having difficulty articulating just exactly what they wanted to do as a group, and I had been suggested by somebody's husband as a "headshrinker who can be trusted."

During my first session with the members, I recognized that everyone except me was a woman. When I pointed to this gender difference, it was initially marginalized as "no big deal" by most of the members, but I sensed the deference may still have come from stereotypical gender-authority themes, and asked if it was okay in future sessions if I might be joined by a female co-facilitator I knew from a local community mental health center. There was some good natured joking about me "needing a skirt to hide behind," but in the end, the members agreed it would be fine, as long as my colleague "cared about fire service families."

The group spent its first months developing and defining itself. The members see the purpose of the group to be social support, but have also wrestled with questions of membership and activity. The members changed the name of the group several times as they allowed the membership to expand. At this point, they've agreed to be open to spouses of any fire or EMS personnel, whether city, county, or voluntary fire companies, and have granted members the liberty to advertise and recruit participation through word-of-mouth. "Spouses" has also been discussed and agreed upon openly to include girlfriends, boyfriends, and partners...as members recognized that some of the service members were women, or gay. (It was all very white and straight at first, but everyone has benefited from a spirit of inclusion, and the difference!). There is one line in the sand at this time, however, and the color of that line is blue.

"No cops or cop wives," said a vocal member in one of the first meetings. "Poe-lice" (she said in a very Baltimoreese accent) and fire just don't mix. Let them get their own group." All the members agreed, and no one had any second thought when I raised a question. I've raised the issue periodically since then, and it always gets shot down. It's fire and EMS. That's how they roll.

This afternoon's group is all abuzz about the big fire from last night. Nobody's direct family members were involved, but everybody knows somebody who knows somebody. I get pumped for details, but just give the briefest of official versions. I know the stories will emerge over time. The theme of "thank goodness nobody was hurt" passed around and then smacked up against the awareness that eight people in the various houses, including children, had died. There was a little guilt, and then a balance about being a part of a "special service." The members were supportive of each other, and there was a welcoming and a little orientation for a new member, a woman whose husband is a paramedic on the east side. Much of the session is spent with members picking up where they left off, doing some thinking about whether they want to get involved with a charity event run by a county auxiliary.

I show up at 30 Company Truck 8 house a little after 2:00 p.m. We are going to do a debriefing before these guys go off on a four-day break. A Critical Incident Stress Debriefing (CISD) is a short-term group psychoeducational crisis intervention that developed out of the experience of a number of clinicians who were involved in some way with the Maryland Institute for Emergency Medical Services Systems—or "the Shock-Trauma"—one of the first centers for trauma care in the U.S. The technique was designed to use interpersonal strengths of individuals who, as part of an emergency services team, such as paramedics, police, or firefighters, had experienced symptoms of stress response following a "critical rescue event." A group is led through seven "phases" of process, and the technique is designed to decrease acute stress effects by creating an environment where the relationship between the critical incident and the personal responses would be identified and discussed within the supportive "family" of a working team of first responders.

The technique built upon a natural part of emergency service organizational life, the "operational critique" or "incident debriefing," which was a routine meeting to discuss the performance of the team during a big event. The difference is that CISD was designed to allow for members to discuss their own personal thoughts, feelings, and behaviors during and after a stressful emergency event, rather than just operational performance.

The CISD group is usually about a one- to three-hour single session facilitated with the natural working team requesting debriefing, a fire company, a rescue squad, and perhaps the associated ambulances or police who were part of the effort. The group leaders are a pair of cross-trained debriefers: a "mental health professional" and one or more "peer support persons"(PSP's). My co-leader, Craig, is a city firefighter who's worked with me dozens of times before.

Entering the fire house for the debriefing, I was prepared for the male locker-room ribbing and kidding that is part of the usual test of authority and sense of respect.

"Hey, Doc! Hey, Craig! Look! We're putting the chairs in a circle already!"

"Yo, Shehan, you better look out! the shrink's here. You better get your game face on or you'll be NFD (not fit for duty)!"

"Hey Doc! How you feeling today? You here to see Shehan? Did you know he's crazy?"

I look at FF Melvin Stewart, the guy announcing my presence. "Hi, Melvin. Good to see you again. No, I didn't know that Lieutenant Shehan was crazy. I'm not shrinking anything today, anyway. I'm a social worker...you know that."

Stewart jives back, "Oh, that's different then. I need to see you then. At the rate I'm getting' paid, I'm gonna need you to help me get some food stamps!"

"Don't mind him, Doc. He don't need no food stamps. And he don't need no head shrinker. He needs a mouth shrinker."

"Ouch!" Melvin shoots out, still sliding chairs into a circle. "I thought you loved me, Goldfarb! Doc! I think Goldfarb has hostility issues. Can you send him to Anger Management?"

I pick a chair from the corner and slide it into the now forming circle of chairs behind the parked engine. "I'm fresh out of management today. I'm too tired from last night. I think we'll just stick to a debriefing this afternoon."

Melvin keeps adding chairs, "You got that right, Doc."

The CISD process follows a format that builds on the natural skills of a working emergency response group. In a sense, the working team will slowly transition into a sharing group that moves from the instrumental details of a rescue operation to the sharing and vulnerability of internal personal emotional and cognitive experience, and then with the support of the natural "band of brothers" and the normalization of the experience, transition back to the working team that they have always been.

Using the process has not been without controversy. I heard an old-timer shake his head once when I came into his house. "Feh, social workers. I remember when ladders were wooden and men were steel. You shrinks have made the ladders steel and the men made of wood." I told him I only was involved with the fire service out of my deepest respect, and the awareness that too many good firefighters had left the service before their time, partly because they needed a chance to "deal." I'm not sure I ever "sold him," but younger generations of emergency service personnel have come to see the process as useful.

The process follows standardized "phases"—first, an "Introductory Phase" for introducing the facilitators and participants, outlining confidentiality and time boundaries, suspending for the time being the importance of rank, and explaining the purpose of the session. Everyone reports their name and role on the squad. We go "around the circle" once, and everybody gets to see that they've been able to participate and nobody got embarrassed. Next, a "Fact Phase" elicits from members of the group what activities they performed at the incident, and their perceptions at the scene. This is key, because a critical incident has so much varied phenomena going on that nobody "can see it all" at the time of the crisis. Adding the brief statements of facts begins to build a larger picture of the incident, and for some, begins to fill in some of the gaps of their memory and perception.

The "Thought Phase" encourages a discussion of the initial thoughts that rescue workers had at the scene. In the "Reaction Phase," the facilitator encourages members to share with others the emotional feelings they had at the scene and feelings they had afterward. Next is the "Symptom Phase," in which the facilitator explores the psychological and physical after effects that the workers have experienced following the incident, followed by a "Teaching Phase," where the group leaders can discuss normalization and stress management hygiene. Finally, a "Re-entry Phase" concludes the group's activities by answering questions and allowing the group to plan some future action if it wishes.

I'm always impressed with how easily the guys fall into the group process. There's usually some initial defensiveness as part of the self-image of being a smoke-eater is to be a superman. It's especially true of truck companies whose job at a fire is to break in and rescue people. But it is also true that the men and women who form fire companies are a close knit, supportive crew who will respond openly and deeply if given some boundaries and trust. Some in this company have been through a CISD before, and they see it in some ways as a ritual, an opportunity to share and bond.

The debriefing goes pretty much according to process. During the fact phase, a number of observations that have not been totally shared are heard freshly for the first time. There is some poignancy to a theme that emerges on the closeness that some of the guys have had to losing their own lives. There is much support shown to the newbies, and respect shared with some old wise hands. A somber grief trickles out about each of the victims, and there is a still-developing rage at the possibility that the whole thing started as an arson. In the end, stories are told, backs are slapped, successes celebrated and families mourned. The looks around the room are appreciative of each other. There is a sense that even in the face of great loss, they have each other's back.

I look up and announce that I think we are done. Seeing agreement, I give my own last nod of appreciation for the risk and the service that each member of the scene has given, and continues to give. Craig echoes me. I tell them they know where to find me if there is anything private that is needed.

Melvin looks at me and laughs. "Heck no, Doc, we got it all out. But C shift is over and I got a date with a girl who wants to go fishin' this weekend. You gotta help us put all these chairs back off the deck."

"My pleasure to help, FireFighter Stewart. I certainly don't want to get in the way of anybody's goin' fishin'."

Goldfarb picks up a chair and puts it into the stack. "That's good Doc, 'cause the only thing Stewart gonna be doin' is fishin'. He couldn't get a date to take his momma to church." Somebody laughs. Stewart smiles. I'm sure the ribbing goes on for at least a few more minutes until A-shift settles in and the firehouse goes quiet on a hot afternoon.

Soon enough, the siren will go off again.

Think About It

1. The narrator of this story calls himself a "generalist." What examples of generalist perspective can be found in the narrative?

2. There are (at least) two different groups described in the narrative. Identify each group and describe how they are alike. How are they different?

Additional Reading

Rogers. O. (2009). *Emergency group crisis interventions,* in A. Gitterman & R. Salmon (eds.). *Encyclopedia of social work with groups* (pp. 72-74). New York: Routledge.

Rogers, O. (2011). *Social work in the ER.* In L. Grobman (ed.). *Days in the lives of social workers* (pp. 29-37). Harrisburg, PA: White Hat Communications.

Chapter 29
Strengthening Leadership, Building Community

IIIIIIIIIIIIIIIIIIIIIIIIIIIIIIIIIIIIIIIIIIIIIIIIIIIIIIIIIIIIIIIIIIIIIIIIIIIIIIIIIIIIIIIIIIIIIIIIIII

by Marci Mayer Eisen, MSW

I drive onto the I.E. Millstone Jewish Community Campus eager to start my day at the Jewish Federation of St. Louis as Director of the Millstone Institute for Jewish Leadership. Even after 30-plus years working in this community, I am excited and feel honored to focus on "community building." Using terms like *developing leaders* and *building community* can sound lofty or vague. It's important that every day I focus on conversations, dialogue, training, networking, sharing resources, and developing programs that will have a direct impact on our ability to strengthen the effectiveness of our professionals and volunteers. We're in the relationship business, and my overriding values are always guided by social group work.

The campus is more than 80 acres and is home to the Jewish Federation and a number of other agencies, including the Jewish Community Center (JCC). I recognize the impact that the JCC has had on my own family and believe we are better group workers when we recognize our own need for belonging to a community. The focus of my work is on training and leadership development targeted to two distinct groups—paid staff and volunteer leaders. There are approximately 60 different nonprofits within our network, including agencies, organizations, schools, and religious congregations. Group work values and skills directly influence our methods for community building. I work with both educational groups and decision-making/task groups.

I go to my office and recognize that to be effective at community building, I can't rely on sitting at a computer all day. I glance at a small piece of artwork I recently purchased that has a girl with her head cocked to one side. The front of her dress reads, "She felt wrapped in the arms of community." That's what I want to provide for others. I believe that every conversation with a colleague or volunteer leader has the power to help that person feel connected to others and the community as a whole.

I check in with my associate, Karen, to see what she has planned for her day. We go over a list of potential participants to launch a new monthly leadership program for emerging and established volunteer leaders. We rely on building trust with senior managers, so that they promote our initiatives and share names of potential participants. We look for diversity of age, experience, geography, occupations, and religious observance, in addition to leadership skills.

My first meeting of the day is with the three officers of our professional association, a decision-making/task group. I work with them to plan professional development programs and build professional relationships. We are meeting to review our last full board meeting and to ensure that we are following through with ideas previously discussed. As their staff person, I support them and provide direction. We focus on the purpose of the association. When they direct a question to me, I stress that it is "their board" and pause to ask, "What do you think?" I want to build their skills and commitments. I intervene to help the discussion stay focused and challenge them to set high goals.

The president, Michelle, raises a concern that one of the committee chairs wants increased responsibility. I know that it is important to listen to each officer's views before I react. I also appreciate that diverse perspectives are crucial for a healthy decision-making group. We want to provide a culture within the board where concerns can be openly shared. We discuss their expectations of how they function as a board. We discuss the importance of continually clarifying roles and responsibilities.

I leave the officers to set up for a staff educational group. Many of our staff development training programs reflect our Jewish mission. At the same time, we want to support and show appreciation to the increasing number of staff who are of different faiths. During lunch time, we sponsor a "lunch and learn" holiday program for staff from different religious backgrounds. I go to the room early to make sure the table set-up allows for interaction among the participants. I move a few chairs around and set out the food. I welcome each person by name as he or she arrives, hand out name tags, and encourage them to take their lunches. There are 12 people for the program. Several who are attending for the first time appear somewhat nervous. I am prepared for participants to experience ambivalence or anxiety. I want to put them at ease. As they take their seats, I introduce them to one another and encourage informal conversation. I explain the ethnic food, knowing it is unfamiliar to some. Before the speaker begins, we take time for formal introductions. I ask them to share their name, organization, position, and their interest in the topic. I want everyone to feel comfortable asking questions about a religion that is not their own, so I bring out the commonalities of the group. I also stress that "there are no bad questions—feel free to ask what is on your mind." The speaker begins and gives an overview of the material.

I am observing the level of engagement. The presenter quickly provides a lot of information. Beth and Matt look interested, make eye contact, nod often, and ask questions throughout the presentation. However, Melissa and Dawn appear distracted. I wonder if they are not interested in the topic or thinking about work or personal issues. At all educational programs, I question how to involve those who appear less engaged. When the presenter pauses, I ask the group if there are any questions, making eye contact around the room. Ann has informed me that she will need to leave early. I recognize how important it is to help participants comfortably enter and leave the room, so I wave and say thank you as she leaves. I continue to observe the participation. I notice Paul has a question that goes unnoticed by the speaker. I get the speaker's attention and quietly point to Paul. Paul seems happy to ask his question. At the conclusion, I thank the speaker. I look around at each person to express my appreciation for the work they do on behalf of our community. I hand out the evaluation form and announce the next educational holiday program. Jane stands back while the others leave. She wants to talk to me about the program and share her perspective from her own religion. I listen with interest. I know that my role continues, even after the formal program ends.

I walk across the parking lot to the JCC to meet with six members of the Annual Staff Recognition Luncheon committee, another decision-making/task group. They are staff members from different organizations and are finalizing details for a community luncheon. We expect 300 staff and guests to attend. The agenda developed by the luncheon chair includes confirming the food, reviewing the trivia game about our organizations, and finalizing the door prizes. My goal is to provide an environment in which the committee members make the decisions and follow through on their commitments.

I am concerned that the trivia game has too many questions about our largest organization and leaves out potential questions about our smaller ones. I pause to think about how I respond. As the staff person, I do not want to take over small details and appear to "micro-manage." Yet, when focused on "building community," we need to appear inclusive of all. I state, "These are really great questions, but perhaps we can include a few about some of our smaller organizations." I am pleased when there is agreement and ideas for other questions are shared. As with all of our decision-making/tasks groups, I thank everyone for their time and ideas and give special recognition to the chair. Before concluding, the chair summarizes what needs to be accomplished in the upcoming week.

The other half of my job is targeted to volunteer leadership development, primarily members of nonprofit boards. I work with experienced community leaders to plan different trainings, including strategic planning, legal issues, financial issues, and running effective meetings. This evening, we are sponsoring a program on board governance. It is an educational group. Unlike the lunch session for staff members, this program is just for volunteers. I have 17 people signed up, but with the forecast of inclement weather, I know that several will cancel. I must be enthusiastic even if the attendance is smaller than planned. I print evaluation forms and materials. I check the PowerPoint and set out beverages and name tags. Just as with the lunch time educational program, I greet and thank each person for attending. When I informally introduce attendees to each other, I bring out commonalities, including, "You're both board presidents," "John is also interested in the arts," and "Janie is also a lawyer."

Even though there are only nine in the room, I recognize that it is time to begin. I welcome the participants and briefly talk about the purpose of our institute. It is important to clarify purpose, especially with a new initiative. I ask for introductions and encourage each person to talk about his or her volunteer role and interest in the topic. Three more people enter the room after the presenter begins. I get out of my seat to hand them their name tags and quietly thank them for attending. I wait until the speaker pauses to ask to take a moment to welcome those who recently entered.

The material for board leaders is at a high intellectual level. Several are engaged in the information, but it appears difficult for others to grasp. I ask a question to specifically help the speaker move on to the next topic on the agenda. As the concluding time draws near, I ask the speaker if there will be time for a few questions. She apologizes for rushing through the material and stops to ask for questions. I recognize that it is important for an educational group to pause for questions and comments. At the conclusion, I thank the speaker and the participants and remind them about the evaluation form. I attempt to converse briefly with each person before he or she leaves. Already, I am thinking about topics we can offer for the series next year.

When the seminar concludes, I spend a few minutes at my desk preparing for tomorrow. The work is satisfying, yet there is much to do to have a long term impact on the culture of leadership in our community.

Think About It

1. What are the similarities and differences between decision-making/task groups and educational groups? Which group work values guide each?

2. What differences are there in developing training for professionals versus training for volunteer board members?

3. How can social workers measure impact when working on long-term community change in areas such as collaborations, improved effectiveness of boards, and staff training?

Chapter 30
Collaboration, Connection, and Community: A Women's Psychotherapy and Psychopharmacology Group

|||||||||||||||||||||||||||||||||||||||||||||||||||||||||||||||||||||||||||||||||||||||||||||||||||||||||||||||||||||||||||||||||||||||||||||||||||||||||

by Ashley D. Davis, Ph.D., LICSW

Tuesday morning staff meetings had become predictable. Sandwiched between making announcements and reviewing cases, our manager updated us on the serious financial squeeze facing the public hospital in which our outpatient clinic was situated. We depended on the state for financial support, and funds had been shrinking more and more as a result of increasing cuts to the budget. Without enough support, the hospital had to make hard choices about how to operate and meet the needs of our clients. I often felt discouraged as we were expected to "do more with less." It felt stressful to be asked to add more clients to my bulging caseload, simply because there were not funds to hire more staff. It felt lousy to have even little perks—like free employee parking or a water cooler in the staff room—taken away as cost-saving measures, despite the impact those decisions had on staff morale. My anxiety and frustration were mirrored in the faces of my colleagues as we sat through those meetings together.

While our work lives were affected by the economic downturn, our clients experienced harsh financial realities on a daily basis. The hospital's mission was serving the diverse, urban community in which it was located. Clients from different socioeconomic backgrounds sought treatment at the hospital because of its well-respected reputation. Many clients with a low socioeconomic status in particular turned to its clinics because their services would be covered by Free Care, the state-sponsored program for people who could not afford health insurance. Few hospitals and clinics accepted Free Care, which limited clients' abilities to seek help elsewhere. Clients' reasons for having a low income varied greatly. Some clients earned little to no money because of their immigration status, physical or mental disability, and/or chronic underemployment. Their financial situations caused significant stress and exacerbated the mental health issues for which they sought treatment.

Clients' financial situations often created practical issues that got in the way of their treatment. They might cancel or "no-show" for an appointment when they did not have reliable transportation or could not afford childcare, when they had an opportunity to pick up an extra shift at work, when they needed to spend a day applying for or resolving problems with their government benefits, or when their illness was too debilitating to leave home. Sometimes I watched my tightly packed schedule crumble from one missed appointment after another. I tried to use my feelings to generate greater empathy for my clients who were burdened by much larger inconveniences, frustrations, and hardship on a daily basis.

I felt the squeeze from both sides, as the hospital and our clients faced hard economic times. I sought to find a way to meet the needs of my multi-stressed clients and to achieve my "productivity" expectations set by the hospital, which stipulated how many hours of billable services to clients I needed to log each week. Initially, it seemed like my clients, the hospital, and I had needs that were in conflict with one another. How could I have clients on my caseload who had spotty attendance when the hospital had a waiting list of people in the community who were seeking services? How could I terminate services with clients whose reasons for missing appointments were related to the very reasons they sought help in the first place? How could I bear these tensions while striving to be productive and efficient in a practice setting that depends on income from billable client services? Necessity is indeed the mother of invention, which is how I came to devise a solution that would strive to meet the clients' needs, the hospital's needs, and my own needs. Group therapy was just that solution.

One Tuesday morning in our staff meeting, I shook off the disempowered feeling that inevitably set in as the hospital's precarious financial situation was discussed. With renewed energy, I floated my idea by my colleagues.

"What if we offered a group for clients who can't make regular therapy appointments but who need ongoing—and even long-term—treatment?" I proposed. I went on to explain how a group could weather clients' inevitable absences, whereas such missed appointments would lead quickly to a forced termination for a client being seen in a valuable hour of weekly individual therapy.

My colleagues helped me hash out the details. We decided to limit the group to women, in order to have one unifying trait among members. We figured that the group would need to be large enough to feel like a group even if several clients missed on the same day, so we settled on a membership of 15 clients. The accommodating attendance policy had some limits—clients needed to be in touch with me about their absences and communicate their intention to remain in the group. This policy helped to keep the group cohesive, as I could inform the group of a particular client's absence, thus acknowledging and "holding" her spot among us.

My colleagues scanned their caseloads to think about clients for whom the group might be a good fit. A fellow social worker, Kathryn, suggested that one of her clients, Debra, might be interested.

"After her mother died, Debra realized she didn't have anyone in her life," Kathryn explained. "When she started therapy, she didn't have a reason to leave the house or even get out of bed. She's in a different place now and might be ready to transfer to a group."

Individual therapy had been a lifeline for Debra through the crisis of her mother's death. As her grief faded, new problems came to the fore: loneliness and isolation. Kathryn saw a group as the next step in Debra's treatment and an opportunity to develop and practice new social skills. More quickly than I imagined, referrals for the group poured in. I arranged intake appointments with potential members to discuss their current needs, review their previous treatment, and answer their questions about the group. I started to form an initial connection with them and to socialize them to the group's structure, norms, and commitment. Once the client and I agreed to give the group a try, I sent my co-facilitator, Dr. Rachel, an internal e-mail to let her know about the new member.

Dr. Rachel's role was another unique feature of the group. At first glance, she and I appeared quite similar. We were both white women in our 30s. We requested that group members call me "Ashley" and her "Dr. Rachel," to differentiate our professional roles. As members got to know us, our personalities and styles differentiated us further. We facilitated the group together and divided up the additional tasks. I managed referrals and met with potential new members; followed up with members who missed group and had not notified me ahead of time, and handled any case management needs that arose for members. Dr. Rachel was the prescribing provider for all group members who took psychiatric medications. Right after the group, she provided individual check-ins with members who needed to discuss refills, side effects, or possible medication changes. These meetings were brief in large part because, after listening to them in the group, she was already aware of their symptoms and the happenings of their lives.

Our group, named the Women's Psychotherapy and Psychopharmacology Group, was a large investment in resources on the part of the hospital, with two independently licensed clinicians present for each hour-long session. Yet, by offering psychotherapy and psychopharmacology services, the group met the treatment needs of most members. Our efficiency benefited the hospital and did not come at the clients' expense. On the contrary, the group met the clients' needs in a way that other modalities would not. Rather than scheduling multiple appointments for services, they had both therapy and psychopharmacology in one appointment, and they could see their prescribing provider as often as they needed. Clients used their initial connection with Dr. Rachel and me to settle into the group as a "holding environment," and then used this "secure base" to form connections with one another (Bowlby, 1988). We hoped the group would eventually come to be their secure base from which they could venture out even further.

The power of the group came from the relationships they formed with each other. They faced different life stressors, upbringings, and illnesses (most often mood and anxiety disorders), but they shared the common experiences of stigma and isolation. For many members, the group helped chip away at the pain of being on the outside of their families, friends, and communities because of their illnesses or life situations. Many members were learning how to live with problems that were not going to go away entirely, such as their ambivalence about taking medications or their hard work to prevent a relapse of their illness. The long-term nature of group allowed clients to have validation, support, and company as they struggled with problems that did not resolve quickly. In one of the earliest meetings of the group, one client, Christine, shared her distress.

"How in the world can they deny my application for disability?" Christine asked with an incredulous tone. "I'm barely making it." After waiting months for a decision about her application for Social Security disability, Christine had received the bad news in a form letter the day before. She sounded outraged and discouraged. Her psychiatric symptoms included panic attacks and paranoia that prevented her from holding down a job, and with her bank account already depleted, she had been counting on the financial support. It was hard for anyone in the group to fathom that she was undeserving of disability benefits, but the rejected application was an all-too-common experience among group members who also had applied. The group responded with encouragement and urged her to remain hopeful and advocate for herself.

"I think they reject everyone's application the first time. It weeds out the people who really need the benefits from those who don't," one member said.

"I appealed my rejection with a letter from my doctor and got benefits," another member explained. "You should, too. Don't give up!"

Group members often had dealt with similar realities, such as lengthy, confusing, and bureaucratic processes to obtain services and benefits. They encouraged each other by sharing firsthand stories and giving advice about navigating the system. They waited out the process with one another and relied on each other's ego strength to persist. Christine pursued an appeal, and the group held her by hearing her updates—or lack thereof—week after week, until one week she came in with good news.

"I knew I couldn't hold down a job, but they didn't believe me. I felt invisible. I was broke and broken," Christine began through her tears. "But now I will have money coming in. Now I know I will be okay. Last night, I let myself order pizza and had it delivered for the first time ever. I felt so normal to be able to do that."

The group collectively breathed a sigh of relief. They understood the dignity and power that come from having a little money and a few more options. Resonating with meaning behind Christine's pizza, they shared how they would celebrate making it through their own hardships or having more stability in their lives. The conversation was playful, poignant, and hopeful, especially for a group of women who find themselves feeling—and being treated—like they are not entitled to much.

Group members' practical or concrete concerns, such as Christine's struggle for disability benefits, were a way to seek and give help. The tangible give-and-take fostered trust among group members, which in turn allowed them to reveal more of themselves to one another and deepen their commitment to the group. Out in the world, group members experienced their symptoms and hardships as barriers to being accepted and understood, but in the group, their illness, limitations, and struggles were entry points for connection. As is a hallmark of mutual aid groups (Gitterman, 2004), a taboo topic is acceptable for discussion and central to group cohesion. It was around their struggles that members' strengths, skills, and inner and outer resources were revealed.

Perhaps the same was true for me. The struggle that I experienced as a clinician in a financially strapped hospital system eventually revealed my strengths, skills, and inner and outer resources. Rather than becoming disempowered, immobilized, and isolated, I identified an efficient way of delivering services to a disenfranchised client population that all too often bears the brunt of hard economic times. Our open-ended, long-term therapy group provided a sense of community that addressed the needs of both the over-burdened clinic and multi-stressed clients. My own needs were met, too. As Dr. Rachel and I reached beyond our individual work, our collaboration helped us to be responsive, adaptive, and invested in doing the challenging, meaningful group work together.

Think About It

1. Can you think of other ways in which group work could meet the needs of multiple members of a system at once?

2. What are the benefits and drawbacks of combining psychotherapy and psychopharmacology treatments in the same group?

3. In what ways might group work not enhance efficiency for workers?

References

Bowlby, J. (1988). *A secure base: Clinical applications of attachment theory.* Florence, KY: Psychology Press.

Gitterman, A. (2004). *The mutual aid model.* In C. Garvin, L. Gutierrez, & M. Galinsky (Eds.), *Handbook of social work with groups* (pp. 93-110). New York: Guilford Press.

Additional Reading

Bronstein, L. R. (2003). A model for interdisciplinary collaboration. *Social Work, 48* (3), 297-306.

Gitterman, A., & Schulman, L. (2005). *Mutual aid groups, vulnerable and resilient populations, and the life cycle.* New York: Columbia University Press.

Roller, B., & Nelson, V. (1991). *The art of co-therapy: How therapists work together.* New York: Guilford Press.

Chapter 31

Group Practice Complexities: A Hospital-Based Group for Persons Living With AIDS

IIIIIIIIIIIIIIIIIIIIIIIIIIIIIIIIIIIIIIIIIIIIIIIIIIIIIIIIIIIIIIIIIIIIIIIIIIIIIIIIIIIIIIIIIIIIIIIIIIIIIIIIIIIIIIIIIIIIIIIIIIIIIIIIIII

by Gregory J. Tully, Ph.D., MSW

When I studied group work in graduate school, I learned abundant theory from expert teachers. They taught me about group work planning, stages of development, member roles, and types of groups. In addition to group work knowledge, I was introduced to material on group work skills and values. As my coursework progressed, I felt confident I could be a successful group worker, fostering mutual aid in the group. I looked forward to helping group members experience the many benefits not gained in an individual session but only found when being part of a well-executed group.

During my graduate school field internships, group work came fairly easily for me with a variety of populations. All the while, however, I kept worrying that one day there might be a group population or a group need I would be unable to effectively assist. What if there was a group of clients whose struggles were too complex for me to help? Could I really work effectively with any group population in any group setting I was assigned?

When I was hired to work in a hospital setting to facilitate groups with persons living with AIDS (PLWAs), these insecurities surfaced. Both the setting and the population posed a great challenge for me in terms of my preparedness and abilities. I had never worked in a hospital setting, and I sensed the fast-paced, complex organizational environment would challenge me. In addition, I had never had a serious health diagnosis, and I wondered if I could effectively serve a population with whom I had little in common. In fact, I had never been ill enough to spend even one day

211

in a hospital, I did not have extended knowledge of AIDS because of the enormous complexity of the disease, and I suspected I had unconsciously avoided thinking too much about AIDS because I feared how overwhelming it would be if I became infected with a virus that could not be quickly "fixed" by a prescription from my doctor. Overall, I had doubts I was a "competent enough" group worker for a hospital setting working with a PLWA group.

Today is Tuesday, the day of the week my PLWA group meets. My day begins with a variety of typical hospital assignments, with my PLWA group scheduled to meet late in the afternoon. Group work in hospitals is complicated. For example, I have been able to reserve a room that is centrally located in the hospital, is always available at the time I need it (4 p.m., when most group members can attend), and is air conditioned, roomy, and reasonably clean; however, I know I am fortunate to reserve this room, because it is not always easy to find a space like this in a hospital. To get this space (and to get support with promoting the group), I made sure I got to know other staff in the hospital. I realized that if I wanted a good space and good attendance at the group meetings, I needed to get the support of various hospital personnel, including administrators, nurses, doctors, aides, and other social workers. My ability to network and form good relationships with hospital staff has been crucial to the successful execution of the group.

My boss originally told me the purpose of my PLWA group should be to provide support for PLWAs who want to discuss their therapeutic issues in a once-a-week open membership group. However, the members of the group have led me in a different direction. Like my boss, I assumed group members would want to talk about emotional struggles, but each week the group has consistently steered the content to be an educational group with an occasional diversion into self-support. The group members want education/information about a variety of topics—topics like the newest medications available on the market; the side effects of medications; how to deal legally with potentially discriminatory work site practices; strategies for communicating with family, friends, and partners about their identity as a PLWA; and the latest information on AIDS research.

I co-lead the group. My co-leader is a nurse whose primary assignment in the hospital is patient education. As a social worker trained in group work, I have the expertise to facilitate groups, and as a patient education specialist, my co-leader has a lot of medical and resource/referral knowledge about AIDS. We are a strong combination; we balance one another in terms of expertise the group needs. On the other hand, we have different personalities when we work. I can get emotional about the day-to-day issues that surface in the group, worrying that I am not helping enough, and concerned that the group members need more support from me. My co-leader is less emotional than I am and feels that one needs to do one's best on the job but go home at night with a clear conscience about separating work responsibilities and worries from home life. Although I am pretty good at making sure I take care of myself emotionally, I also recognize that my co-leader's approach is a wise one, especially when working in an intense environment like a hospital with a population like PLWAs.

When my co-leader and I arrive for today's group at 4:00 p.m., I look around the room to get a sense of who has decided to attend our open membership group this afternoon. As usual, there is diversity in the group in terms of gender, race, and age. AIDS does not discriminate, and this fact is manifested each week (and today) in our group composition. One consistent PLWA diversity theme in the group composition each week is "method of contracting the disease," and today's group is no different. There are nine group members who are present in the room today.

The theme for today's group emerges within a few minutes. Two members have brought up concerns about existing medications they are taking and their continuing frustration with a lack of development of new medications. Some group members have been using medications for many years, and others have begun taking them more recently. Everyone seems focused and engaged as the conversation unfolds. My co-leader shares information about new research on current treatments and new medicines in development. I use my group work skills to enable members to verbally participate. A few members are silent, but I leave them alone, noting to myself that the majority of the group members are participating and the silent ones are not withdrawn but are quietly focused. At times, I am tempted to steer the group members away from their intellectual discussion of medications, and move them toward a greater expression of feelings about concerns and frustrations. However, I remind myself that it is best to let the group members slowly find their way to their thoughts and emotions without my interference.

Mid-way through the session, my mind wanders somewhat to two countertransference concerns I am struggling with in the group today. One concern: *Is there anything I can do or say to help relieve their anger, worries, despair about certain medicines being unavailable or seeming inadequate?* A second concern: *Can I fully help/understand the group members' current struggles with medications when I have no personal experience with taking medications for a serious illness?* As I continue to facilitate the group interaction, I gradually find resolution to my two concerns.

Resolution to my first concern: What can I say or do to help relieve their anger, worries, despair about certain medicines being unavailable or seeming inadequate? As the group progresses today, I am reminded of the power of mutual support. Do I, as group facilitator, need to worry about finding a solution to fix their struggles? No. The group members are sharing their universal issues with AIDS medications, and they are finding their mutual voice of support and action through interaction with one another. Some are offering advice to others about managing medication side effects, while others are suggesting alternative meds or therapies. One member offers to bring in an article about a new drug that is soon to be released. I don't need to have the answers for them; I need to facilitate their experience of finding the mutual support and sharing of knowledge that only a group can provide.

Resolution to my second concern: Given my lack of experience with medications for a serious illness, can I relate to them? As the conversation in the group moves toward a discussion of frustration at the government's support of research and treatment for certain illnesses and not others, the members talk about the government spending large amounts of money on heart and cancer research while limiting funding for other diseases like AIDS. It dawns on me that I can relate to them to some degree. I watched my mother suffer for 10 years with a slowly destructive diagnosis of Alzheimer's. She had little awareness of where she was or who was near her (me, my father, my siblings, and lifelong friends), and we were forced to watch her continuously cry and moan in her bed most hours of each day for nearly five years until her death. Each day I was with her, I would wonder with frustration why more was not being done to offer relief to her and other Alzheimer's patients, and why there was limited research planned to find a medication or a cure for such a devastating disease. Thus, I had some sense of the emotions motivating the group members' discussions about the limits of medications. I had lived with my own pain and frustration related to the limits of medication and the government's complex, inadequate relationship with healthcare. I could relate to the group members to some degree.

The group ends for today, and the members leave. I remain in the room with my co-leader for a few minutes. We like to process the group session immediately after each meeting. My co-leader believes it is helpful to talk about the group briefly before going home for the night, and I find it is very helpful for achieving my goal of better separating my work day and my home life. We both agree that the topic today was worthwhile, and that our group members succeeded in gaining information and support for one another.

As I leave the room, and make my way through the busy hospital floors, I exit the building and I smell the fresh air outside. I reflect on my ongoing but gradually diminishing worry that I am still not the most perfectly qualified group worker for this assignment, and I decide to reframe my thinking more positively. I remind myself I am using every bit of the group work knowledge I possess, and I am certainly succeeding in providing my group members with the many benefits of being in a group. Group work in a hospital setting with PLWAs is complex, and I need to give myself some credit for being a pretty good group worker. This new way of thinking suits me better. It has been a good day.

Think About It

1. A question: What are one or two strategies for separating your personal life from your social work life when facilitating groups in stressful workplace environments with complex populations?

2. A point to ponder: Is it best to have a group facilitator who has personally experienced the group's issues, or is it good enough that the worker is well trained as a group facilitator?

Additional Reading

Gitterman, A., & Salmon, R. (2009). *Encyclopedia of social work with groups*. New York: Routledge.

Chapter 32
Family Caregivers: Services for Unsung Heroes

IIIIIIIIIIIIIIIIIIIIIIIIIIIIIIIIIIIIIIIIIIIIIIIIIIIIIIIIIIIIIIIIIIIIIIIIIIIIIIIIIIIIIIIIIIIIIIIIIIIIIIIIIIIIIIIIIIIIIII

by Kim Lorber, Ph.D., LCSW, MSW

Caregivers of older adults and others who cannot function independently are the invisible rope holding together families, relationships, histories, and cultural values, very often at the cost of extreme personal sacrifice. As a result of an absence of funding and alternative resources, many suffer financially, losing employment and relationships while experiencing dire personal health and family challenges.

A New York City hospital provided a program for seniors, offering many free social work services such as caregiver and bereavement support groups. I facilitated existing groups and developed new ones, in traditional and new formats, while providing individual therapy, telephone and in-person crisis counseling, visiting hospitalized members, and designing and contributing to two newsletters. My part-time schedule included a 10½ hour day accommodating early morning paperwork, evening groups, and individual therapy sessions.

I would usually respond to at least one caregiver crisis. Although some elements of my day were scheduled, there was usually something urgent that came up. On this day, it was visiting Ann, a patient I had come to know, who wanted to know what death was like as she correctly anticipated her own imminent demise. I do not think she expected an answer; she wanted someone to care about and remember her. The majority of my day was spent facilitating several 90-minute groups between a few short-term individual 45-minute therapy sessions.

I learned about some new telephone technology and developed a reminiscence group for homebound elderly members. This group was unique among all I have ever facilitated. Participants were recruited through the newsletter. This eight-session morning group was the first of my day. The group was comprised of homebound women whose isolation was due to fragility; ambulation challenges; and spouses, family members, and friends who had died or were geographically distant. The special telephone technology called members a few minutes before the start of the group, one by one. I was called last. The program I prepared involved history, by decade, to create a reminiscence agenda for discussion among the visually and physically separated members. New rules applied: names were given before sharing, as visual and other cues were absent in this telephone environment. It would take time to discern voices.

The urgency of the isolation experienced by these strangers accelerated their connections as if they were reunited friends talking about shared experiences 60+ years later about their old neighborhoods, schools, and events. From day one, it became clear that my agenda was unnecessary and, frankly, distracted them from what they hungered for—friends with whom to share life stories about what was important to them, not about historical moments. This verbal-only environment removed any stigmas about disabilities, appearance, socioeconomic class, weight, and age; the telephone connected equals.

The participants were immediately engaged and shared family, war, and neighborhood memories; recipes; family traditions; and more. Stories about late husbands, grown children, and grandchildren seemed not so different from what might happen in an in-person socialization group at an adult day program, absent photos. The hunger to connect was great with whoever was in attendance, and there was no curiosity about anyone missing on a particular day. (I followed up with missing members after each meeting.) When a member's telephone was disconnected—a self-described delicate and petite woman who had once been blown over by a strong wind while walking to a mailbox—I only knew she had experienced a drastic life change and would not return. Some members wanted to stay in touch with new friends and asked to exchange telephone numbers during a session. Immediately, I would receive calls as to who could or could not have a member's contact information. I repeatedly discouraged any group disclosures and encouraged inquiries to be made through me after securing specific contact permission.

The most interesting element was the deceptive label of reminiscence. This suggested to me the absence of an urgent connecting issue key to this group's purpose. However, there was an intense urgency of the immediate intimacy, skipping typical group developmental stages. Separated from too many, for too long, members shared contact beyond a wrong number, confirmed doctor's appointment, or blaring television. Although generationally less disposed to sharing very personal information, they connected via anecdotes and memories. This encapsulated the group's essence that might never have materialized had it been labeled a group for people who are stuck at home, of fragile health, absence support systems, and desperately lonely. The whole-hearted storytelling, and absence of even a moment of silence, showed the need for connection shared by each person who had answered the phone to participate that day. The use of telephone technology predates Internet social networking and uses equipment that is accessible and familiar to all.

I was, admittedly, confused about my role. I occasionally engaged someone who had not participated. One suggested, to the hearty agreement of many, that they should use Access-A-Ride to meet for lunch. I had not anticipated the intense connections between members and was deeply moved.

I had previously developed a lunch time group to offer a convenient drop-in resource for caregivers. Interviews and member commitment were not required. The challenge of caring for someone in the hospital, with medical practitioners dropping in to check on patients, prohibited caregivers' participation. This group, although well-intentioned, did not meet participants' needs.

The early afternoon closed caregiver group was an offshoot of a successful long-standing evening group. There was much prep work involved in establishing a new group, including advertising, interviewing prospective members, and booking meeting spaces. More men participated. It is often the case that caregivers will be women, sometimes the daughter, spouse, or in-law. One husband was caring for his dying wife, and his daughter was in the evening group. Sheila had moved in with her parents after losing her job, quickly becoming a full-time caregiver while craving a new job and independence. Her brother would fly in annually bearing many opinions, and she would disagree and become very angry. Grace grieved her mother's declining health, eventual move to hospice, and death.

In both closed open-ended caregiver support groups, some members would ultimately lose the person for whom they cared, experiencing a state of limbo. Their support system of other group caregivers was long-standing, but their circumstantial needs made a bereavement group more relevant. We, the facilitators, felt the organic moment of moving to another group would come to the bereaved members when they were ready. It did.

My bereavement group colleague and I discussed our respective groups as time permitted. He felt Martha had not grieved long enough, but he was unable to define the right amount of time. (I was seeing her individually.) Martha had been married to her great love for 35 years. He had been experiencing physical losses over the preceding 10 years. Their doctor told her if she did not put him into a nursing home, she would have a stroke. Martha made the hardest decision of her life. To me, his 10 years of declining health, organ by organ, memory by memory, and physical dependence at the expense of her health, were all mourning stages. My colleague and I debated whether her lack of obvious grief was healthy or not. In fact, it was what it was.

I had become the co-facilitator of the open-ended closed caregiver evening weekly support group when I started this job. It had a well-educated and articulate membership of 12. New members were interviewed in person. The group participants often went to dinner afterwards. Group rules—inclusive of disclosure, confidentiality, and taking turns/not overtalking—were shared with new members.

An important part of co-facilitating is determining respective roles and identifying methodological commonalities to resolve differences. Members would come in filled to bursting. Somehow, the most pressing of issues would prevail, with all participants focused on the most distressed member(s). Such organic prioritization and attention to one another left others' needs unspoken and some members silent. My co-facilitator and I had differing views as to how to attend to the latter. I advocated for a last 10-minute check-in with those who had not participated; he felt group members should practice reciprocal care. I disagreed with this parallel process of asking caregivers, stressed beyond their very seams, to attend to others. The check-in prevailed, and eventually, I facilitated the group alone. One woman, attentive to another's priorities, disclosed during the member check-in her husband's stroke since the previous week. Group members gasped. Another woman shared her decision to take her severely demented husband off of dialysis following a lucid moment when he looked into her eyes and said he wanted to die. Somehow, the pressing issues and limited time to address the needs of family caregivers did not change the dynamic. Each member was at a unique crisis point.

Cultural promises, family dynamics, and health issues provided many challenges for group members. Esther, the daughter of Holocaust survivors, promised her parents she would keep them in their home and never move them to a nursing home. Her sister was uninvolved, and Esther experienced guilt about the abuse the 24-hour nursing staff suffered from her father's Alzheimer's uncensored outbursts and fits of violent behavior. Selena, of a traditional South American culture, lived with her non-English speaking parents in a one-bedroom apartment. She had been a bank manager, but her parents' medical needs consumed her time, resulting in divorce, unemployment, and her daughter's refusal to visit. Family caregiving was the only culturally acceptable option. Sarah's husband left her when she became her Alzheimer's diagnosed mother's caregiver. She paid out-of-pocket for a caregiver while she worked (after having first bathed her mother who would stand, hands at her sides, under the streaming shower, completely disconnected). Sarah slept on the couch while her mother used the only bedroom. Her sister lived in the same city, but was frequently traveling or redecorating her numerous homes. She did not help in any way, a typical sibling dynamic.

Maria enjoyed a wonderful marriage and planned retirement in the Caribbean in the house she and her husband built. Suddenly, he was diagnosed with an aggressive, debilitating disease that affected his motor control and ambulation. He could not leave his doctors. Expenses required delaying retirement and giving up their Paradise plans. Depressed, and in individual therapy, she responded to a hospital depression trial. Maria was not accepted—she was too depressed and was not given any referrals. She came straight to group with this day's topic.

Groups are a powerful resource for members. My most successful groups require little intervention, as members interact with reciprocal respect. I facilitated another group that remains dear to my heart.

During my social group work internship, I asked to develop a new group. I chose to start one for HIV sero-discordant couples. Sero-discordance refers to different HIV statuses of partners within a couple; one member is HIV positive (HIV+), and the other is HIV negative (HIV-).

I mention this group because I think it was one of the first, if not *the* first, of its kind in New York City, in the mid-1990s. It was the beginning of my experience working with the stress of caregiving. I ran it for 18 months, until work and doctoral studies prohibited my ongoing volunteering. The group was comprised of couples I interviewed by telephone, including one heterosexual, one lesbian, and the rest men who had sex with men. The group members were committed to each other and even met while I was on vacation. One HIV- member had been the psychiatrist of one of the HIV+ members—awkwardness was quickly overcome via confidentiality reminders. When one HIV- partner wanted to become pregnant by her HIV+ partner, all group members vehemently protested the risk of HIV infection. Members shared commonalities in different ways. Some couples had been in long-term committed relationships pre-dating the HIV+ conversion of one partner, and other couples were newly dealing with intimacy and risks of HIV contraction. In other dynamics, HIV- partners could share their thoughts and feelings instead of the more frequent discussions about couples' issues. HIV+ partners could share their fears of infecting their partners.

I remember one session vividly. A new couple had joined. HIV+ Michael, of one of the two original couples, explained he had just been released from the hospital after almost dying. He looked ter-rible, very thin, weak, angry, and scared. It was important to Michael and Peter to attend. Filled with emotion, Michael, who had known me for almost 1½ years, attacked me verbally. I listened; he vented. I did not seek clarification. I wanted to see what would unfold. I observed myself vividly not taking anything personally. We all left together, as usual.

The new members privately told me they would not return because of how I had been treated. I thought it might be something else, perhaps experiencing the fear and witnessing the face of near death. I called during the week, having sought permission first. They did not return.

The following week, Charles, the HIV+ partner of the other original couple, too sick to attend the previous session, who had been filled in by his long-term HIV- partner, took Michael to task, demanding his apology. I remained silent. Michael apologized and shared his insight that his anger was not with me. He had been scared, and I had been there for him for so long that he did not fear losing me. I found his insight profound and a glimpse into the fears shared by all group members. As with the caregiver groups, I found it a privilege to bear witness to such deep insights.

My typical day with caregivers of older adults comprised a variety of tasks, including handling telephone or in-person care-giver crises, as well as providing individual therapy and facilitating groups. Often, I did not know what the day or a group would bring. Caregivers, who had shared so much in their groups, sought tools of comfort and survival, returning to their own lives, seeking a bal-ance between grief and relief.

Think About It

1. What are some of the cultural issues that affect caregivers?

2. What is the difference between self-help groups and those facilitated by social workers or other professionals?

3. These groups took place in New York City. Do you think the issues of caregivers are different in other parts of the country?

Additional Reading

Ness, D. (2011). Women, caregivers, families, and the Affordable Care Act's bright promise of better care. *Generations, 35* (1), 38-44.

Obama, B. (2011, November). *Proclamation 8748—National Family Caregivers Month, 2011.* Daily Compilation of Presidential Documents,1-2.

Tolkacheva, N., Van Groenou, M., De Boer, A., & Van Tilburg, T. (2011). The impact of informal care-giving networks on adult children's care-giver burden. *Ageing and Society, 31* (1), 34-51.

Resources

Alzheimer's Association: *http://www.alz.org/*

Department of Health & Human Services Administration on Aging: *http://www.aoa.gov/AoA_programs/HCLTC/Caregiver/index.aspx*

Family Caregiving Alliance: *http://www.caregiver.org/caregiver/jsp/home.jsp*

National Alliance for Caregiving: *http://www.caregiving.org/*

National Family Caregivers Association: *http://www.nfcacares.org/caregiving_resources/*

Chapter 33
The Caregiver Support Group

||||||||||||||||||||||||||||||||||||||||||||||||||||||||||||||||||||||||||||||||||||||||||||||||||||||||||||||||||||

by Denice Goodrich Liley, Ph.D., ACSW, LCSW

As I am sitting here, it is hard to believe that the caregiver support group will be ending in two weeks. This group is one of the "extras" I have in my work week as a geriatric social worker. It was initially started to help out family caregivers, but in the end, it has been one of the most educational and eye opening experiences of my work with geriatric patients and their family caregivers.

Today's group has not been remarkable in and of itself, but when I look at each of the members, it is truly hard to believe that they are now able to come out each week and discuss their challenges. They listen to each other, sometimes offering ideas but many times just nodding, acknowledging, and validating what another has said. I am a part of the group, but also not seen as an official member. I serve to assist and coordinate activities as the group asks me. I regularly joke that I am the hostess. Today is no exception.

The caregiver support group came out of a desire to recognize the role of the caregiver. Family caregivers often feel as though they are responsible to see to everything themselves, and they may be reluctant to seek help or to inquire about assistance. This reluctance about seeking outside help can, and in many cases does, lead to caregiver isolation, depression, feeling overwhelmed, or complicated health concerns that could lead to premature placement of the patient. As the medical social worker, I heard similar stories from so many of the family members providing care. This led me to believe that if I could get a group of the caregivers together, it would help normalize their feelings, and they would provide support for each other.

In my mind, it seemed so easy. Serving as a social worker for a geriatric medicine service within the Veteran's Affairs Medical Center, I had a caseload of patients and many family caregivers. So I thought just set up a time, a place, and start inviting people, and magically I would have a "Caregiver Support Group." Well, let me tell you, it has been anything but easy to get where I am today with a feeling of satisfaction and a successful group experience.

The caregiver support group is two hours long each week for eight weeks. This is the third year that I have been offering caregiver support groups. I have learned that it works best if I run one group session for eight weeks with a fixed group of caregivers and then offer a new group with new members. Within the two months the group runs, group members grow supportive of one another and do not appear to require the formal group atmosphere to get together. By this milestone, members begin planning their own activities and/or have more frequent contact with select members of the group. Most commonly, when one group comes to an end, I schedule a new group to begin, with about a month's break between groups. Caregiver support groups don't typically occur in December and January, because snow is always a possibility in my part of the country, and roads may be icy, making it unlikely that caregivers would attend. My current group is the first one of the new year, and I think that having the nearly three-month break from caregiver support groups makes this group seem better. At least it makes me more aware of how much I gain from being with the family caregivers.

Saying my caregiver support group is two hours long is very misleading. It isn't like the caregiver support group takes roughly three hours of work each week—prep work for a half hour before the group, the group happens, then a half hour after group to wrap up everything. Recruitment of family caregivers is ongoing. The need to talk with patients and families probably takes an additional half hour on top of each meeting I am already having with the patient and family. It takes time to explain what the caregiver support group is about, ways that the family member might benefit, and then helping to problem-solve care for the patient if the caregiver is going to be away at the support group. Getting members for the group requires that I listen and sell the group as having something to offer the caregiver. At least that was what I initially thought.

What I learned is that the caregiver support group works best with very little of me and most of "them" doing what they decide they need to do. Today, all I had to do was mention that we would be meeting for two more weeks, and the group took over organizing the weeks ahead, as well as talking about where we began six weeks ago. They made suggestions of topics that they were interested in and some programs that they wanted more information about. I have learned that these family caregivers are quite competent in organizing and getting things done.

I now approach my "sell" of the caregiver support group from the point of view of what the family caregiver has to offer other family caregivers. When I visualized the caregiver support group, I saw the goals of the group as the group members being supportive of each other, learning about community resources, normalizing their feelings, and providing alternatives for handling situations. The key benefit of the group is the peer experience. The members themselves provide the voice of those in the trenches, thus validating that the caregiver is "not alone, is not crazy, and that many of their feelings are in fact normal." Additionally, as the social worker, I get to learn more about the people who provide care to the patients I serve. What I did not know until I had done a few groups is that the caregiver support group provides an entirely different view of the home dynamics—a view from an entirely different perspective. The family caregiver gets to be the focal point. So much of the care, the services, and needs all center on the patient—the caregiver support group provides a voice and validity to those who are doing the care.

Today as I listen to the stories of "what has been happening" this past week, I hear of struggles with daily care needs for the patient, the concerns of caregivers that they may not be able to continue to care, worries about the cost if outside services are used, and fears of the unknown. Before I participated in the caregiver support groups, many times all I "heard" or interpreted that I heard was a caregiver concerned about care needs of the patient. As I listen in the caregiver support group, I have learned that much more is not being said.

The caregiver support group targets family members who provide ongoing day-to-day care to an older adult. The vast majority of caregivers live with the older adult and are on call as a caregiver for 24 hours a day, 7 days a week. The majority of members of caregiver support group are wives, significant others, daughters, or daughters-in-law. The caregivers are not only providing the 24 hours a day, 7 days a week care—they are trying to cope with care needs as well as grieving the changes and losses of the loved one for whom they are caring. Listening today, I hear stories of better days. I learn things about patients I have known for years that surprise me. The caregiver support group provides me with much richer texture to the lives of the patients I am working with, as well as those who are providing the care to the patient. I hear of things that they wish to share with others, rather than merely the regular routine check-up questions.

Today's group has eight members. I think this is the perfect group—eight weeks for eight people! When I began having caregiver support groups, I had the groups weekly, and they were open to anyone and everyone. My largest group was nearly 20 people. The members ranged from those with patients in the hospital to family caregivers providing 24/7 care. The diversity was too much, and the size was horrific, as it didn't allow much talking time to individual members. My smallest group has been one family member! Other than happening at the scheduled time of the Caregiver Support Group, not really much of a group experience. This group of eight caregivers ranges in age from late forties to over eighty years of age. All the caregivers are wives. This provides common ground around issues of "in sickness and in health," as well as struggles with children, parents, and in-laws. One would think of the forty-year difference from youngest to oldest member as a challenge, but these two members are probably closer to each other than to other group members.

My caregiver support groups are now closed membership. The first two weeks are open to come and try out, but by the third week, I have found that family caregivers are either committed or not. Introducing new members after the second week prevents the group from developing cohesiveness. The longer the group meets, the stronger the bonds within the group. If someone new were to come to today's group, the person would feel like an outsider and most likely would perceive all the people in the group as being "very close to each other."

I schedule the caregiver support group for early afternoon in the middle of the week. Part of the reason for this schedule is that the group has to fit around my scheduled activities within the medical service. The early afternoon has proven to be the most popular with caregivers. Frequently, as time goes on, some group members meet for lunch before group, go to a movie after group, or plan an early dinner for anyone interested in the group. Today, the group is going to a nearby local restaurant to have pie afterwards. When I was planning and developing the program for the caregiver support groups, this would never have entered into my planning. In the three years that I have been leading the groups, all but the first group have scheduled their own activities outside of the support group. Sometimes, I am invited, but frequently I am not "formally" asked to join in. At first, I felt somewhat slighted, but one group member said, "We'd invite you, but you have work to do." It reminds me that I am part of the group, but I am not one of the caregivers.

Today, after the group has ended, I am rewinding the group in my mind as to what happened, what was said, what I think was not said, and what I need to follow up on. I honestly spend more time in following up after the caregiver support groups than in preparing and anticipating for the next group meeting. This is probably the most different aspect from any of my other group experiences. Prior to beginning the caregiver support groups, programming and planning took a big part of my time. I felt I needed to be prepared, to have materials for the group, and to be sure that every group offered "something" to the family caregivers, so they felt that the group was worth their time. I now know that the family caregivers are the "gold" of the meeting. Initially, I may need to help start the group and break the ice, but these family caregivers are very competent and capable people who can direct the group. The caregiver support group is truly a perfect model of a self-help group.

I am fortunate that the geriatric medical service I work on is located on the ground floor of the hospital. The medical service also provides outpatient clinic visits at this location. There is a conference room located right off the lobby that we use for the caregiver support group meetings. Patients and families frequent our area of the hospital regularly, so the location is familiar and there is ease and convenience in parking. This has helped when talking to caregivers about attending the support group. Many see the group as part of our medical service. Today, a group member was telling others that she was recommending the group to a wife of a patient she met in outpatient clinic. "I told her that she needed to get into the next group. She did not know what she was missing. Of course, I told her that she would meet lots of wonderful people, but they could not be as wonderful as the people I have met." Former and current group members are part of the recruitment force for future groups.

Today's group has ended. I feel a sense of accomplishment and satisfaction. Eight family caregivers have expanded their circle of resources outside of themselves. These family members no longer look to me to be a conduit to resources, problem solving, or validation. Each caregiver support group has a unique atmosphere that comes from the individual members of the group, as well as the "synergy" of the group. Each week, I learn something new. I may learn something about a patient, a family member, a challenge that someone is reluctant to share, or some way to handle a caregiving problem. What amazes me each week is the strength and courage of the family caregivers and their readiness and willingness to share with others.

The personal benefits to caregivers are numerous. The decrease in stress and isolation, increase in support systems, and education about resources available are only a few to mention.

The patients, residents, clients, and consumers whose caregivers participate in these groups are much less likely to face premature institutionalization resulting from burnout or illness of the caregiver. Less isolated, less stressed caregivers are able to problem solve and to provide more ideal care.

As a social worker, I can see the benefits of leading a caregiver support group in the faces of the participants. One family member, who later assisted as a co-facilitator, said it all: "My participation in the caregiver support group has reformed me from a DO IT ALL MYSELF into someone who can ask for help and has some help to offer others." The caregiver support group truly models that we all need some help, and that others are willing to help when asked. It is the best resource for family caregivers that I know of!

Think About It

1. There are currently more than 50 million people in the United States caring for loved ones 18 years of age and older. As the population continues to age, what are some ways to assist those in caregiving roles?

2. What could be considered "unmet needs" of caregivers? What are some possible solutions to helping to meet these needs?

Resources

National Alliance of Caregiving: *http://www.caregiving.org*

National Association of Social Workers. Caregiving Current Trends— NASW releases Standards of Social Work Practice with Family Caregivers of Older Adults: *http://www.helpstartshere.org/seniors-and-aging/caregiving/caregiving-current-trends-nasw-releases-standards-for-social-work-practice-with-family-caregivers-of-older-adults.html*

National Family Caregivers Association: *http://www.nfcacres.org*

Chapter 34
Pet Loss Support Group

llllllllllllllllllllllllllllllllllllllllllllllllllllllllllllllllllllllllllllllll

by Juliet Sternberg, LMSW

Thursday is my Monday, the start of a busy four days of work. As the practice director of Hope Veterinary Clinic, which I run in collaboration with my veterinarian partner, I walk to work on Thursday mornings anticipating all the tasks that need to be accomplished. These include meeting with staff members, responding to client e-mails and voicemails, managing the finances, and ensuring that the environment is in good shape.

We do not charge for my counseling services—they are instead part of the comprehensive services that Hope Vet provides. Rather, I am paid to manage the practice. This works well unless there is a billing dispute involving someone I have been counseling. In this event, I delegate the issue to one of my assistants—the office manager or head receptionist—rather than enter into an awkward and ethically conflicted exchange with a client.

It is not until early evening, when I take a walk to collect my dog from daycare, and stop at home to feed him and my cats, that my thoughts turn to the evening's Palliative Care and Grief Support Group. I wonder who will come. Because it's a drop-in group open to anyone (Hope client or not), and to people nursing their pets through end-stage diseases, as well as people experiencing loss, participants vary each week. However, similar issues recur no matter the number or demographics of the attendees. Most people come once or twice, and occasionally someone will come for many months. Sometimes, people will return after a break or seek individual therapy from pet-sensitive social workers to whom I refer them.

231

I still have a little performance anxiety and worry that I won't be of adequate help, but after 10 years of running this group, I reassure myself that the magic of the group will prevail.

Although animals have lived around the human fireplace and grain store for thousands of years, it is only in recent decades that pets have been recognized as integral members of the family. Sadly, the social work profession seems to be lagging behind our clients in this regard. Numerous bereaved clients have reported that their therapist has stated something to the effect of, "You should replace your lost pet and realize that it was just an animal." Needless to say, this does more harm than good, and clients end up feeling even more isolated and unbalanced when, in fact, they are experiencing a very normal response to a profound loss. I apologize too often for my profession and hope that the next generation of social workers, recognizing pets as family members, will be more empathic.

This evening, three people attend the group. Josie is in her 70s. She walks using a shopping cart for stability, the result of a stroke a decade ago, which robbed her of her dancing career. In the interim, she and her husband divorced, and she has recently lost her 12-year-old dog, Mikey, to cancer. As she speaks, it becomes clear that the impact of the cumulative losses is wearing on her. Josie has been coming almost weekly for five months and says that the group is helping her find community and support. For the first four months, she was focused entirely on her stated inability to get over this loss. "I miss him so much," she repeats. "I should be over this by now." Encouraged by the other participants, Josie is gradually acknowledging the multiple losses and that "getting over this" would mean not needing the group anymore and giving up the last identity of being a loving pet owner. Finally, she acknowledges that she doesn't really want to work on "getting over it" at all, and that this is okay. She is convinced that she didn't love Mikey enough, and is berating herself for this, in spite of doing things like wrapping gifts for him and putting them under the Christmas tree. We know her well enough to tease her gently about her perceived lack of love, and she laughs.

People commonly express feeling guilty that they didn't do enough—and the group finds itself discussing what is "enough." The participants conclude that it is indefinable, and animals thankfully have remarkably low expectations about "enough" where love, care, and quality of life are concerned. For a moment, Josie can acknowledge that she wouldn't be feeling this much pain if she hadn't loved Mikey, and the others reassure her that Mikey certainly experienced that love. I expect Josie to attend the group for a long time.

Amanda is a new attendee tonight. She reports that she lives alone and has recently lost her cat, Sammy, the admitted love of her life. "I had to wait all my life for the right man, and when he came, he was a cat!" she says. The group laughs, easing any tension she has about being here for the first time. Amanda expresses her spiritual beliefs about Sammy being in heaven and worrying that he might not know how much she loved him and that she wanted only the best for him. This leads to a more general discussion about the spirit world and animals' place in it. This is a common theme, and I am often reminded of my social work training to "meet the client where the client is." This means never imposing my own spiritual beliefs, but always trying to support clients in exploring their beliefs and thoughts. Ritual is often meaningful for clients, and Amanda talks about doing something to honor Sammy's memory. The group helps her with suggestions about making a scrapbook of photos and memories, writing letters to Sammy telling him how important he was to her, and inviting friends to a memorial gathering. All have been used in the past to good effect depending on circumstances and appropriateness

Monica is the third attendee tonight. Her border collie, Jackson, is in the end stages of intestinal cancer, and she is here for support during this intense nursing and caretaking experience. We used to separate people whose pets are in the throes of palliative care from people who have lost pets, but we have found that combining the groups can be cathartic. And so it was tonight—Josie and Amanda helping Monica to make quality of life decisions, and Monica reassuring Amanda and Josie that they were indeed great "pet parents." We talk with Monica about the paradox of this experience—becoming intensely closer to her beloved Jackson, all the while knowing that she will soon lose him. Amanda says that this has been a life-changing experience, and Monica is agreeing with this. She is using the time of reflection and intensity of emotion to consider a career change to work with animals, or volunteering at an animal shelter after she loses Jackson.

The participants all say how helpful the group experience is to validating their feelings and being able to share similar experiences with one another. I find this to be the essential power of the group over an individual counseling session—the sharing of common experiences helps normalize feelings that they may have believed to be abnormal, and it decreases the isolation so prevalent after a profound loss. And no matter how dissimilar participants might appear at the outset, ultimately the common bond of love and loss makes for a potent and moving group experience.

Typically four consistent themes emerge in pet loss groups:

1. Clients need reassurance that they aren't crazy for feeling so devastated about the loss of their close companion, and the loss of their caregiver role.

2. People need reassurance that they made good decisions and need not feel guilty about treatments they decided to pursue or the decision to euthanize their pet.

3. Clients are sometimes angry after a pet has died. If they are angry with the doctors at our clinic, I have to try hard to not take it personally, but rather to recognize that it is a normal part of the process of trying to rationalize their pet's death.

4. The emotional pain of the loss will eventually not be so intense but will never completely fade. New pets may be adopted and may become equally as loved, but can never ever replace the lost pet.

I am often tired and have low energy when I come to group. It has almost always been an exhausting day. But when the group ended tonight, as in most weeks, I am left feeling what brings us all to this profession—the satisfaction of using my skills and experience, of helping people to feel a little better, and giving them some supportive tools to use to help them during the coming months. And I am warmed by the participants' gratitude of finding a supportive social worker and a group of pet owners who understand the importance of their relationship with their pets and the deep pain of their loss.

Social work students often contact me enquiring about working with animals. While I believe that there is a tremendous need for social workers to work with animals and people, and that animals are a largely underutilized social work intervention, the most challenging aspect of obtaining work in a private veterinary clinic is the difficulty of getting paid for doing clinical work. I am paid at Hope to be the administrator. Other social workers have obtained veterinary nursing degrees or sought training in animal-assisted therapy. Provided that new social workers demonstrate self-reliance and creativity, there is no reason why they shouldn't seek to make a career in this emerging social work field.

Think About It

1. Think of someone you know (perhaps yourself) who has lost a pet. How did you respond to that loss? Being perfectly honest, did you consider that the pet was a family member? If so, why? If not, why not? And how did this feeling influence your response to the loss?

2. How do you feel about death, loss, and grief? It is something we will all experience in our lives, but is something with which few people are comfortable. What can you do to feel better prepared to help yourself and other people cope with the experience of loss?

3. How might pets be of benefit to people with various needs? How could pets be used at your internship placement or in your social work practice?

Resources

Pet loss support for clients: *http://www.petloss.com*

SWAHAB: Social Workers Advancing the Human Animal Bond. Based in NYC, monthly meetings and a mailing list at *swahab@yahoogroups.com*

Veterinary Social Work list: *[VETSW@LISTSERV.UTK.EDU]*

Chapter 35

Children Facing Loss: Renewing Hope Through Group Sharing

IIIIIIIIIIIIIIIIIIIIIIIIIIIIIIIIIIIIIIIIIIIIIIIIIIIIIIIIIIIIIIIIIIIIIIIIIIIIIIIIIIIIIIIIIIIIIIIIIIIIIIIIIIIIIIIIIIIIIII

by Kenna Liatsos, MSW, Ph.D.

Nowhere am I more fully grounded in my beliefs about children than when I listen to their experiences of loss and their feelings surrounding the death of a loved one. This is the opportunity and privilege I have as co-leader of a children's bereavement group.

My work with bereaved children began years ago when I was unexpectedly invited to interview for a part-time position in a pediatric hospice. At that time, I was working full time as a social worker in a public elementary school and had just begun a part-time private practice. I had no intention of taking on any more work! Encouraged by a friend, however, I scheduled the interview.

Little did I know that this would be a moment that would change my professional direction and add deeper meaning to all of my relationships. I felt an instant connection with the nurses at the interview, as they identified that the greatest need for social work services was not with the dying child but, rather, with the young, well siblings in the family. They described many services available to parents and the ill child, but the same were not readily available for the siblings they described as "lost." Most of these children were young, in pre-school and primary grades. The nurses could see the questions on the children's faces, and despite all good intentions on the part of caring adults, often the explanations given to them about their brother or sister's illness or death were abstract and confusing. Parents were overwhelmed with their own grief. They were often uncertain about the best way to approach the topic with their children or felt they were protecting their children by not discussing the death. They were grateful for additional support.

The nurses were sensitive to the parents' struggles and understood that these youngsters needed honest and reliable information. We shared the belief that children were capable of feeling deeply, of understanding what was happening in the family, and of participating fully in the family's experience. We discussed the need for children to be offered reliable information from a developmentally appropriate approach, and that they would benefit from the opportunity to express their feelings within the context of a trusting relationship. And so began my work with bereaved children.

Currently, I work part time for Cranberry Hospice and Palliative Care, an organization that is located in Plymouth, Massachusetts, and provides hospice services for patients and families living on the South Shore and Cape Cod. One of the programs offered through the hospice is called Fragile Footprints. It is dedicated to the needs of children and has two special missions—a pediatric palliative care component providing help and support for families with a child with a life-threatening illness, and a bereavement program committed to offering individual and group services to children and their parents. Although I also value my time teaching graduate social work students, it is this clinical work that continues to be the center of my professional life.

In this role, I serve as co-facilitator of a children's bereavement group. Children are referred by local schools, hospitals, pediatricians, and various community service organizations. The group bereavement services are offered free of charge and are open to all families in the surrounding communities.

Groups are ongoing throughout the school year. The number and composition of groups are determined by the age of the children. Ages range from pre-school through high school, with 6- to 12-year-olds accounting for the majority of group membership. Families are free to attend any and all sessions. Therefore, the composition of groups may change from one session to the next. We acknowledge that this structure presents challenges for group planning, but we also understand that after a death, families may feel overwhelmed, overscheduled, and uncertain of direction. We believe that they will come if the need becomes clear. We trust this process.

Our goal is to provide a safe environment where children can share their feelings and experiences. We have found that, in addition to discussion, expressive art activities such as drawing, painting, sculpting, and body awareness exercises have been effective modes for expression. Furthermore, we work to strengthen the relationships among children and their parents. The parents meet together in a group while the children's groups are held. The parent and children's groups are facilitated by professional social workers with assistance from trained volunteers.

The following description of the structure and content of our group process is a composite of actual group sessions.

The groups meet every two weeks from 6:30-8:00 p.m. I arrive at our group site with other staff members and volunteers about 45 minutes before the group begins, to arrange furniture and organize materials that we plan to use that evening. We then meet together briefly to review the activities for the evening, clarify directions for the volunteers, and answer questions that may arise.

Families arrive at 6:30, and we begin with a meal of pizza and a beverage. This time offers us an opportunity to talk informally with children and parents and to greet new families. Although parents have registered and the group process has been explained, family members may feel anxious on their first night. We use this time to answer questions and help them feel at ease.

The groups begin at 7:00 p.m. As the parents leave to join their group, the children gather together in an activity room for an opening circle. We briefly discuss the common experience of all group members, that of the death of a family member. We introduce ourselves, and the children identify the person in their family who has died. Usually this is a parent or sibling. Next, I lead the group in a brief activity. We encourage children to participate, but also support children if they wish to be quiet observers.

For the beginning activity this week, I am presenting "Rocket Ship Blast Off." We stand on a parachute with our hands over our heads and palms facing each other. We imagine that our bodies are powerful rocket ships and that the parachute will help to lift us. Each child is given a turn to choose a place where they would like their rocket ship to go. We count down from five, lowering our bodies with each count. When we reach number one, we blast off by jumping straight up into the air. The goal is to provide an opportunity for children to participate in any way they wish, imagining that some children may use this to relate to an experience with the deceased. First it is Bobby's turn, and the 6-year-old says he would like to go to the park to play. We pretend we are at the park with him as he describes the slides and swings and the joy he feels there. Next it is John's turn. He is 11 years old and says that he would like to go to heaven to see his brother. He imagines what this looks like and what they would play, and expresses how much he misses his brother. Next, 9-year-old Mary says that she would like to go back in time before the death of her father. She talks about her sadness as she recalls the joy she felt with her dad. Paul remembers holidays and wishes he could play the game that he and his mother played every Christmas.

After each child has had an opportunity to "travel," we divide into groups according to age. I work with the youngest children as we begin our group activity. This week we are creating bowls with Model Magic®, everyone designing their bowls with the colors and shapes they imagine. The bowls serve as vessels for feelings that they will write or draw on small cards, discussing which feelings they prefer to keep inside (in the bowl) and which emotions they feel comfortable expressing. As they continue the activity, group members talk about the feelings they have in common, some of which are easy to share and others that are not. For instance, Paul, whose mother is deceased, says that he feels confused when kids in school ask him what his mother and father do for a living. He doesn't know what to say. Mary suggests that Paul give an answer only about his father's job. Another child says that maybe Paul can simply explain that his mother died. Paul says he thinks about that, but it makes him feel different from the other kids, so he doesn't say it. He says that he doesn't know anyone else in school whose mother has died. I ask if anyone else has felt "different" like Paul. Another child immediately joins in saying he too feels different having only one parent. Paul says that he's glad that at least here other kids know what that feels like. This leads to another conversation about the many ways in which children in school may feel "different."

Another feeling that is discussed is "confused." As one child states that she was confused about the happenings surrounding her father's death, another says that he was present when his father died and also has unanswered questions. The focus of the discussion now becomes how to get the information they need—who to go to, how to ask the questions, and what their worries are about asking their parents. (Children often say that they worry about upsetting their parents if they bring up the topic of the deceased.).

As the conversations continue, I notice that it seems difficult for Bob, nine years old, to name positive feelings. He is new to the group, and although he has participated in our discussions, this is hard for him. As other group members offer suggestions, he seems suddenly surprised as he discovers the word "confident." We discuss the meaning of this word and affirm all of the strengths everyone here possesses.

It is soon time to end the activity and join the older children for our closing circle. Children are asked to show their bowls to the group and share feelings they have expressed. John proudly shows his colorful bowl and adds that he often feels "distracted" in school. Other children respond that this sometimes happens to them. Bob discusses his feeling of "confident" that he has found for the first time tonight. Other children show their unique creations and name more feelings that they discussed in their smaller groups. We end the evening by acknowledging that all feelings are important. Because we have talked about some easy and some hard feelings, we want to leave them with warm feelings from the group by offering them a "warm and fuzzy" pompom to take home. Every child takes one or two or three!

We invite parents to join us for our favorite good-bye song. Holding hands in a circle, we sing *Three Little Birds* by Bob Marley.

Finally, when parents and children have left, the staff and volunteers review the evening. We discuss strategies that were successful, what we might change, and most importantly, our observations of how the children are feeling. The social worker who facilitates the parent group shares topics of importance. We know that the causes of death in these families include illness, accidents, and suicide. We also know that in some cases, the children have not been told the cause of death. This presents a challenge, especially since we have observed some behaviors of children that may be symptomatic of trauma.

We know that grief in a family is often unspoken. Parents want the best for their children and frequently worry about them after a death in the family. Often, however, their own suffering makes it difficult for them to communicate with their children. They may find themselves emotionally unavailable to their children, or they may be uncertain about the words to use. If the children are very young, parents may think the children wouldn't understand or will forget. In our groups, we continually see the capacity of young children to know the truth through their feelings and experiences, to express what they know and feel, and to support one another. They need honest, age-appropriate information. We work to help parents and children give voice to pain that may be buried in silence, grief that if left unresolved may continue to burden relationships in the future. We believe that this sharing is the key to renewing hope and strengthening relationships. We brainstorm how we can create a bridge of communication among parents and children. We decide to begin by scheduling an evening for the professional staff to meet with parents.

Our open group format provides people with the freedom to attend the group, leave, and return to participate once again. Despite the challenges that this structure presents, we believe that this approach respects their process, allows space, and encourages continued growth as human needs and lives change. These families are my best teachers as they share their most intimate experiences. I know that this is a privilege experienced by few, and I am grateful for all they continue to teach me.

Think About It

1. In what ways did the expressive art work facilitate the children's feelings of belonging and break through feelings of isolation?

2. How might the challenge of silence in the families be addressed with children and parents?

Additional Reading

McClatchy, I., Vonk, M., & Palardy, G. (2009). Efficacy of a camp-based intervention for childhood grief. *Research in Social Work Practice, 73* (3), 405-422.

Schuurman, D. (2004). Literature for adults to assist them in helping bereaved children. *Omega, 48* (4), 415-424.

Schuurman, D., & DeCristofor, J. (2007). *After a parent's death: Group, family and individual treatment to help children.* In N. Webb (Ed.), *Play Therapy with Children in Crisis: Individual, Group and Family Treatment* (pp.173-196). New York: Guilford Press.

Webb, N. (Ed.), (2002). *Helping bereaved children: A handbook for practitioners.* New York: Guilford Press.

Resources

National Child Traumatic Stress Network (NCTSN): *http://www. nctsnet.org*

Chapter 36
Grieving Daughters

||||||||||||||||||||||||||||||||||||||||||||||||||||||||||||||||||||||

by Margot Wilson Jurgensen, MSW, LCSW,
and Kay E. Whitehead, MSW, LCSW, CT

This group was born out of the felt need we experienced in our community, as well as the interest that was nurtured in the strengths-based practices in our group class work in undergraduate and graduate school. Later, as a hospice social worker already doing grief groups, my colleague Kay, who worked in the bereavement department in our hospice, asked me to join her in the development of a grief group for women who had lost their mothers to death. I jumped at the chance. As a woman whose mother had died five years earlier, I was aware of the unique and complex mother-daughter relationship and how central it can be to our sense of self.

Women come to this group to share their stories and to receive affirmation and validation that the grief they are experiencing is "normal." They learn that they are not alone on this journey, and the journey is healing itself. So often, the bereaved say, "How many times can I tell my story to my friends or family? I am wearing them out," or, "No one gets me." They report people saying to them, "Surely you must be over it by now." A grief group normalizes their experience of a variety of intense emotions and grief reactions.

In developing this grief group, the rhythm of each of the 6-week sessions became a template for the rest of the groups that we developed and co-facilitated. It is a combination of learning more about self, sharing of stories, and discovering and expressing feelings. Other tools, such as exercises in writing, art, and music, are introduced to find expressions for grief that at times does not have language. It is a psychoeducational and process group.

The week we have chosen to write about is Week 5 of the 6-week group, in which we share "Memories of our Mothers." Kay and I meet for 30 minutes to an hour before each group, to discuss any concerns we have about group members and go over the plans for the evening. This week, we have concerns for two women. Wendy has lost her mother within the last two months, and we learned in the intake that their relationship presented as enmeshed and dependent. "How will I ever live without her? We did everything together," she would lament. Kay and I have had concerns about having a woman in the group whose grief is so fresh, but we have been encouraged by professionals who know Wendy to accept her into the group. Although she presented as grieving deeply during the intake process, she has participated appropriately during the first four weeks. (If someone is not ready or a good fit in the group and decides to withdraw after the group begins, we, as facilitators, validate the woman's sense of self and decision to drop from the group.)

Rosa, born in South America, whose mother died and was buried there, has discussed in previous weeks how difficult sharing memories has been, and this week is all about memories. Kay and I have discussed how we might handle both these women if they need extra support in the group.

We also set up the room—tables with chairs in a circle, name tags, tissues, a CD player for soothing music as they enter the room, and any handouts that we will use for the session. We talk about who is opening and closing, and who is leading which exercises.

As we begin week five, we open with a brief breathing exercise, encouraging the women to put the cares of the day aside and to be present to each other for the next two hours.

After the breathing exercise, we do the weekly check-in, asking if there are any loose ends from last week, when we discussed "Forgiveness and Healing." Wendy talks about wondering anew, "Did I do enough for my mother? Was there more I should have done?" Others in the group express feeling the same way. As facilitators, we "normalize" these feelings and encourage her to share what she was able to do for her mother. When the women are ready to move on from the general check-in, we shift our attention to the actual sharing of memories.

We discuss some of last week's session and why we share our memories. First week, we shared the stories of the death of our mothers verbally, and the next week we wrote our history of losses. Week 3 explored creative expressions about our feelings through drawings and the ways we coped. Week 4, we did some work around remembering the painful moments we hoped to forgive, heal, and release. In this fifth week's session, we remember our mothers in a more tangible way, with an item to share that was their mother's or reminds them of their mother. Telling one another our stories differently helps us integrate her death into our life.

We encourage each person to share her memory one at a time, not interrupting each other. We encourage and suggest gentle questions from the other women in the group about the items each has brought, and encourage them to respond if they choose.

Before the sharing begins, I am noticing that Wendy is tearful, trying to control a sob. Then she wonders aloud if she can go to the restroom "to get control."

Kay and I look at each other, and I signal her that I am going to go out with Wendy to see if I can invite her to walk with me and talk to discharge her emotion. (Some therapists would keep the member in the group.) I chose to honor her request to leave the room and trust the process. The fact that I went with her proved to be the right thing to do. The group was comfortable when I encouraged Wendy to step out and go for a walk down the quiet hall. The group continued to share their memories as Kay facilitates. On our walk, Wendy sobs freely and talks about missing her mother and the changes in her life, but also how she appreciates the support of the group. "We are all in a similar situation," she says through tears. After a few minutes, she says she is ready to return to the group. She is gently acknowledged as the group continues to share their memories.

When it comes to Wendy's turn, she is able and willing to share a favorite picture of herself and her mother, taken when she was five years old, around the time her father left the family...and yet she reports how she and her mother made a life for themselves. "We made it!" she reports. She is appropriately and understandably tearful as she tells her story.

The group continues in its sharing, and Rosa is next. As she talks, it becomes an increasing challenge to understand Rosa, as tears choke her already difficult to understand English, her second language. She tells the group the story of how her mother sang a lullaby to her in Spanish when she was a child. She loved hearing it, and all the children in the family had the same lullaby sung to them growing up. Now she is a new mother, and she is longing to sing this same lullaby to her daughter. She knows all the words, and she knows the tune by heart. And then, she breaks down and sobs, saying, "I can't sing it because my mother is not here anymore. I just can't do it!" The whole group just sat there for a moment in silence while she sobbed. Then, one by one, the women asked questions about the song, what it was about, what she remembered, how many children in the family did her mom sing it to, and did she have any kind of recording of the song. She answered all their questions, and as she did, the stories contained in the answers are what comforted her.

We thanked them for sharing their memories with us and asked, "What has it been like for you to share memories? Does it make you feel closer to your mother, or does it feel more distant and difficult?" Wendy responds that she is feeling closer, more settled, as she is beginning to experience herself as a separate woman from her mother. Rosa stated she felt "the pain of her longing even more," as she remembered anew that she was not able to be there with her mother at the time of her death.

We begin closing the group by discussing our final week together. We asked them to please come with a gift your mother gave to you, and one you gave to your mother. It is to be a non-tangible gift, like a character trait or a value. We would be using this as part of our final candle lighting ritual. Additionally, we encouraged everyone to bring finger food to share after the ritual. There would be a celebration after completing the six weeks.

There was a touching end to this Grieving Daughters group the following week. At the candle lighting ritual, Rosa brought a recording of the lullaby to the group. We played it near the end of the service, at the suggestion of one of the group members. Rosa began to weep quietly as we all listened, and as she did, instinctively the women gathered around her, and a couple of the women put their hand on her back as the lullaby played. Everyone hummed along with the second verse, affirming her, hoping to give her newfound courage to sing to her daughter the lullaby sung to her by her mother.

After the group was gone, we spent a few minutes putting the room back together and debriefing with each other. This group had some challenges—each group does in its own way—but it affirmed to us anew the value and healing of the group process.

Some brief thoughts for facilitators—It became apparent, by trial and error, that the group functions best with eight to12 members, meeting for two hours each session for six weeks. Following a stated and predictable rhythm for the evening provided a safety that was important to the participants. It was our experience that it was important that the facilitators' mothers had also died. Being on this journey longer gave hope. We learned it is not in the best interest of the group/members if sisters or other family were in the same group. They tended to compare stories. And we found it was best to have women who had lost their mothers at least three to six months before taking the class, so they could be present to themselves and to the others and not stuck in their acute fresh stage of grief.

For Margot, whose mother had struggled with depression and was often distant, telling the story over and over again in the group helped to reframe the stories of the good and the not so good of that relationship, and come to a deeper peace, place of gratitude, and understanding of her mother.

Kay's mom had had brain aneurysms and strokes at a young age. Telling her story was recounting feelings of loss from the perspective of a child, caregiver, and friend. And it moved her to a place of healing and acceptance. The mother she had in all phases of life was the mother she loved.

Co-developing and facilitating the group provided for us the heightened awareness that in this mother-daughter journey of grief, there is much that is different and some similarity in our mother stories. But, gratefully, we do not feel so alone and isolated.

Think About It

1. Grief affects us differently and on many levels of our being— emotionally, physically, cognitively, behaviorally, and spiritually. As someone who might lead a grief group, how might you prepare yourself as a facilitator dealing with these issues? What resources might you use?

2. What can you do to provide for your own self care, as you are working with the bereaved?

3. What is your view/perspective of death and loss? How do you think this might influence your work in a bereavement group?

4. How could you become more comfortable "sitting" with the bereaved and the expressions of their loss?

Additional Reading

Ainsley, R. (1994). *Death of a mother: Daughter's stories.* San Francisco: Harper Collins.

Brooks, J. (1999). *Midlife orphan: Facing life's changes now that your parents are gone.* New York: Berkley Books.

Commins, P. (1999). *Remembering mother, finding myself: A journey of love and self-acceptance.* Deerfield Beach, FL: Health Communications, Inc.

Edelman, H. (1994). *Motherless daughters: The legacy of loss.* New York: Dell Publishing.

Kidd, S. M. (2002). *The Secret life of bees.* New York: Penguin Books.

Kottler, J. A. (2001). *Learning group leadership: An experiential approach.* Boston: Allyn & Bacon.

Neimeyer, R. A. (1998). *Lessons of loss: A guide to caring.* New York: McGraw Hill

Whitehead, K. E., & Jurgensen, M. W. (2007). *Grieving daughters: A grief support group for women who have lost their mothers to death.* Indianapolis: Self Published Manual.

Yalom, I. D., & Leszcz, M. (2005). *The theory and practice of group psychotherapy* (5th ed.). New York: Basic Books.

Zimmermann, S. (2002). *Writing to heal the soul: Transforming grief and loss through writing.* New York: Three Rivers Press.

Chapter 37
Group Work: A Means for Consultation With Schools

IIIIIIIIIIIIIIIIIIIIIIIIIIIIIIIIIIIIIIIIIIIIIIIIIIIIIIIIIIIIIIIIIIIIIIIIIIIIIIIIIIIIIIIIIIIII

by Robert Blundo, Ph.D., LCSW

G roup work is applicable to a wide range of systems and levels of practice. One way that is different from working with treatment groups is my use of groups to address challenges in agencies and organizations. I have been using group work as a means of consulting with individual schools around challenges that teachers and administrators face. Rather than meeting with a member of the administration, I ask for teachers and others in the administration to be involved in a group process. The group is usually focused on one or more issues the teachers and administrators are attempting to address.

On one occasion, I was asked to help with some problems an elementary school was having with students and their families. The principal asked if I would come to talk with her about the "struggles" her teachers were having with the kids. She seemed very frustrated and determined to make some changes to take care of the problems. Using a solution-focused approach (Jackson & McKergow, 2002; Metcalf, 1998), I was prepared to engage the teachers and administrators in a process that focused on what might be working already but in too small and fleeting a way in the midst of the chaos to be appreciated and expanded upon. The basic concept is to discover what is already working or taking place that is part of the desired outcome, even if in small ways.

I did not come with a predetermined set of actions to address problematic children. As with any group, from treatment to agency work, I never know what is going to be presented. I do have some comfort in recognizing some basic group work process and skills to help me engage and work with the members of the group.

The meeting started off with the principal listing and asking the teachers to list the types of problems they were having in the classroom. The teachers were exasperated by multiple problems and issues. It was like they were turning on a valve and all the problems and issues came flowing out. They shared story after story of what the children were doing to disrupt the class while the parents were not cooperating to make things better. Their frustration grew as they described difficult situations—"Then she got out of her seat and started fighting with another child, and I just lost it. She never gets her homework done, and her parents refuse to come to the school. These families don't care what their children do—the morning was wasted with trying to get those two to stay quiet until I had to send them to the vice principal."

The teachers all wanted to vent their frustrations. It was building to a crescendo when the principal asked everyone to write down all the problems they were having so they could give them to me. Now, this did not take very long. From the start to this moment, it could not have been more than eight or ten minutes. When given a chance to vent, the teachers were more than happy to oblige. The room was very tense, and frustration was dripping off the walls. Now it was my turn.

It was time to disengage from the problem-saturated session and the frustration that was building. I was not thinking about the problems, but about how the group might change direction toward finding what might be working—a solution-focused perspective. I paused for a moment, took a deep breath, and asked the group to take a deep breath with me. They laughed and tried to follow my lead. I shared my appreciation of the struggles they were going through and how frustrating it had been for them.

I then asked them to try something a little strange. It was a little experiment I would like to have them do with me. They seemed intrigued by the "strange" request and agreed. I said, "Imagine, after you go home tonight, you take care of things at home and then go to sleep. But this night is different—tonight a miracle happens, and of course, you do not know it happens because you are asleep. When you wake up tomorrow morning, you take care of things around the house and come to school. But a miracle has happened while you were asleep. The miracle is that when you arrive at school, you start to notice something is very different. The miracle has transformed the school and your experience with the children into exactly what you would have wished it could be when you first decided to become a teacher—what you dreamed teaching could be like. A miracle has happened."

I asked them to picture this in their minds—what they would see—and notice the school and the children in their class. Now, I asked each teacher to write down some of the things they would notice that told them "a miracle has happened." I asked them to describe in as much detail as possible what the class would be like with the children they had just described. I asked them to imagine what the children would be doing differently and what they, as teachers, would be doing differently in response to the miracle responses of the children. I asked them to try to create a very clear picture of what this would look like and to write it down. After a few minutes of writing down this picture, I asked them to think back over the past several weeks and think about a time, even a small amount of time, in their classrooms that something like any of this had taken place—just a small example of the miracle (DeJong & Berg, 2008).

The atmosphere had changed dramatically. The tension and stress had lifted from the room. A weight had been lifted off our shoulders. There were even a few smiles around the large table. Each teacher was able to recall a moment or longer when something like the miracle had taken place. This was followed by me asking them to think about what they had done or what had happened to make this time just a little better, like the miracle. It was somewhat strange to hear them talk about these "miracle" moments, what are referred to as exceptions in solution-focused work, given how the group conversation had started (DeJong & Berg, 2008). They were able to recall incidents or times during class that some of the miracle had taken place and how it might have been created. I was amazed at the teachers' ability to recall some of the things that they and some of the children had done to make the day or situation better. One teacher commented:

> *I was tired by that time of day and was not sure how I would go on, The kids had been a handful so far that day [there was general laughter and recognition from all around]. I decided to ask the kids how we should do the next lesson. As I spoke, I had this thought that this was not the right thing to do, but it came out anyway [more laughter and acknowledgment from the others in the room]. Then Anthony said, "Groups, do the group thing!"*
>
> *Others chimed in. "Groups! Yeah, do the groups!" This was some-thing we had done several weeks before...the kids work in groups and compete with other groups. At that point, I was willing to try anything [more laughter around the room]. They really got into*

it, and the lesson went pretty well. Most of them were actually involved in the work...maybe it was the competition...anyway. I actually felt better myself.

In another situation, a teacher had decided to engage the students by making a game out of a math lesson and appointed the biggest troublemaker to lead the game, commenting that he was good at math, even though he did not pay attention during class. The experiment worked for longer than she had expected. Even though things broke down at a point, she recalled the difference it made for the lesson and the student she had asked to lead the exercise. She also speculated that the time required of the students to stay focused during the math period might have been too long. But something had made a difference for a period of the day. After other teachers told their "miracle" stories, I asked how they might make these small miracles happen again and if they might keep a diary of the times when the class is better, even just a little. Rather than listing all that would go wrong on a day, the assignment was now on what goes a little better and what happened to make that possible.

The group meeting went well, and the feelings were much more positive and filled with possibilities. There was laughter and smiling all around. It was a real shift from feelings of frustration and resignation that had started the meeting. Of course, in this type of work, I never know what is going to happen. Maybe I was just lucky. In this case, I believe it was the use of a group process based on my solution-focused group work practice model that helped create a shift in focus for the group (Metcalf, 1995, 1998). Solution-focused group work focuses on desired outcomes and shifts the conversation toward the future and goals, which brings about a sense of hope and possibility. The moods change when the focus is shifted from problems to possibilities. Possibilities create a sense of energy.

I have learned not to try to "fix" things, but to open the door through group process for the possibility of change. The hoped-for outcome for me as a solution-focused group worker is the possibility that if even one of the teachers can grasp the idea and run with it, then there is success. Change takes time and effort. When acting as a consultant and using group sessions, it is hard to predict what the outcome will be with only one opportunity to meet, as was the case here. In the case of an agency or organization, it is a matter of maintaining support within the agency or organization for change to take hold.

Think About It

1. What do you think about the idea of focusing on the desired outcomes (the miracle question) rather than spending time discussing the many problems faced by the teachers?

2. Given the limited amount of time and the fact that this was going to be a one-session group, what do you see as the value in this group solution-focused session for the teachers?

3. What do you think might happen in the group if we had had an opportunity to meet on a regular basis while doing this work?

References

DeJong, P., & Berg, I. K. (2008). *Interviewing for solutions.* Belmont, CA: Brooks/Cole.

Jackson, P. Z., & McKergow, M. (2002). *The solutions focus.* London: Nicholas Brealey.

Metcalf, L. (1995). *Counseling toward solutions: A practical solution-focused program for working with students, teachers, and parents.* West Nyack, NY: Center for Applied Research in Education.

Metcalf, L. (1998). *Solution-focused group therapy: Ideas for groups in private practice, schools, agencies, and treatment programs.* New York: Free Press.

Chapter 38
Gloria's Casserole: Group Social Work at a NORC

IIIIIIIIIIIIIIIIIIIIIIIIIIIIIIIIIIIIIIIIIIIIIIIIIIIIIIIIIIIIIIIIIIIIIIIIIIIIIIIIIIIIIIIII

by Kristen Marie (Kryss) Shane, MSW, LSW, LMSW

I hadn't planned to work with older adults. As a former high school teacher and as an LGBT activist, I'd always focused on the adolescent and LGBT populations. For my final MSW internship, however, my school assigned me to the Alliance for Aging in Miami-Dade County, Florida. As someone who didn't know many elders and who certainly had never been one, I was admittedly quite nervous about this placement. My gregarious personality and true curiosity about the lives of others proved to be great attributes as I learned on my feet. I also discovered that it was quite helpful to learn not to take a client's reaction personally, and that older clients were often coming from a place of battling long-standing physical and/or emotional pain. Realizing this allowed me to not only be more accepting overall; it also taught me that sometimes just listening was far more important than any agenda I'd planned to discuss. This lesson in quickly reading a client and in being able to adjust to his or her needs has served me well in numerous settings, including my time as a NORC director.

NORC is a newer term, coined in the 1980s, and is an acronym for Naturally Occurring Retirement Community. In contrast to a nursing home where a person goes to live after reaching a certain age or need for care, NORCs happen when any small area of housing has a large number of people over the age of 60 who just so happen to live there. The goal of a NORC is to contribute to the lives of these seniors and to facilitate happy and healthy lives within their own homes, to prolong the clients' independent lives whenever possible. This benefits clients in that they are happiest in their own environments. It also benefits the government, as it remains less expensive for someone to live at home compared to living in a managed care or nursing facility.

The NORC in which I've been working is located in Astoria, New York, in the New York City area. This specific NORC is located in the middle of 40+ apartment buildings that house people who qualify for Section 8 housing. First built in 1951, many 20-somethings came here when the buildings were new to raise their families, and they have remained, providing us with more than 1,200 building residents over 60 years old. The demographic includes a population that is fairly equally divided: whites, blacks, and Hispanics. As is typical in New York, different cultures group together but live next door to each other, making it common for a Haitian woman to live next to a man from Florida who lives next to a woman from Puerto Rico. In this community, people often do not socialize across groups, which has presented in the NORC space as clients who were self-segregating with the race or ethnicity most like their own.

In some ways, a NORC is much like any other social service agency. Staff work as a team to help clients be as self-sufficient as possible, working with a goal-specific plan, and stepping in only when requested by the client or the client's family. The biggest challenge in working with NORC clients, though, is the difficulty of maintaining confidentiality. Although the staff is trained on HIPAA laws, the office location is both in the middle of the housing community where the clients reside and is located within the local senior center. This means that anyone coming to see a NORC staff member is seen by others entering and exiting the office, and those who see them also happen to be the client's neighbors. This often makes a person in need hesitate to request our services, refuse options that involve a staff member coming to their home, or find other ways to hinder their success, all in an attempt to protect his or her privacy. These extra roadblocks are frustrating for all involved but often feel insurmountable, since clients are unlikely to move and the office doesn't have a secret entrance. I also began to discover that the gossip in the housing community was worse than I thought, because a person's social group was quite small with the self-segregation of races and genders. I began to search for ways to combat this, recognizing that clients who felt more secure in privacy would be more able to benefit from our agency's services.

Group work with this population follows this same line of being both incredibly beneficial to participants and very difficult to pass through the initial stages of group formation. Through trial and error, I discovered that an open group worked best in this setting, as members often wanted to join only after hearing from others that it was a safe and fun place to be. In addition, since seniors tend to have more medical appointments than younger clients and may choose not to attend based on the day's weather forecast, a closed group of 10 may result in two members attending on a rainy morning.

I spoke with longtime NORC clients shortly after becoming the director of the agency, and I discovered that previous attempts at having groups failed because clients were uncertain whether they could trust the other members. Some reported feeling forced to attend, and others didn't feel they had anything worthwhile to contribute. Knowing that clients came from a variety of backgrounds and many were not formally educated past middle school, it was understandable that the majority could be fearful of being asked to complete tasks in front of others that they felt unable to accomplish, let alone feeling this discontent in a room full of peers/neighbors.

Eight weeks ago, as a test group, we began to offer a group gathering, which we called "Senior Circle." This took place in the back room of the common space, in a quiet yet open area. One of the last clients to enter was Gloria, a lovely woman in her late 70s who had no living relatives. Although she was one of our kindest clients, her fear of bothering anyone led her to a mostly solitary life. The staff would often introduce her to other clients, but Gloria's fears and shyness made others wary of her quietness, and they often shook her hand and then excused themselves to return to their friends. When Gloria entered the room, she could see that the chairs were prearranged into a circle and that clients were asked to introduce themselves by name before speaking. As is common in many group types, the more outspoken clients offered to speak first. As the group leader, I would encourage the more quiet folks to contribute. Soon, the more vocal group members were taking ownership of the group, directing questions to the quieter people, and telling longer and longer stories of their lives when it was their turn to speak. Clients began to notice that Gloria took a great deal of encouragement to speak but that, when she did, she told wonderful stories.

In addition, it was known among the clients that I come from the Midwest and am not fluent in Spanish. I was often able to use this to further the conversations, asking some of the quieter members who were nervous about speaking to me in English to help me understand the geography or traditions of their countries. It seemed that being the "expert" helped those clients to feel more comfortable in the role of educating me than they did in volunteering their own stories. These questions often led to multiple members talking to each other to try to collectively answer my questions. We also discovered that there were experiences in common between

Dominican women and their same aged peers who were raised in the southern United States. Sometimes, Gloria would quietly tell me that she'd wondered the same thing but had been too shy to ask. Before we knew it, the hour had flown by. I always closed the group with a request that the conversations continue throughout the week and that the clients share their experience of being in the group with others. I also asked that they let me know if they had future group topic ideas.

Today's group was based on the topic "Food From My Childhood." I was pleasantly surprised when 30 clients arrived, more than triple the average number for previous sessions! I learned that some of the members were so excited about this topic that they'd been discussing it all week with friends, and that those friends had decided to join to see what the fuss was about. At group time, we discovered that approximately half had brought items to share— including some staff members—to the delight of all. I noticed that Gloria was especially thrilled to be in the company of so many people, a rare treat for her.

We began by sitting again in a circle and by sharing our names and the story behind what we chose as our favorite meals. Although I made a point to let the members take ownership of the group and initiate the conversations, I sometimes would inquire whether a dish from one person's home country was similar to another's chosen food. This often led to discussions about food preparation, food storage, and commentary about how much times and food options had changed since they were children.

Gloria shared a story about the dish she'd brought, a casserole that had been common in her house while she was being raised in New York. For the first time, her peers heard her stories of being the youngest of three girls whose parents died young, and the fact that her two sisters had both succumbed to different forms of cancer. Gloria spoke of being protected by them all throughout her life and how lost she felt to live alone, both in her family home and in the world. It was immediately clear from clients' behaviors that they suddenly felt closer to Gloria, handing her a tissue when she cried. One reached to hold her hand, and another shared that she'd grown up with a similar casserole dish in her own childhood home in Puerto Rico.

After each had shared, we had a pot-luck style lunch, tasting bites from each member's contribution. Again, my Midwest background was brought up as the Latin dishes were foreign to me. So many clients were thrilled to have the opportunity to introduce me to new flavors and cooking techniques. Surprisingly, the discussion wasn't about teaching me something as my elders, but rather it was about someone with little education teaching something to someone with degrees framed on her office wall. It was a lovely way to give the clients power without causing anyone to feel looked down upon. Most everyone had a dish that someone else hadn't heard of, so there was education between folks from different countries, different states, and different times in history. Clients from Mississippi explained their dishes to women from Puerto Rico, who described an ingredient to a man from Ecuador, who helped us to understand that the dish he'd brought was commonly prepared in the 1930s but was considered outdated to serve in the 1940s, when some of the younger members were growing up. We quickly discovered that each person had both something to learn and something to teach, and all of us were excited to participate in both.

After our lunch group had ended, it was time for the clients to return to the larger main room for the afternoon activities. The mixing of ethnicities became more obvious in the dining room that day, and Gloria was suddenly finding herself invited to join other groups. Although she had been coming to the NORC for several years, this was the first time Gloria had company to sit with, many of whom invited her to join them for activities outside of the NORC as well—a wonderful sight for the staff!

Although a group of low-income elders likely has many shared experiences relating to aging and financial difficulties, the lesson in this for me was to recognize how to start where the clients felt comfortable, not where I felt prepared. As much as textbook chapters and classroom discussions teach us how to conduct groups in more formal settings, the ability to adapt to the clientele's surroundings and abilities is far more important for client happiness and group success.

Think About It

1. How might working with NORC clients differ from working in a nursing home or other senior housing facility?

2. Is it beneficial or detrimental for a social worker to admit to not knowing about something the client is an expert on (such as geography of a client's home country or familiar food)? Why?

3. How might you help a shy client become more involved without pushing him or her too far from her comfort zone?

Additional Reading

Greene, R. R., Cohen, H. L., Galambos, C. M., & Kropf, N. P. (2007). *Foundations of social work practice in the field of aging: A competency-based approach.* Washington, DC: NASW Press.

Hill, R. D. (2005). *Positive Aging: A Guide for Mental Health Professionals and Consumers.* New York: W. W. Norton.

Chapter 39

Tapping Into the Creative Parts: Art Therapy With Older Adults

IIIIIIIIIIIIIIIIIIIIIIIIIIIIIIIIIIIIIIIIIIIIIIIIIIIIIIIIIIIIIIIIIIIIIIIIIIIIIIIIIIIIIIIIIIIIIIIIIIIIIIIIIIIIIIIIII

by Jennifer Clements, Ph.D., LCSW

I remember very clearly when I was in my social work master's program taking an elective in art therapy. I was so excited about this type of work and at the same time had a sinking feeling that I was in the wrong field. I was quickly reassured by my instructor that clinical social workers are more than qualified to use the techniques and interventions of an art therapist. As the semester rolled on, I knew that I would want to use art therapy in my career. I just was not sure how.

My typical day includes working a full-time job in a large child welfare agency. I work part-time at a nursing home facility on the weekends. The agency contracts with me to provide art therapy services as a licensed clinical social worker. Since I do not work with older adults on a full-time basis, this part-time work is usually a refreshing change from the day-to-day struggles of child welfare. The agency has asked me to provide services to a small group of clients referred to as "end stage" residents. These residents are in the final stages of various diseases, and their doctors have given them less than six months to live. When I agreed to take this job, I had no idea how powerful and life changing my experiences would be working with these older adults.

I am responsible for facilitation of two groups, as well as individual sessions with the residents. The group members were chosen based on their interest in participating. All of the group members are engaged in a 12-week mutual aid group that centers on the use of art therapy to develop memory books as part of a life review process. Many of the residents were initially very resistant to the art work, but as the sessions continue, their confidence builds.

It is Saturday morning as I begin to pack up my supplies for the day. These include the usual items you would expect, like paper, markers, and pastels, but I do have some very special supplies that help me to aid the residents through their sessions—patience and positive encouragement! As I arrive at the home, one of the nurses tells me that John, a resident in the group I facilitate, passed away just last night. This is an expected loss, as John was dealing with end stage cancer of the stomach and lungs, but no less painful. Death is something that I do not have to deal with on a regular basis at my other job, so I am not sure how to handle this as I head over to my group.

I have about a half hour to prepare for group. I am gathering everyone's lifebooks, additional supplies, and my composure. Ideas run through my head about how we can process the loss of John. Should I bring it up, should I wait for one of the group members to do it, or should I just not mention his death? I rationalize in my head that the nursing staff will be dealing with this and that there are other social workers there to help them. Right at that moment, I find John's lifebook—full of his art work, memories, and not yet completed. This feels very sad. I decide to head over to the activity room to get set up.

Several residents are already there and begin to ask me what they will be drawing today. I tell them that we will be working on the page in their books about their fondest memory. As the staff help several residents get situated, I begin to hand out everyone's lifebooks. As I get to John's book, I carefully place it back in the box when Aggie, another resident, asks me if that is John's book. I answer her truthfully, with a knot in my stomach. She asks me what will happen to his book, and I share with her and the group that I am not sure. The group then begins a discussion about John, as they remember their times with him at the home.

The group is bursting with mutual aid, as they support each other through the process of losing John. Some of the residents are tearful, but most of them enjoy the stories of John. Then the subject of his lifebook comes back to me. The group asks me if it is possible to get his book to his family. Ellen, one of the residents, says that John has a son who visited him pretty regularly. I agree with the group's idea of getting his book to his son and decide to make a phone call to him after the group is over. Another suggestion by the group is to help complete his book with artwork of the stories they have of him. I am amazed by the great ideas and agree to help them add to John's book.

Each of them begins to draw—some of them with my help, some independently—their memories of John. Fran, a group member, yells out that John was the youngest of them in the group. Statements like "It just seems unfair," "It will be one of us tomorrow," and "I feel like I need more time" come out of members' mouths as they draw and process. The process is cathartic. Many of them cry, laugh, and yell out to the point that staff checks in on us a few times to see if we are okay. I check my watch, and we have gone well over our two-hour time frame. I ask the members to begin to wrap up what they are drawing.

As the artwork nears completion, I carefully add their pages to John's book. Many of them have used pastels, so I need to apply a fixative (basic hairspray) so the pages won't smear. This has to be done away from the residents, since many of them are on oxygen. The group wraps up and the residents head back to their rooms. Once the room is clear, I get to my work of preserving John's book. I am moved by the content and the submissions of his peers.

I check in with the nursing staff first to see if they have made contact with John's son. It turns out that the son will be arriving at the home later today to retrieve a few important belongings of his dad's. I ask them to inform me when he arrives, so I can pass on the lifebook. I have several individual sessions scheduled today, which I am now very late for, but all of the residents understand.

I hear my name being paged over the intercom. I am sure that this is about John's son. As I arrive at the front desk, John's son is standing there with a box of personal items. I introduce myself to him and ask him if he has a few minutes to chat. We walk over to the family room, and I begin to explain the lifebook and how John was working on this in group. I also explain the final pages and how they were contributions from the group based on memories they had of John. The son looks over the book and turns to the page we developed weeks ago about "a day I knew I was important." It is a picture of John, holding his infant son in his arms. I had written out at the bottom what John had asked me to write. "I knew the day my son was born that I was important—not because I had a child, but because I was holding a gift from God. A gift that was on loan to me and that I better take good care of him." John's son cried as he read that page, and I sat there with him in his grief. I do not remember how we wrapped up that moment, other than the fact that he thanked me and the staff as he walked out the door.

I walked back to the activity room and gathered up my supplies. I would need to go back to my office and write out some case notes of the session. As I finished up the paperwork and filed it away, I decided that I should thank John. I learned a lot about social work today and especially about myself.

Think About It

1. In what ways did the artwork facilitate the social work helping relationship?

2. Are there challenges to using art therapy with older adults that need to be considered?

3. Check out the Web site for the American Art Therapy Association and print out a resource you could use in your own practice.

Chapter 40

Some Things Just Have To Be Lived: Drumming in Group Work

IIIIIIIIIIIIIIIIIIIIIIIIIIIIIIIIIIIIIIIIIIIIIIIIIIIIIIIIIIIIIIIIIIIIIIIIIIIIIIIIIIIIIIIIIIIIIIIIIIIIIIIIIIIIIIIIIIIIIIIIIII

by Kyle McGee, II, LMSW

Some years before I was a professional social worker, I lived in the San Francisco Bay Area working as a clinical case manager by day and a musician by night. Like many of my peers, I was in my late twenties and trying to find that delicate balance between making a living and creating a life that would prove fulfilling. I loved my work as a case manager, but it was very hard. I was working at a community residence with transitional age young adults living with serious mental illness and helping them to negotiate transitions that were extraordinarily difficult for any young adult, let alone one with a tragic history of trauma, recent onset of schizophrenia, or bipolar disorder. In fact, the truth was that I had only one step ahead of them in age, so the parallel between our life courses was so very familiar.

At one point as I was nearing burnout, I decided to approach my clinical supervisor about taking a 6-month leave of absence so I could go study drumming in West Africa. One of the blessings that had entered my life at this time was a master drummer from Senegal, Abdulaye Diakite, with whom I had begun studying in Oakland over the previous year. Abdulaye was going to take a group of his students to his home village in Senegal for a few months to learn and experience firsthand the culture and history of the rhythms he was so generously giving us in class. I was granted this leave and met with such support from my superiors that it still seems unbelievable, especially when thinking about all the demands that case managers face in today's agency climate. But that's another story.

I went to Africa and returned to work six months later both transformed and rededicated to my work and to my life purpose. I had realized when I was away that I truly did love each of my two passions, social service and music, but that I had to find a way to bridge them together if I was going to actually maintain my sanity on any long-term basis. So I did just that. Again, I approached my saintly clinical supervisor, but this time it was with a proposal to start a drumming group for the members of the agency. To my relief, I received very positive and enthusiastic approval and within a month, I was set to start the group, which would soon come to be called, "Offbeat." I was both anxious and incredibly excited to finally have an opportunity to put in place what had become my present dream.

The group began, and over the next several months, it became a huge success for the members. I incorporated several simple rhythms as our main content, based on variations of West African rhythms that I had learned. Although I wasn't a professional social worker at this time, let alone familiar with mutual aid or other group dynamics, I could feel that these elements were in motion. It was exhilarating and, to my pleasant surprise, the members were not only enjoying the experience but they were getting GOOD! After each rhythm we played, I would always incorporate a debriefing with them to see how we all experienced it. Themes such as stress relief, invigoration, self esteem, and communication all began to surface on a regular basis. We would sometimes spend up to half of the group time discussing these themes.

Unlike some of the socialization skills group work that I had done before with the young adults, Offbeat's membership was open to consumers agency-wide and thus our composition included older adults as well as younger. The members all lived with mental health conditions and some had physical handicaps ranging from limited mobility to our one member, Madeline, who was deaf.

Madeline was in her late 50s and had been deaf throughout her entire life, a result of a pre-birth complication. She was generally very shy and quiet, and I found myself regularly preoccupied with her well-being during group. I believe this was due to the fact that my mother is legally blind; hence, the role of caretaker and being vigilant for her needs was ingrained in me. Madeline was very gracious and patient with my overcompensating toward her, and she always participated in group, even though it was hard to assess how much she actually enjoyed it. She was incredibly sweet, and although she was able to speak and read lips, she often would keep silent because of her anxiety around how others perceived the sound of her voice.

The group's success continued, and one day the issue was raised of possibly creating a video of the ensemble performing each rhythm. I thought this was a great idea and we started to brainstorm how we could put this plan into action. This is when our special "guest member," Suzanne, chimed in. Suzanne had taken a keen interest in our Offbeat group after I had presented about it at our agency's annual "Wealth of Health" conference—a local event that was mutually planned by both agency staff and consumers. My workshop showcased the success of our Offbeat group and the positive treatment benefits of drumming. Suzanne had spent years as a professional woodwind player for various orchestras and was currently retired and also the Board President of my agency (something I didn't realize was so special at the time). The group had agreed to allow her regular participation, as she expressed how wonderful and positive the experience was for her, and how it helped her feel a direct connection to what truly motivated her to perform the leadership role she played in the agency as a whole. Suzanne graciously volunteered her video camera and her husband to film the group in action.

We gathered for group that week with a wonderful sense of excitement and energy. The group was buzzing about how each of them would look on video or how they would sound, and I was feeling more nervous than usual as the leader, yet feeling as proud as ever. But what was most exciting was that we all knew this could be something wonderful. Something about having the opportunity to be on TV was heightening all of our senses and willingness to dream. Personally, I was really beginning to think about how I could expand this type of group activity to more of a business proposition. I remember that at that time I even met with the Deputy Director of the County of San Mateo Mental Health Agency to talk about a proposal for me to facilitate drum circle groups with all the youth under mental health auspices in the county. I had visions of our video becoming something of an instructional tool that could be marketed for all of us to benefit from, if it were to catch hold. Simply put, it was a moment of dreams.

The group started, and we played our rhythms with such energy and precision that I just couldn't help shouting out traditional exclamations and sounds that are typically done in traditional African drum circles. It was truly exhilarating, and I could also see everyone keeping a corner eye out for Suzanne's husband Perry, walking about with the camera in the room. After ending one of our favorite rhythms, we all clapped exuberantly and then fell back in our chairs to begin our reflection of the experience, which had become our tradition. Staying true to form, I had been tracking Madeline's behavior and demeanor during the group with extra vigilance to see how she was doing. To my pleasant surprise, she was more animated and jubilant than I had ever seen before in group. It was as if she let go of any inhibition! I could tell this was on the minds of others in the group as we went around the room talking. One of the other members soon commented about Madeline's positive energy and how that had given him an extra sense of energy and joy himself. (Madeline was able to read lips and, therefore, able to follow along with the conversation about her.)

Other members quickly chimed in with similar feedback and, finally, I looked at Madeline and asked her what it was like to hear this from everyone. She paused for several beats and then looked around at all of us as she began to get tears in her eyes. After a minute or so of comfort from all of us, she said, "I feel like I have found my own voice through this drum." The best she could describe it was to say that the vibrations from the drum, in combination with the singing and emotion, led her to a feeling like she could understand a voice, HER voice, for the first time ever. It was one of the most profound things I've ever experienced in my life, and we all began to sob—even Perry.

That day in group and the impact of the experience with Madeline has stayed with me throughout my career. The notion of group work activity being connected with finding one's voice has served as an anchor for me in almost all the groups that I have done, and even when I achieved my MSW in group work some years later, I think my ability to absorb the complexity of mutual aid was somehow enhanced by what happened in group that day with our beloved Madeline.

I don't recall much more detail of how we ended group that day as the emotional catharsis was so high. However, I do remember the phone call I received later from a mortified Suzanne, who ultimately explained to me that Perry had forgotten to press "play" on his video recorder for the entire session. I guess in life, there are just some things that have to be lived.

Think About It

1. How does the idea of "finding one's voice" relate to social group work concepts and the engagement of a group in activity? How can this be strategically incorporated as part of the purpose?

2. What other benefits do you think drumming has to offer as an activity? What would you need to consider if you were to

implement this in a group? Remember, if you can talk, you can sing, and if you can walk, you can dance!

3.   Check out the Web site Drumming About You with Bob Bloom *(http://www.drumming-about-you.com/)* and find out some tips on how you can get started with incorporating drumming into your own groups.

Chapter 41

Reaching Out and Outreaching: Connecting Rural and Urban Groups Through Technology

||||||||||||||||||||||||||||||||||||||||||||||||||||||||||||||||||||||||||||||||||||||||||||||||||||||||||||||||||||

by Sue Foley, B. Soc. Stud., MSW, MA, M.Ed.

Group work as a professional activity was a compulsory part of my undergraduate social work course. I was able take part in formal and informal groups for young mothers, children, and foster parents. The goals of these groups were very different, but before beginning social work, I had been involved informally with groups as a leader in children's holiday camps. I think this experience helped me to be comfortable in groups and teams in professional settings. It probably also helps that I am a fairly extroverted person who enjoys engaging in creative activities and what I now call generative discussions. I think this type of discussion seeks to engage a group of people in solving a problem or developing further understanding a particular issue.

My first foray into writing about my work as a social worker was a description of an innovative group for late teens who had been sexually assaulted (Mason, 2001). The culture of the group was "therapeutic." I was the new coordinator and social worker in a hospital-based social work sexual assault service. At that time, there were no models for me to follow. I worked with another social worker, and we developed a program by using the knowledge and skills of therapeutic groups that we had developed in both our initial training and in post-graduate short courses, including social skills, gestalt therapy strategies, narrative therapy approaches, and psychoeducation about symptom management and about the dynamics and effects of sexual assault.

Turn the clock forward, and my current professional role is as the coordinator of an outreach telemedicine program in the psychological medicine department of a large city pediatric hospital in Australia.

This program operates out of a large city and connects with rural and remote government community health settings. My particular role focuses on use of the videoconference process for educational activities, including clinical supervision and case discussion. In the past 30 years, I have undertaken postgraduate adult education master's studies, as well as postgraduate social work studies. I am a bit of a "technology person," so this position suits me well. It also allows me to be innovative and put into action the important social work values of social justice, service to humanity, competence, and integrity.

My typical day includes some face-to-face clinical work as part of a child and adolescent mental health team of psychiatrists, psychologists, nurses, occupational therapists, and me, the sole social worker. My role varies in that some weeks I have a lot of face-to-face acute clinical work, and sometimes very little. In the down time, I prepare reports, write evaluations, and plan strategically for the year ahead.

Today, I arrive at the hospital early to prepare for the 50-minute videoconference based "Trauma Think Tank," a group I facilitate every second week on Wednesday at 8 a.m. Mostly, this group takes place from the departmental conference room, which is equipped with a big screen and videoconference equipment. I also have videoconference equipment on my desk, but this is more difficult to manage with several groups of people on the screen and in the room.

I "dial up" to four groups of health, education, and child welfare professionals, including psychologists, social workers, and school counselors who attend four rural health sites. Our purpose in meeting is to increase our knowledge and skills about working with complex trauma. Following e-mail consultation, we choose an issue to discuss, such as "understanding the therapeutic window in counseling," or "working with attachment difficulties for traumatized children." I have access to a range of resources through the hospital's library. We watch a 30-minute video segment together before stopping the film, at which time I facilitate a discussion across the screen.

This open group has been meeting for 18 months. Those attending need to tell me ahead of time, so that the technology can proceed as smoothly as possible. At times, we have also had people joining by telephone. The feedback from the group has been very positive. The main concerns are usually about the technology faltering because of weather or equipment issues.

I have been excited to hear how members of the group have used the material they watch and hear, to create or construct their own understanding and then directly apply it to some of the clinical or systems situations with which they are struggling. From my discussion with them, I am aware that rural and remote practitioners do not have access to the "corridor conversations" that city teams can engage in.

Today in the hospital conference room with me are two social work students, a social worker from a community agency, a psychologist, and two other hospital social workers. The multi-site videoconference medium is challenging, but with time, the group has developed a significant level of comfort. The technology actually allows the rural sites to turn their microphones off and have discussion among them while watching the film material.

I still find it challenging to manage many remote controls at once, and the good relationship I have developed with the technology support staff means that we can usually problem solve very quickly. I describe my experience as being like a conductor. I seek to ensure everyone gets to contribute to the discussion and usually offer additional reference material, which may be e-mailed or posted later. The group takes place at the start of the day, so the equipment is more readily available and staff can get on with their day. When caseloads are high and meetings are many, professional development is often forgotten. The timing does reduce accessibility for some staff, so I have planned for the possibility of another time and another day.

The participants in this group range from students to highly skilled and highly competent practitioners. We are learning together from another expert and seeking to consider what we as a group learn that can enhance our practice. Such interactions are beneficial for me as I learn from others and also for rural clinicians who often speak of finding the interactive discussion helpful. It is sometimes a disjointed discussion, as the multi-site set up makes it difficult to pick up the cue of who is speaking next. However, the group seems to tolerate this, and I try to do the conductor role of identifying who would like to speak next. I find this process difficult at times, because in group work terms, I am trying to be many types of leader—process, task, emotional, and technology!

From speaking with my rural colleagues, I have learned how much rural clinicians and rural clients are often disadvantaged and unable to access these development opportunities. Telemedicine attempts to address the injustice that this situation creates. I am fortunate to be able use my social work and my education knowledge and experience to implement such processes.

After the telemedicine group ends, I head to my office to send e-mail invitations to the next session of this group. I make a note of where we are up to on the DVD, and I write myself a "remember" note for any resources I have offered to find. I head to the hospital coffee shop for a quick "social work secret business" meeting and coffee. I meet with my departmental social work colleagues to both discuss professional issues and catch up personally every two weeks. Social workers are the minority in this department, and it is good to keep our connections and maintain our value-based identity. I like to be inspired to remember our values and practice principles.

By mid-morning, it is time for another videoconference group that I usually co-facilitate with Lil, a junior staff member and a clinical psychologist. The department has been funded to provide these outreach services, and as coordinator, I seek to ensure that the program reaches out to rural colleagues in a way that meets their needs. This session takes place in my office, which is brightly covered in photos, books, and craft activities, providing an interesting backdrop to our videoconferenced picture.

The next group is situated about 1,000 kilometers away in a medium sized coastal rural town. Some conflicts in this rural team have had an impact on the supervision process, so I have joined Lil and the rural group to try to understand the difficulties for them. Sometimes it is hard to see everyone in the rural group, because of the room set-up. So, I ask them to rearrange the camera on the remote end and check the sound. I then suggest that we spend some time discussing how the rural clinicians would like to use their telemedicine time. I am well known to the clinicians and have met many of them in person when I have visited the centers in which they work.

The outreach program was established to be based on relationships and on collaborative exploration of issues. I also conduct regular surveys or evaluations to ensure I understand what is helpful and what is not about the outreach programs. Today, one of the key, strong personalities is not present at the session, and together we identify how today's session can be used, without too much difficulty.

One of the participants, Rose, identifies a struggle she is having with assisting young teens who have a diagnosis of Asperger's

Syndrome and are self harming. Fortunately for me, we have a new staff member, Jodie, sitting in on the session, and she has significant experience in this area.

In order to not establish an expertise hierarchy, the telemedicine group tries to use reflective processes. I use terms like "I was wondering about" or "that reminds me of." I have found that this process seems to inhibit the tendency for "ping pong" type conversations across the technological divide. Some groups are better and more comfortable with this process than others.

Today, Lucy, one of the rural clinicians, turns to Rose, her colleague, and says, "That is just like my client, Paul." I have found it really hard to engage him and he won't talk to me." Rose comments that they have not had trouble with engagement but when it comes to talking about feelings, it is really hard and the client changes the subject.

At the hospital site, I turn to Jodie and Lil and ask if they have any ideas or thoughts about how these issues are particularly affected by the Asperger's aspect of the person's function. Jodie comments that she has also struggled with these two issues. She has found a particular book helpful, and she has used a specific set of "feelings cards." She also acknowledges how difficult this kind of work can be.

When the hour and a half is coming to a close, I suggest to the group that each person, including the hospital staff, comment on what they have learned from the session. Jodie also promises to pass on some references by e-mail through me. When we end the videoconference call, Lil, Jodie, and I briefly discuss how difficult it is for rural clinicians to have in-depth discussion and to admit that they are having difficulties in their local settings. Lil and I are very appreciative of Jodie's input to this supervision group session.

I find the telemedicine process exciting. This session felt as if the process was empowering for all participants and supportive for rural clinicians. I hope that this will help them in their confidence, reduce some of their isolation, and add to their knowledge and skill level.

It is nearly lunch time and I hear my page go "beep." There is a new ward referral, and it is my turn to begin the information gathering process. It is a little girl with epilepsy who is refusing to walk for fear of having a seizure. The medical team needs help from the psychological medicine team. I pass the information on to the team medical officer, who will clarify the medical issues and then speak further with our multi-disciplinary team.

There is time for a quick lunch break before meeting with my student social worker, Lynda, and prepare for a project team meeting. This project team is a group of social workers, one doctor, one health education expert, and one psychologist. I have been a member of this group for nine years, and now I am a key leader and organizer as we continue to carry and develop a project that has now become international. Lynda has been conducting some online research to help with the next stage of the project. We have produced a three-minute animated film about responding to a crying baby and are in the process of developing postcards with key messages, which we hope to distribute to men. Usually only 50% of members (usually the social workers) attend the meetings, and we connect with the others by e-mail or by phone during and after the group meeting.

The project team is a creative and informal group. I enjoy the group's enthusiasm and vibes. We often share what is happening in our lives, as well as bounce around our ideas, or reconsider decisions we have made. Today we are meeting with the graphic designer and deciding in how many languages we want to produce the postcards. Lynda has already consulted with men's groups and colleagues, both nationally and internationally, and has produced a report of these activities for us to discuss. I often think of this group as more like those depicted in movies with creative advertising people, rather than as a group of social workers.

We have stayed together as a team in this project because it is very worthwhile to prevent serious injuries or even death of babies and toddlers, and we are committed to enhancing the wellbeing of families. I have a lot of experience with abuse and neglect and have seen many tragedies. I feel very privileged to be able to engage in this prevention activity. I also have a part-time role in providing reports for courts about the capacity of families to keep their children safe after an injury has occurred. This group does not keep minutes, although we usually have action plans. We often work together to present information sessions to colleagues, and on this day, I remind the others that we are presenting a session in two weeks' time. We negotiate who will be there and how to proceed with the organizational aspects and with finalizing the PowerPoint presentations.

In my office, I send e-mails about the project, and then two colleagues knock on my door and ask for my thoughts about a complex case that looks like "factitious illness by proxy." In particular, they want to talk about how to manage the hospital systems associated with these concerns. I have long had an interest n this area of work and in particular in the polarization among professionals that occurs as we try to understand the motivation and underlying anxiety and trauma difficulties that parents and sometimes children contribute to this situation (Kozlowska, Foley, & Crittenden, 2006).

It is now about time to head home, but then I remember that I promised to telephone Beverly, a mother. She is suffering from depression and is struggling with the complex and challenging behavior of her little girl. Usually, this phone call is a conference call with members of the team. I discover that Jenny (the pharmacist) is at her desk, so the three of us meet by telephone, identifying issues to follow up with other colleagues, the occupational therapist and psychiatrist. We clarify questions about medicine and behavior strategies, affirming, coaching, and reflecting with Beverly about her daughter.

I thoroughly enjoy working with colleagues and clients in the context of ongoing development. I thoroughly enjoy the range of activities my day brings and the opportunities to apply professional theory and practices and enact my social work values. I enjoy the opportunity to engage in many layers of our health, social, and service system, working in a systemic way to influence helping systems. In my opinion, that is what social workers are especially able to contribute to multidisciplinary teams and thereby promoting social justice.

Think About It

1. What ethical and confidentiality issues exist for social workers when discussing clients with other professionals? Are the issues the same when technology such as videoconferencing is involved?

2. In what way does professional development through ongoing learning enhance social justice?

3. What are the challenges for social workers in a multi-faceted practice, dealing with a range of situations, including managing crises? What skills are needed to ensure that patient needs can be addressed safely and adequately?

4. Look up Web references and journal articles about "reflective practices in supervision" to discover ways in which this is different from directive consultation and administrative supervision.

5. Look up your professional social work organizations and identify the values that influence social work practice.

References

Kozlowska, K., Foley, S., & Crittenden, P. M. (2006). Factitious illness by proxy: Understanding underlying psychological processes and motivations. *Australia and New Zealand Journal of Family Therapy, 27,* 92-104.

Lazar, M. C., & Mason, S. M. (2001). Group counselling for victims of sexual assault. *The Australian Journal of Sex, Marriage, and Family, 3* (2), 131-134.

Additional Reading

Fontes, L. (1995). Sharevision: Collaborative supervision and self-care strategies for working with trauma. *The Family Journal, 3,* 249- 254.

Starling, J., & Foley, S. (2006). From pilot to permanent service: Ten years of paediatric telepsychiatry, in *Telemed Telecare, 12,* 80-82.

Tolliday F., Simons M., Foley S., Benson S., Stephen A., & Rose D. (2010, December). From inspiration to action. *Communities, Children, and Families Australia, 5* (2), 31-47.

Chapter 42

Technology in Social Work: Moderating Online Support Groups for Cancer Patients

IIIIIIIIIIIIIIIIIIIIIIIIIIIIIIIIIIIIIIIIIIIIIIIIIIIIIIIIIIIIIIIIIIIIIIIIIIIIIIIIIIIIIIIIIIIIIIIIIII

by Rachel Odo, LCSW

I began my social work training as a second career. I loved working with groups of people, and I was (and remain!) passionate about life and thinking about what makes life important for each of us—how we, as human beings, learn to live fully and well, even in the face of an acute, chronic, or life-threatening illness. While working on staff at a comprehensive cancer center in New York City, I rotated through different treatment areas, working with in-patient, out-patient and post-treatment teams. There, I honed my group work skills, developing and leading face-to-face psychoeducational support groups for patients, caregivers, nursing staff, and medical residents. The power of group process and the deeply healing role of forging connections in our lives, especially when faced with an experience like illness and treatment, which can otherwise be alienating and isolating, came into clear focus as I ran these weekly and monthly groups. And, although I loved hospital work—the fast pace, the intellectual stimulation, the camaraderie of working with dedicated and caring interdisciplinary teams—I needed to transition to a more flexible, part-time career. As I was considering the transition, I searched for a way to maintain my group work practice, and in the end, I found it online.

I left the hospital setting to begin work in a social service agency dedicated to meeting the needs of cancer patients and their family caregivers. Because I am a part-time online support group moderator, I telecommute, which means that I rarely go into an actual office. The bulk of my working hours are spent at a computer at a desk in my home. I can run my groups from anywhere. When traveling for work, for example, there are no disruptions in my groups, because I can get online from any location. I can also fit my group work into my schedule, at times that are most convenient for me. I tend to "think" better and more clearly at night, so I often work then when things in my own home are quiet! The downside to the untraditional schedule is that, when crises within a group do arise, I do not automatically have a colleague or supervisor to turn to for discussion. Newer social workers might find it more comfortable to work during regular business hours, when they can seek supervision as needed. Working online, for telecommuters at least, also has the drawback of being professionally less "connected." I am not at an office seeing my colleagues on a regular basis, so it is important for me to put effort into maintaining relationships with my professional contacts and friends in the field.

The online groups that I run are actively moderated, with clinical social workers providing psychoeducation and supportive counseling, as well as helping to facilitate group discussion and to manage the space in ways that are therapeutic for everyone involved. However, they are not "live." When they are in session, they are run as asynchronous groups, open continuously, so that members can read and post at any time of the day or night. This works well with groups whose members come from all over the country (and sometimes beyond). Group members know that responses are not posted in "real time." They are assessed via e-mail, prior to the group and throughout the session, to be sure that there is a good fit between their needs and the kind of support that this type of online group can realistically provide.

These groups are organized by disease type and/or situation. I've run groups for gynecologic cancer patients, ovarian cancer patients, colorectal cancer patients, men with cancer, women with cancer, pancreatic cancer caregivers, general (mixed) caregivers, and the bereaved.

Members participate by reading the messages that others post and then responding, either directly or simply by sharing their own thoughts, questions, concerns, and issues. I never meet my group members in person. I never even speak with them by phone. I know them strictly through their writing in the group and, for those who do reach out directly for one reason or another, via e-mail contact. The written word is our singular mode of communication. As a social worker, I've learned to interpret narrative text in much the same way that I might interpret speech patterns and body language, appearance and eye contact, tone of voice, and spoken word when working face-to-face.

As I sit at my desk this evening, writing, in the same space where I sit to run my groups, I am thinking about what it means to communicate through the written word in this age of social media. And, I am thinking about the day-to-day experience of clinical practice through text-based relationships. Some days, I sit down and log on, quickly scan my e-mail folder to be sure that no one has written me "offline" with a particular issue, then head over to the group space itself, notice the number of new posts in each group, and settle in to read. Perhaps someone is writing about her anxiety in anticipation of an upcoming scan to determine whether or not a course of chemotherapy is working, and other members of the group have already posted in response, sharing words of support and setting down some of their own fears and worries about treatment or recurrence. In another group, a member may be talking about how hard it is to plan for the future when her husband's disease is so unpredictable. Should she encourage her daughter to move her wedding date up so her father can be there? "But when? When is the right moment? How do I know whether or not he'll be too sick to make it? Or make it at all?" Another member may be facing a transition from active treatment to hospice care and writing about what it means to watch her husband go from being a "big, healthy, strong man" to "skin and bones and pain with hardly any time awake and none of it good." A homebound member of another group, who would have almost no social network if it weren't for an online group like ours, might share a link to a video he's taken of his new kitten, a gift from his far away son. Still someone else may be posting inspirational quotes or jokes to help everyone "make it through the day."

I will sit with all of this, let it percolate for a bit, and then, a day or two later, having gone through this daily ritual of sitting and reading and absorbing, I will sit down once again, only this time, after logging on and reading the latest posts, I will begin to write.

I will write to everyone who has written since my last post, and I will answer queries that haven't already been answered by other group members. I will support healthy coping strategies, point out similarities and differences, teach about emotions and moods, help people grieve their losses and changes. I will share my enjoyment of the kitten, "laugh" at the jokes, encourage the mutual aid and support that flows from post to post, member to member, and help to negotiate the conflicts that sometimes arise. I will speak to the strengths that the group members share. I will write and write and write, and then I will read and re-read what I've written. Checking my "facts" and listening to how the words sound, I wonder whether they will convey what I want to say. I won't know immediately. I won't know until members have posted in response, so I choose my words and phrases carefully, perhaps even more carefully than I did when I was speaking them aloud in a face-to-face setting where I could see, at a glance, how my comments were being received and make subtle changes in the moment. I will post my thoughts to the group and hope that they will resonate, as I hope that some of what I'm saying here resonates with you.

My days are filled with reading and thinking and writing. An average group of this type may include 15 to 30 members posting about 20 to 50 messages each week. Very active groups may post upwards of 80 to 100 messages weekly, and quieter groups can go for weeks at a time with just a handful of new posts. As the moderator, I craft a new post once or twice a week on average. These weekly posts may run anywhere from a few hundred to 1,500 words or more and take anywhere from 15 to 90 minutes to properly craft. When there are larger issues in the space—a recurrence, a death, a new diagnosis, other bad news—I may be more "present" through more frequent, though generally shorter, posts for a period of time. When new members enter the space, I respond within a day to welcome them. On average, I spend about two to three hours each week with each group that I run.

Like any support group leader, I work to make a direct thera-peutic connection with each member while simultaneously fostering and nurturing the connections that members make with one another. When we are face-to-face, visual and aural cues and responses are some of the main ways that we do this. Online, we lose the aural cues and have to modify our understanding of the visual. For example, every time I post, I address each member of the group by name. The visual cue of using their names and carving out a separate "space" for each individual within the frame of my posts not only reinforces members' sense of belonging in the space, but also helps others "put names to stories" in more meaningful ways as I synthesize multiple posts by each member and highlight the core issues they are raising.

With text-based relationships, writing style itself becomes a powerful tool. It can be used to better understand individual members (how formal is it, what kind of vocabulary is used, what kinds of punctuation, does a person use emoticons?), and it can be used to clarify roles or encourage a positive countertransfer-ence by adjusting one's own style according to the message—more formality in a strongly educational post for instance, or mirroring the style of a group member in a supportive response. In the text-based counseling relationship, text as narrative and text as tran-sitional object become particularly powerful. This is storytelling made concrete. One group member put it this way as she opened a lengthy, emotional post: "This will be a long update, as I am using it to kind of consolidate where I am at mentally. On the one hand I feel weird exposing so much about where I am at mentally.... But it helps me, so I do it." Here, the written narrative itself becomes a crucial healing factor.

For other members, what they gain from the group might look more like this: "The reason I joined this group is because I had reached the limits of my ability to cope with my sister's behavior toward me. I have been visiting her and giving her moral support since she had a gall bladder attack and removal last February. She has always been difficult to deal with, but the pancreatic cancer diagnosis and subsequent surgery, colon injury, and chemo have really made her angry and hostile toward the world in general and toward me in particular. Had I not joined this group and received the support, wisdom, and kind words of Rachel and my fellow travelers, I would have abandoned M some time ago, which I really did not want to do. Since joining the group, I've learned to make changes in my own behavior toward M, and I have also learned important information about drugs and side effects and antidotes that others here may know about and which I am able to at least suggest to M and her medical team from time to time. I also try to show support toward others on this board as we journey together, and sometimes I just blow off steam if I need to. No one is judging. Today, my relationship with my sister is better, and I am hoping we will continue to progress."

The therapeutic potential of the online support group is tremendous. For social workers who like to read and to express themselves through writing, online modalities can be incredibly powerful and highly rewarding. Working in this way has not only broadened my ability to reach people through the sheer impact of technology, but enhanced and deepened my clinical skills in every setting.

Think About It

1. What skills are crucial for an online support group moderator?

2. How are therapeutic relationships nurtured online?

3. Visit *http://www.cancercare.org/* to read cancer survivors' stories online for yourself. What is your response?

Additional Reading

Bloom, J. W., & Walz, G. R. (2000). *Cybercounseling and cyberlearning: Strategies and resources for the millennium.* Alexandria, VA: American Counseling Association.

Bolton, G., Howlett, S., Lago, C., & Wright, J. K. (2004). *Writing cures: An introductory handbook of writing in counseling and therapy.* New York: Brunner-Routledge.

Chmiel, A., Sienkiewicz, J., Thelwall, M., Paltoglou, G., Buckley, K., Kappas, A., & Hołyst, J. A. (2011). Collective emotions online and their influence on community life. *PLoS One: 6* (7), e22207.

Colon, Y. (2004). *Technology-based groups and end-of-life social work practice.* In J. Berzoff and P.R. Silverman (eds.), *Living With the Dying: A Handbook for End-of-Life Healthcare Practitioners.* New York: Columbia University Press.

Eysenbach, G., Powell, J., Englesakis, M., Rizo, C., & Stern, A. (2004). Health related virtual communities and electronic support groups: systematic review of the effects of online peer to peer interactions. *BMJ, 328,* 1116-1121.

Joinson, A. N. (2003). *Understanding the psychology of internet behaviour: Virtual worlds, real lives.* Hampshire and New York: Palgrave Macmillan.

Klemm P., Bunnell, D., Cullen, M., Soneji, R., Gibbons, P., & Holecek, A. (2003). Online cancer support groups: A review of the research literature. *Computer, Informatics, Nursing, 21* (3), 136-142.

Lepore, S. J., & Smyth, J. M. (2002). *The writing cure: How expressive writing promotes health and emotional well-being.* Washington DC: American Psychological Association.

Meier, A. (2004). *Technology-mediated groups.* In C.D. Garvin, L.M. Gutierrez, M.J. Galinsky (eds.) *Handbook of Social Work With Groups.* New York: The Guilford Press.

White, M., & Epston, D. (1990). *Narrative Means to Therapeutic Ends.* New York and London: W.W. Norton.

Chapter 43

On Group Work for Social Justice: Intergroup Dialogue

||||||||||||||||||||||||||||||||||||||||||||||||||||||||||||||||||||||||||||||||||||||||||||||||||||||||||||||||||||

by Relando Thompkins, MSW

Peace is not the absence of tension; it is the presence of Justice.

Dr. Martin Luther King Jr.

E ven before I began my training for my MSW at the University of Michigan, my process of coming into the knowledge of intergroup dialogue and later learning how to teach the skills to others for the purpose of working toward increased intercultural understanding began when I was an undergraduate student at Oakland University. It was there that I became increasingly interested in exploring issues of privilege and oppression, and how those things can show up in social identities such as race, class, gender, sexual orientation, and others. It was also at Oakland that I decided I wanted to pursue a career in social work.

My interest in social justice group work became even more solidified when I took a course there on "Multicultural Social Work Practice." As a result of taking this course, I learned even more about how our social identities interact and intersect in our everyday lives interpersonally and systemically. Having the experience of being able to be in a classroom and honestly talk about my experiences with racism and my experiences with being discriminated against in other areas of my life, and having the opportunity to be able to hear others share their stories as well, further reinforced my interest in exploring issues of privilege and oppression.

When I began grad school to study for my MSW and began looking for an internship, I came across a program called "Intergroup Dialogue Social Change Agents" that was connected to the School of Social Work. The program works with high school students in the Ypsilanti and Ann Arbor area of Michigan. After I learned that this program involved conflict resolution and was focused on bringing people together and communicating across differences, I jumped at the chance to become involved. It seemed to me that many of the experiences that have excited and inspired me in the past in terms of how I felt that I could best use myself in service to others seemed to be leading up to working with the program as the next natural progression in my development. So, I became an intern in the program and also took a class on dialogue facilitation for social justice. Now that I've graduated, I've returned to be a facilitator for the program.

My focus in learning about dialogue started from a desire to improve race relations; mostly because of my experiences with racism and being discriminated against. However, as a result of participating and learning the skills of facilitation, I can see how my focus has expanded. I'm still very passionate about improving race relations, but now my lens has expanded to include other social identities, as well. My focus shifted from specifically improving race relations to wanting to improve intergroup relations. For me, this is much more of a collective and inclusive approach to working toward social justice.

If someone were to ask me how this change in my development occurred, I would respond by telling them that having continuous opportunities to be able to share my experiences with others, listen to theirs, and to confront my own privileges was a great catalyst. A quote from my training that still resonates with me says, "Because oppression is so systemic, people tend to absolve themselves of blame, but unless someone chooses to identify with institutions and systems, the act of honest confession will never take place." Yes, I experience oppression in many forms as an African American male, but I also carry with me unearned privileges that can be found in my gender and in aspects of some of my other social identities, as well. We are all implicated somehow in the web of privilege and oppression. Some aspects of our identities can place us in positions of privilege, while others can leave us vulnerable to discrimination.

Understanding that "my hands aren't clean" gives me an increased ability to remain self aware, which helps me to be better able to work collaboratively with others. I think it is easy to look outwardly in terms of oppression and privilege, but I think that we can all benefit from choosing to continually look inward at ourselves to find ways that we contribute to oppression, so we can change any oppressive thoughts and behaviors that may be present and use ourselves to be better allies. Working to do so in my own life is an ongoing process.

This is a great lesson that I have learned that I think can play a very important part in peace building. I hope to be able to spend a great deal of my time creating opportunities to engage current and future helping professionals in conscious efforts to enhance our self awareness, because I believe that knowing ourselves is truly critical to our work. I can also see how transformative dialogue can be when used in communities, as well, and will continue to incorporate it into my style as a practitioner.

Dialogue work is highly interactive and depends on the ability of facilitators to work collaboratively with participants while engaging them in the process. It can be very challenging personally, and it is really necessary for facilitators to develop self awareness, awareness of others around them, empathy, and comfort with managing conflict. Facilitating also takes a great deal of courage and a willingness to fully invest oneself in the process. One of the ways to do this is to tell your truth. Facilitators can be catalysts for determining how other members of the group will participate. I can't tell you how many times I've normalized feelings, expressed discomfort during dialogue, or shared personal experiences that have affected me, and have seen other group members come alive with excitement because I caused them to think of something differently, or because they could personally relate to what I had shared. There's something liberating about telling your truth. Some other characteristics that I think are useful to hone in doing this kind of work are attentiveness, good listening skills, and a willingness to recognize and confront one's own privileges and triggers. Continually invest time in getting to know your social identities and the roles you play or can play in the web of privilege and oppression. This isn't the kind of work you do "on other people"—it's the kind of work you do along with others. We are all teachers and learners. I know that I've only scratched the surface here, but I really think self awareness is very important.

I use the process of intergroup dialogue to work with high school and college students and contribute to creating safe spaces where participants can engage in respectful dialogue across differences. The overall purpose is to help participants to be able to increase their ability to manage conflict in peaceful ways, build relationships with people with whom they might believe they have nothing in common, and to gain better understanding of larger social issues that can fuel prejudice and tensions between groups. Throughout this process, we share our personal experiences in dealing with issues of race, class, gender, sexual orientation, religion, age, ability status, and other social identities. Dr. Martin Luther King, Jr., once said, "True peace is not the absence of tension; it is the presence of justice." A part of my job as a facilitator is to intentionally create tension to disturb complacent or unquestioned attitudes about social justice issues. Throughout this process, conflict can arise on the road to gaining a better understanding of ourselves and others, but after thinking of his words, and connecting them to my experiences, I see dialogue as being the "presence of justice" among the tension that can arise, because it is truly a way to negotiate conflicts peacefully and non-violently.

I work with a co-facilitator, as well. There is an educational component to the program in which we teach participants about social identity development, stereotypes and their effects on groups, and how privilege can manifest itself in society. We also facilitate and participate in consciousness raising skill building activities with facilitated dialogue that allows us to look at how we are connected to privilege and oppression, helping us to increase our understanding and work through any conflicts or resistance that might appear. Throughout the program, we teach peace by teaching participants methods of communicating and collaborating across differences, empowering them to be able to apply the skills they learn in their everyday lives. I think this is particularly important, because I believe that even with all the education in the world, education without application gets us nowhere on the road to becoming social change agents. This is why I really appreciate the intentionality of really working to empower people to act on what they have learned.

Participants can take action in a variety of ways. Some participants, in my experience working with students in the high schools, have presented to the teachers and administrators at their schools on what they learned throughout the year, and why they thought having safe spaces to communicate across differences was important for their school and communities. In my experience in working with college students, some have taken action in the form of challenging oppressive attitudes in their homes or among their friends by speaking up against racist comments or jokes, homophobia, and other things that they would not have even thought about previously.

I do dialogue work primarily with high school students in the Ypsilanti and Ann Arbor areas, but since completing my MSW, I also still return to the School of Social Work to facilitate dialogues. I do this primarily through a group called "Making Race Heard"—a forum that was started by a group of my former classmates to bring people of color and their allies together to discuss how issues of race intersect with other social identities and have an impact on our lives in the School of Social Work and beyond.

Every session is different, and before each session I always wonder to myself, "How is this going to turn out?" or "What's going to happen today?" It gets easier, but those familiar butterflies never completely go away. I've been told that the occasional nervousness just means that I really care about what I do. After thinking about it, I'd have to say that I agree.

A typical day of work with the high school students includes me meeting with my co-facilitator an hour beforehand to take a temperature of where we are personally, as well as planning strategy for the coming session. Although the particular activities we do vary every week, our sessions typically begin with a fun and engaging icebreaker that helps to get participants talking and ready to share. After that, we expose the students to a thought-provoking experience through an activity, and spend the rest of our time processing our experience. After the session is over, we stay behind and process how things went, as well as plan for the next session.

One day we played a game called "Win all you can." This was a game about getting as much as you can out of a situation. The key to this game could be found in defining what "you" meant. Would it mean defining "you" as an individual or "you" as a group? Participants were split into separate teams and were given the opportunity to make a simple choice between choosing the letter X or Y. There were several rounds and rules involving points, but to summarize, the general pattern was that the more everyone worked together, the more points everyone could gain. Conversely, the more individual students would choose for themselves, those students would gain points, while the others who worked together would lose points. The game started off with everyone working together, but eventually a couple of students began choosing for themselves. Other students began to notice that only a few students were gaining points while many others were losing them, so more students began choosing for themselves in hopes that they would gain, as well. However, the other side to this game was that as more people chose for themselves without considering the wider group, the more points everyone would lose as a whole. We began the game with the possibility of everyone finishing with positive points, but by the time the game ended, all of the participants finished with negative points!

Students were able to share their experiences with the game during our dialogue afterward. One student shared that she realized early on that if they all worked together, they would all gain points, but after seeing a few people gain points at the expense of everyone else, she got tired of "losing" and wanted to get some points, too, so she began choosing for herself. Another student shared that he was all for himself from the very beginning. During this activity, many of the students defined what "you" meant in different ways. Some defined it individually, and others collectively. During this dialogue, we were able to make parallels about how this "game" works in the reality of their experiences not only in their school but in their personal lives and communities. We were able to talk about privilege and oppression and how this game also shows up in our social identities and in society in terms of the ways that our different privileges cause us to gain things at the expense of others who do not belong to our group.

As we were wrapping up the session for the day, a student said something that continues to resonate with me—something that I have no doubt will remain close to my heart for many years to come. He said, "I understand the game; I just don't understand the players." It caused me to pause and think. We know that helping other people and sharing resources can lead to collective success, so why don't we do it? What's keeping us from getting there? I think exploring those questions is a part of what social justice group work is all about.

Think About It

1. What do you think is important in creating a safe environment to have dialogue about difficult issues?

2. How aware are you about your social identities? (Examples include race, class, gender, age, ability, sexual orientation, religion, national origin.)

3. Can you name any unearned privileges you have at your disposal every day? How important do you think it is for helping professionals to be aware of their own privileges, and areas of oppression?

Additional Reading

Dessel, A., Rogge, M. E., & Garlington, S. B. (2006). Using intergroup dialogue to promote social justice and change. *Social Work, 51*(4), 303-315.

Lorde, A. (1996). *There is no hierarchy of oppressions.* In J. Andrzejewski (Ed.), *Oppression and social justice: Critical frameworks* (5th ed.) (p. 51). Boston, MA: Pearson Custom Publishing.

Schatz, M., Furman, R., & Jenkins, L. E. (2003). Space to grow: Using dialogue techniques for multinational, multicultural learning. *International Social Work, 46* (4), 481-494.

Chapter 44
From Group Member to Hero, Husband, and Father: A Long-Term Reflection

||||||||||||||||||||||||||||||||||||||||||||||||||||||||||||||||||||||||||||||||||||||||||||||||||||||||||||||||||||||||||||||||||||||||||||||||||

by Andrew Malekoff, LCSW

I turned 60 in 2011. I was 23 in 1974 when I worked with my first adolescent group. It feels like yesterday, but much has changed. Then I was single and living in Nebraska. Now I am married, have two grown children, and live in New York. In the intervening years, both of my parents, and many other dear ones, died.

To my wife's chagrin, I am the same weight today as when we were married in 1980. I had a full head of hair then and have almost none today. For most of my 60 years, I have been in near perfect health. Recently, a few things caught me by surprise that now require special attention.

My first assignment as a group worker was with teenage boys and girls. My group work today is primarily with accomplished men and women—members of my staff, board of directors, and the local community. Although much has changed over the years, one thing that has not changed is my belief in the power of groups.

The lessons that I learned and honed by working with groups of children and teenagers over four decades apply to my work today as chief executive of a children's mental health agency. Despite a dramatic change in role from volunteer to CEO, group work informs my everyday work. It influences how I see, think, feel, and do.

In today's world of increasing needs and diminishing resources, my identity as a group worker influences me every day. This does not mean that I practice group work, in a formal sense, every day. It means that I see the world through a group work lens, and I respond accordingly. More specifically, I often look for and try to advance empathic connections, mutual aid, and social justice.

As a chief executive, I attend many functions where I am expected to speak to large groups of people.There is rarely any give-and-take in those situations. Rather, it is me at a podium trying to educate and inspire people to join our cause. Often, what works best is when I can find someone to speak who has used our services and who can give testimony as to how it helped. In my role as CEO, the first person who I asked to do this is someone who is an adult today and who, years ago, was a member of one of my groups.

John and I have maintained contact over many years. More recently, I saw his photo on a United Way poster in the kitchen of our headquarters. I must have passed that poster a dozen times before realizing that I knew the person whose photograph was featured. One day I stopped and looked more carefully and said to myself, "That's John!" I called him immediately and invited him for lunch to catch up and to find out how he came to be the "poster boy" for United Way.

To make a long story short, his business supported the United Way, and when a representative went to his place of work, John asked if one of the agencies that the United Way supports is North Shore Child and Family Guidance Center. When he learned that it was, he said that he was "all in."

I was so impressed with John's ability to express himself about his fondness for his time with the Guidance Center that I asked him if he would think about speaking at one of our annual fund-raising events. Without any hesitation, he said he would do it. I told him that we wanted people who were attending the event to know why they were there, to know that the services that we provide are vital, and to understand that their support is essential, especially in this economy. He got it. He prepared his own remarks, which I helped him to "tweak." Following (with his permission) are John's verbatim remarks. In parentheses and italics are some of my reflections about the group that John referred to in his remarks to about 250 people.

"Good evening and thank you. When Andy asked me to come and speak tonight on behalf of North Shore Child and Family Guidance Center, I was both flattered and honored. So when I sat down and thought about how to express the importance of this organization and how effective it is, I came to the conclusion that the best way to do that is tell you a little bit about myself.

My father lost his fight with cancer in May of 1988, when I was 11 years old. This was a devastating blow to me and my family. My mom, a housewife and mother of five and now a widow, was left to support the household and keep us in some sort of order. This was no easy task for her. My oldest sister was in an abusive relationship; both of my older brothers were dealing drugs, and my other sister was quickly becoming a recluse. I, on the other hand, as you might expect of any confused child, was scared and especially angry.

And so, I acted out. I looked for fights and I sought ways to instigate confrontations. It was me against the world. I was lost. I felt as though my world had fallen apart when I lost my father. I felt as though I was cheated by God. To me, nothing was fair and nothing could make it better. At least that's the way I felt about it. It wasn't long before the school district couldn't handle me any more, and only a matter of time before I would end up before a juvenile court judge. And then I was sent to a special school outside of my community.

My mother had no clue what to do at that point. I was destined to end up like my brothers—dealing drugs, running the streets, or worse. At the suggestion of a school counselor, my mother took me and my youngest sister to the Guidance Center. The sliding scale payment program provided by the Guidance Center made it possible for my mother to afford counseling for her, my sister, and myself.

That's when I first met Andy Malekoff and became part of what was, at the time, a counseling group for children. It was by being a part of this unique hodgepodge of kids my age with an array of troubles that I slowly started to realize that my problems weren't so big and that there were others worse off than me. I also found a positive male role model."

(As I recall, the group John is referring to was composed of early adolescent boys who were referred to the agency for having engaged in some kind of destructive behavior. The purpose of the group was to put a reflective pause between impulse and action. When John first joined the group he told the others about his problems in school following the death of his father. There were daily fights with other students, often provoked by cruel "jokes" about his deceased father. John spent lots of time in the principal's office and in the detention room. He had been no angel before his father died. However, it become evident to me that the emptiness that followed him, in the wake of his great loss, had not been met with compassion but, rather, by insensitivity. In a short time, he was transferred to an out-of-district "special education" setting composed of a population of teens with serious behavioral problems).

"Andy, and my new friends in the group, encouraged and challenged me to do things to help steer me in the right direction and off my path to destruction. Eventually, when I told Andy about my idea to join the Mineola Jr. Fire Department, he encouraged me to sign up and get involved. I believe that that was a turning point for me."

(One of the more memorable moments in the group happened shortly after John joined the Jr. Fire Department. He demonstrated to his fellow group members (and me) how a fire sprinkler system works. I recall him standing on a chair in my office and explaining what he had learned. Another group member reached up with his Bic Lighter, lit it, and waved it nearby the sprinkler head. I did nothing. I did not want to interfere with John's lesson. He seemed to be so proud of what he had learned. The moment was memorialized forever on film, as I used to videotape the group sessions with the boys' (and their parents') permission. I have since used that film clip for training purposes. Of all of the video that I use for teaching about group work with adolescents, the clip of John standing on a chair under the sprinkler head, with another group member "flicking his Bic," is among the most controversial. It creates great anxiety in aspiring group workers who want to know why I didn't stop them from getting so close to the sprinkler head with a lighter. After much discussion, my answer is always that it was important for John to show the group what he learned and to feel proud about it. I did not want to interfere with that. I trusted that the others, despite their provocative behavior, would not ruin the moment for John. And, they did not. I often cite the brilliant Fritz Redl who, in addressing difficult behavior in kids' groups, differentiated between permitting, strategic tolerating, signal interference, and preventive planning. I recall Redl saying that there are times a group worker wants to stop certain behavior; however, there is good reason under certain circumstances to let it go by. That is precisely how I felt when John was teaching the group about fire sprinkler systems—a lesson that, it turns out, was just the beginning of his fire-fighting "career.")

"My father was a member of the fire department, and it was good for me to be around the men that my father knew and was friends with. They took me in and treated me as one of their own. Through the years, I eventually left the special school and returned to the school district in my community. I played on the high school football team. I also became a full-fledged member of the fire department, moving my way through the ranks of the department and becoming the youngest Lieutenant in Mineola fire department's history and receiving multiple county awards both as an EMT and firefighter. My awards were for valor and life saving. I also set a record by becoming the only firefighter in Nassau County history to receive two life saving awards from one fire.

I became involved in the community, acting as a Republican committeeman. I have had the honor to work for a state senator and a state representative. Straight out of high school, I worked for a food distribution company traveling the country and overseeing site builds and establishing vendor contracts. I am currently the operations manager of the New York City market for a multi-billon dollar international power tool company, Black and Decker. And, my greatest achievement of all—I am a husband, and a father of two beautiful boys, with a little girl due in April.

I still have my moments of doubt as a man, a husband, and a father, but I have been fortunate to have the support of my wife and the availability of my friend, Andrew Malekoff. This past year hasn't been easy on anyone, and there is not a single person in this room that can say they haven't been affected by this economy. In these times, it is especially hard to find room in your budget for charities but I ask you to consider my mother's situation 21 years ago—working two part-time jobs just to make ends meet. If it weren't for the supporters of this remarkable agency, my life and the lives of others with even worse life stories, could have gone in a completely different direction.

In reading the program for tonight's festivities, I have noticed that many of you here have been long time supporters of this agency. I would like to thank you personally, for I truly believe you have helped to change my life. And for those new supporters, think of the endless possibilities for the countless children's lives you will be affecting. I would like to thank North Shore Child and Family Guidance Center for giving me the opportunity to speak here tonight, and I would also like to thank Andy Malekoff for being my friend and mentor for over two decades. Good night and happy holidays to you and your families."

(When John first joined the group, he shared a poem with me that he wrote and that was published in the school newspaper. He gave it the title, "The Man Upstairs." Although he said that it was not about his father, the poem was about death and loss. When John's time came to leave the group, several years later, I pulled out a copy of the poem and handed it to him. He said, "I remember this." He read it to the group before they said their final goodbyes.)

After John spoke at the fund-raiser, he was approached by many people who told him how moved they were by his story. Naturally, I was proud that a member of my years-ago boys' group had developed into such a fine man who had the character to give back in such a meaningful and powerful way. As John stood at the podium, I knew immediately that the spirit of group work was in the house.

John's impassioned speech spurred empathic connections and a sense of fellow feeling in the room. He demonstrated the power of mutual aid by testifying about how important a supportive group was during an excruciating time in his young life. In fact, by telling his story, many in the audience who had stories of their own were comforted by hearing how his story unfolded.

By "going public," with local legislators and powerful business people in the room, John fought for social justice by validating that services like ours, in this economy, face the threat of severe funding cutbacks every day. He implored the audience, through his personal and very public testimony, that they could not let this happen.

The night that John spoke was one of the best days in my life as a group worker—to see an 11-year-old boy who lost his father transformed into a man with such heart. Now that's evidence-based practice!

Think About It

1. What ethical issues might arise in asking a former client to support the social worker's agency in this way?

2. What factors do you think may have played a part in John's turn-around from "troubled" child to "hero"?

Appendix A—Organizations, Web Sites, and Resources of Interest to Social Workers With Groups

This is a partial listing of resources that may be useful in exploring social work with groups. These include professional associations, publications, Web sites, videos, and other resources.

American Group Psychotherapy Association
http://www.agpa.org/index.html

American Self-Help Group Clearinghouse
http://www.mentalhelp.net/self-help/

Association for Community Organization and Social Administration (ACOSA)
http://www.acosa.org

Global Group Work Project
http://globalgroupworkproject.com/

Groupwork (Journal)
http://www.whitingbirch.net/cgi-bin/scribe?showinfo=ip001

IASWG on Facebook
https://www.facebook.com/groups/42099491548/

Inside a Men's Group (YouTube video)
http://youtu.be/A6XxjcUco4c

International Association for Group Psychotherapy and Group Process
http://www.iagp.com

International Association for Social Work With Groups (IASWG)—formerly AASWG
http://www.aaswg.org

Irvin Yalom Inpatient Group Psychotherapy (YouTube video)
http://youtu.be/05Elmr65RDg

Journey Into Self—Carl Rogers (YouTube video)
http://youtu.be/LgdjeNZtqPQ

Mental Health America Support Group Page
http://www.mentalhealthamerica.net/go/find_support_group

Mutual Aid Based Group Work (blog)
http://mutualaidbasedgroupwork.blogspot.com/

Social Group Work (YouTube video by Shamika Medaries)
http://www.youtube.com/watch?v=Yunbt4u9uWg

Social Work With Groups (journal)
http://www.tandfonline.com/loi/wswg20

Social Work With Groups (Wikipedia article)
http://en.wikipedia.org/wiki/Social_work_with_groups

Standards for Social Work Practice With Groups (available in English, Spanish, and German)
http://www.aaswg.org

SupportGroups.com
http://www.supportgroups.com/

Appendix B—Standards for Social Work Practice With Groups

ASSOCIATION FOR THE ADVANCEMENT OF SOCIAL WORK WITH GROUPS, INC.
An International Professional Organization (AASWG)

STANDARDS FOR SOCIAL WORK PRACTICE WITH GROUPS
Second Edition

PURPOSE

These standards represent the perspective of the Association for the Advancement of Social Work with Groups, Inc., on the value and knowledge and skill base essential for professionally sound and effective social work practices with groups and are intended to serve as a guide to social work practice with groups.

INTRODUCTION

The Standards focus on central distinguishing concepts of social work with groups and highlight the perspective that social group workers bring to practice. By design, the standards are general rather than specific and descriptive rather than prescriptive. They are applicable to the wide range of groups encountered by social group workers in a variety of practice settings. These groups include treatment, support, psycho-educational, task, and community-action groups. The Standards draw heavily on the Code of Ethics from the National Association of Social Work (United States), group theory from the social sciences, knowledge of individuals and the environment, the historical roots of social group work practice, current practice with groups, and practice research. Thus, they are based on practice wisdom, theories of group work practice, and empirical evidence. They emphasize the understanding and use of group processes and the ways members help one another to accomplish the purposes of the group. The role of the worker, as articulated in the standards, reflects the values of the social work profession generally as well as the unique features associated with social work with groups.

Overview of the Standards

Various comprehensive perspectives of social work practice provide a broad underpinning of the values and knowledge bases of social group workers' practice. Values and types of knowledge that have particular relevance for group work practice are addressed in Section I.

Sections II through V identify the required knowledge and major worker tasks and skills in each of the phases of group work practice, from planning to ending. These sections are structured around the understanding that groups change and evolve over time, thus requiring changes in the worker's tasks and responsibilities. For example, certain worker actions enable group members to start to work together in a new group; other actions enable members who have already developed relationships to engage in work to achieve the purpose of the group. Thus, as groups develop, the nature of the workers' responsibilities change.

The phases and the associated tasks described in these standards are guides for practice. They represent the wisdom that has been acquired from practice, theory, and research. However, each group is different and practitioners must apply these standards in terms of their appropriateness for each group and its particular members.

Section VI examines ethical considerations for social group work practice.

SECTION I

CORE VALUES AND KNOWLEDGE

The group worker should understand the history of group work and the evolving visions of group workers as they faced the challenges posed by each historical era. During this evolution, the following values emerged as those that were essential to the practice of group work.

A.   Core Values

1. Respect for persons and their autonomy.

In view of the equality of persons, people are to be treated with respect and dignity. In group deliberations no one person should be more privileged in a group than another, not a worker, a group member or the agency director. In a group this occurs when a worker helps each member to appreciate the contributions of the other members so that everyone's ideas are heard and considered. This principle is stated while recognizing that the worker, by virtue of his or her position in the agency and his or her expertise, is likely to have a great deal of influence. This requires the worker to use his or her influence prudently.

A major implication of this principle is a respect for and a high value placed on diversity in all of its dimensions such as culture, ethnicity, gender, sexual orientation, physical and mental abilities and age.

2. The creation of a socially just society.

The group offers an opportunity to live and practice the democratic principles of equality and autonomy and the worker should use his/her knowledge and skills to further this. The worker should be mind¬ful of the quest for a society that is just and democrati¬cally organized one that ensures that the basic human needs of all its members are met. This value is presented to the group whenever it is appropriate and reinforced when members articulate it.

B.   Core Knowledge

There are special areas of knowledge that enable group workers to more ably serve the group. This includes knowledge of the history and mission of our profession as it impacts group work with poor people, minorities and other disenfranchised people. Understanding when group work is the practice of choice is important. The skills needed to carry out the profes¬sional mission emerge from our values and knowledge and requires specialized education.

1. Knowledge of individuals.

a. The nature of individual human growth and behavior, utilizing a bio-psycho-social perspective and a "person-in-environment" view. The forces impacting the person and the group are important factors in group work assessment and intervention. This includes viewing the member in the context of the group and the community.

b. The familial, social, political and cultural contexts that influence members' social identities, interactional styles, concerns, opportunities, and the attainment of their potentials.

c. The capacity of members to help one another and to change.

d. The capacity of members to contribute to social change in the community beyond the group.

e. Using competency-based assessment, the group worker places an emphasis on members' strengths, in addition to their concerns. The worker also must understand protective and risk factors that affect individuals' needs for services and their ability to act.

f. The worker has an appreciation and understanding of such differences as those due to culture, ethnicity, gender, age, physical and mental abilities and sexual orientation among members that may influence practice.

2. Knowledge of groups and small group behavior.

a. The worker understands that the group is an entity separate and distinct from the individual members. The group has its own dynamics, culture and other social conditions.

b. The worker understands that the group consists of multiple helping relationships, so that members can help one another to achieve individual goals and pursue group goals. This is often referred to as "mutual aid."

c. The democratic process in a group occurs as the members develop a sense of "ownership" of the group in which each member's contribution to the group is solicited and valued.

d. The group can develop in such a way that members, individually and collectively, are empowered to act on their own behalf as well as that of the group.

e. Groups can develop goals that members are committed to pursuing. These goals may be for individual member growth, group development and/or social change.

f. Group members as well as the group-as-a-whole can seek changes in the social environment.

g. The phases of group development influence change throughout the life of the group.

h. Group processes and structures encompass all transactions that occur within the group and give meaningfulness to the life of the group. These consist of such conditions as roles, norms, communications, expression of affect, and the nature of interaction patterns. These shape and influence individual member behavior as well as the development of the group and also determine whether and how the group will accomplish its purposes. The members can come to understand how group processes and structures shape and influence individual member behavior as well as the development of the group.

i. Groups are formed for different purposes and goals (e.g., education problem solving, task accomplish¬ment, personal change, social action) and this influ¬ences what the worker does and how the group accomplishes its goals as well as the nature of the contract between the worker and members, among the members, and between the group and the sponsoring organization.

3. Knowledge of the function of the group worker.

a. The worker promotes individual and group autonomy.

b. The worker helps the group members to select means of achieving individual and group purposes.

c. The worker's assessments and interventions are characterized by flexibility, sensitivity and creativity.

d. The worker should have a clear understanding of the stages of group development and the related group character, members' behavior and tasks and worker tasks and skills that are specific to each stage.

e. Practice should be based on currently available knowledge and research and should represent contemporary practice principles.

f. The worker has responsibility for ongoing monitoring and evaluation of the success of the group in accomplishing its objectives through personal observation as well as collecting information in order to assess outcomes and processes. The worker seeks the involvement of the members in the process of evaluation. Specifically this means that members should be involved in evaluation of outcomes throughout the life of the group. Workers should systematically evaluate the achievement of goals. The worker should be knowledgeable about methods of evaluation of group work and ways of measuring or otherwise determining accomplishment of group and individual goals. The worker should use all available evidence regarding effectiveness of particular interventions for different groups.

g. The worker should maintain appropriate records of group processes and outcomes and ensure their confidentiality.

h. The worker should have a commitment to supporting research on group work and to disseminating knowledge about effective practices through professional meetings, education and scholarship.

i. The worker adheres to professional, ethical, and legal requirements generally associated with social work practice as well as those specifically associated with social work with groups. The worker seeks to prevent any action in the group that may harm any member.

j. Workers should have a commitment to engage in reflective practice in which they assess their own practice and seek supervision and/or consultation in order to enhance their practice.

SECTION II

PRE-GROUP PHASE: PLANNING, RECRUITMENT AND NEW GROUP FORMATION

A. Tasks and Skills

1. The worker should identify aspirations and needs of potential group members as perceived by members, worker and agency.

2. The worker should obtain organizational support for and affirmation of the group.

3. The worker should select the group type, structure, processes and size that will be appropriate for attaining the purposes of the group.

4. The worker should reach out to and recruit potential group members.

5. The worker should obtain consent from potential members and relevant others as required by ethical guidelines and organizational requirements.

6. The worker should clarify potential group members' goals and expectations of the group work service and use this information to assess prospective members' potential investments in the pursuit of group goals. The worker should help members specify these goals in terms that can lead to the determination of their attainment.

7. The worker should establish an appropriate meeting place and meeting time that will be conducive to members' comfort, safety and access to the group.

8. The worker should prepare members for the group in ways that are appropriate. This will differ depending on the extent to which the group is intended to attain individual goals or to accomplish task purposes in the agency and community. The worker should be empathic in identifying members' feelings and reactions to joining the group.

9. The worker should know how to select members for the group in relationship to principles of group composition, although this principle may not apply to some task groups in which other bodies determine the group's membership.

10. The worker should develop a clear statement of group purpose that reflects member needs and agency missions and goals. This is often done cooperatively with the group members.

11. The worker should consider potential contextual, environmental, and societal impacts on the group.

12. The worker, as appropriate, should explain group purposes and processes to non-members such as other agency personnel, relevant community entities, and parents or referring agencies in the case of groups promoting individual change.

13. The worker should appropriately enhance group content (what will go on during sessions) as well as the use of activities, supplies and other resources.

14. The worker should identify methods that will be used to track group progress (e.g., group progress notes, formal and informal evaluations).

15. After each session, the worker should debrief and plan with the co-facilitator (if there is one) and arrange for consultation and/or supervision on a regular basis. If there is a co-facilitator, they should consider together the implications of their similarities and differences with respect to such issues as approaches, styles and communication.

B. Required Knowledge

1. Organizational mission and function and how these influence the nature and development of group work service.

2. Social and institutional barriers that may impact on the development of group work service.

3. How to assess the impact on the group of the community and agency context.

4. Issues associated with group composition (e.g. gender, education; socio-economic status, previous group experience, occupation, race, ethnicity, age and presenting problems.)

5. The influence of cultural factors on potential members' lives and their ways of engaging in group interactions and relationships with others, the agency and the worker.

6. The importance of diversity in relationship to how a group attains its goals.

7. The theoretical approaches utilized by group workers and how to select the ones most appropriate and effective for the proposed group.

8. Issues associated with group structure (e.g. group size, length of sessions, duration of group, meeting place, open or closed to new members, resources, supplies and transportation).

9. The impact of human development/life cycle factors on potential members' needs and abilities and group goals.

10. Types of groups (e.g., task groups, treatment groups, psycho-educational groups, socio-recreational groups) and their applicability to individual, organizational and community needs.

11. Issues related to group content such as discussion processes, and purposeful use of activities and simulations. Such issues include how these kinds of content are affected by stages of group development, capacities of members and the purposes of the group.

12. Contracting procedures including the identification and clarification of group purpose and behavioral standards and norms needed to actualize group goals as determined by potential members, the worker and the agency.

13. Recruitment procedures, such as community outreach and referral processes.

14. How to identify and develop resources required for group functioning.

15. Group monitoring and evaluation procedures (e.g., pretest-posttest measures, group process notes, questionnaires) to track worker interventions, group progress and the group work service.)

16. The importance of consultation and supervision in enhancing the quality of group work service.

SECTION III

GROUP WORK IN THE BEGINNING PHASE

A.   Tasks and Skills

1. Task: Establishing a Beginning Contract

Skills/Actions:

a. The worker and members collaboratively develop a beginning contract for work that identifies tasks to be accomplished, goals to be achieved and the process by which the work is to occur.

b. The worker identifies the community's and/or agency's stakes in the group, the group purpose and process and clarifies worker and member role.

c. Confidentiality and limits thereof are clearly identified.

d. The worker assists members in identifying and clarifying individual goals and group goals.

e. The worker helps the members to link individual goals with group purposes.

f. The worker invites full participation of all members and solicits member feedback on the progress of the group.

g. The worker employs special skills in working with mandated members and understands the impact on group dynam¬ics of member's mandated status.

2. Task: Cultivating Group Cohesion

Skills/Actions:

a. The worker establishes rapport with individual members and the group as a whole.

b. The worker also aids the group members in establishing relationships with one another so as to promote group cohesion.

c. The worker highlights member commonalities, links members to one another and encourages direct mem¬ber-to-member communication.

3. Task: Shaping Norms of Participation

Skills/Actions:

a. The worker seeks to aid the group in establishing norms for participation that promote safety and trust, facilitate a culture of work and cultivate mutual aid.

b. The worker is active in modeling these norms and instructing members when needed about productive group participation.

c. The worker appreciates the impact of various psychological, socio-cultural and environmental forces on these norms.

d. The worker promotes group exploration of non-productive norms when these arise.

e. The worker demonstrates respect for socio-cultural differences, promotes autonomy and self-determination, and encourages member empowerment.

B.   Required Knowledge

1. An understanding of the dynamic interaction be¬tween the community, agency, group and individual members of the group with which he/she is working.

2. The relevant theories and evidence-based practices regarding the developmental, psycho-social, and clinical needs of the group members and how this informs beginnings.

3. The group type and technology being employed and the ways such may impact group functioning in the beginning stage.

4. The characteristics and needs of the group in the beginning stage of group development and the related skills. Knowl¬edge is needed regarding such variations as working with mandated members; replacing a previous worker; and receiving new members into an on-going group.

SECTION IV

GROUP WORK IN THE MIDDLE PHASE

A. Group tasks and worker skills/actions:

1. Task: Assist group to make progress on individual and group goals. When group goals are a major focus, as in task and community groups, the worker encour¬ages individual members to use their skills in pursuit of group goals.

Skills/Actions:

a. Reinforce connection between individual con¬cerns/needs and group goals.

b. Offer programmatic ideas and activities that support group purpose and assist in helping members achieve individual and group goals.

c. Assess progress towards individual and group goals.

d. Identify difficulties and obstacles that interfere with the group and its members' abilities to reach their goals.

e. If obstacles are related to the specific needs of an individual member, when appropriate, offer individual time outside of group.

f. Ensure that the group has attended to any special needs of individual members (e.g., physical, cognitive, language or cultural needs).

g. Assist members to engage in problem-solving, in making choices and decisions, and in evaluating potential outcomes of decisions.

h. Summarize sessions with the group.

i. Plan next steps with the group.

j. Re-contract with members, if needed, to assist in achieving individual and group goals.

2. Task: Attend to group dynamics/processes.

Skills/Actions:

a. Support members to develop a system of mutual aid.

b. Clarify and interpret communication patterns among members, between members and worker and between the group and systems outside the group.

c. Develop, model and encourage honest communication and feedback among members and between members and workers.

d. Review group values and norms.

e. Assist members to identify and articulate feelings.

f. Assist members to perceive verbal and non-verbal communication.

g. Help members mediate conflict within the group.

h. Assist members to make connections with other group members that may continue after the group ends, if this is appropriate.

i. Use tools of empowerment to assist members to develop "ownership" of the group.

3. Task: Use best practices within the group and utilize resources inside and outside the group.

Skills/Actions:

a. Assist members to identify and access resources from inside and outside the group.

b. Include knowledge, skills and other resources of group worker, group members and sources outside the group.

c. Use group approaches appropriate to the popula¬tions served and the tasks undertaken as demonstrated in the literature, worker and agency experience, and other sources of professional knowledge.

d. Use record-keeping techniques to monitor leader¬ship skills and group process.

e. Access and use supervision.

B.   Required Knowledge

1. Group dynamics.

2. Role theory and its application to members' relation¬ships with one another and the worker.

3. Communication theory and its application to verbal and non-verbal interactions within the group and between the group and others external to the group.

4. Problem-solving processes in groups.

5. Conflict resolution in groups.

6. Organizational theories.

7. Community theories.

8. Developmental theories.

9. Evaluation theories and methods.

10. The impact of diversity: class, race, gender, sexual orientation and ability status.

11. Knowledge about the group's relations with its environment.

12. Specific knowledge of issues being addressed in the group.

13. Awareness of self.

SECTION V

GROUP WORK IN THE ENDING PHASE

A.   Tasks and Skills

1. Prepare members for the group's ending in advance.

2. In a direct practice group help members identify gains they have made and changes that have resulted from their participation in the group. In a task group, members may discuss what they have learned from this experience that will be useful to them in other task groups. This involves a consideration of how achiev¬ing group goals will contribute to the functioning of the organization and/or community.

3. Discuss the impact of the group on systems outside the group (e.g., family, organization, community).

4. Discuss the movement the group has made over time.

5. Identify and discuss direct and indirect signs of members' reactions to the group ending.

6. Share worker's feelings about ending with the group.

7. Assist members in sharing their feelings about ending with one another and with the worker.

8. Systematically evaluate the achievement of individual and group goals. Routine and systematic evaluation of the group experience could/should occur over time rather than in the ending stage alone.

9. Help members make connections with other agencies and programs as appropriate.

10. Assist members in applying new knowledge and skills to their daily lives.

11. Encourage members to give feedback to the worker on the worker's role and actions in the group.

12. Help members apply new knowledge and skills to their activities outside the group.

13. Prepare record material about the group for the agency, for individual members and for referrals as needed.

B.   Required Knowledge

1. Group dynamics related to endings. These will be different depending on the type of group (e.g., long- term, short- term, open-ended, single session). There are also special issues when a member or worker ends but parts of the group continue or there is a new worker.

2. Formal and informal resources that maintain and enhance members' growth.

3. Influence on endings of past losses and separation in lives of members and the worker.

4. Agency policies related to worker maintaining connections following ending of a group or member service.

5. Various forms of evaluation, formal and informal and of evaluation measures, both qualitative and quantitative.

SECTION VI

ETHICAL CONSIDERATIONS

National and/or regional social work organizations typically have codes of ethics to which social workers must adhere. For example, social group workers in the United States of America are expected to be knowledgeable about and responsive to the ethical mandates of the social work profession, as explicated in the National Association of Social Workers (NASW) Code of Ethics. While the entire code is important, there are items with particular relevance to social group work.

Similarly, Canadian social workers must follow the Canadian Association of Social Workers Code of Ethics/Association canadienne des travailleuses et travailleurs sociaux (2005). The expectation of AASWG is that social workers will respect the code of ethics relevant to their locations of practice wherever in the world, as long as these codes call for respect of all persons.

Other social work/ethical guides exist and may be more relevant for specific countries. Each needs to be considered in the context of work with groups and may call for some modifications or additions that reflect the different situations of group work.

A.   Elements of Ethical Practice in Social Group Work.

1. Knowledge of and use of best practices that reflect the state of the art and knowledge and research evidence regarding social work with groups.

2. A basic discussion with prospective members of informed consent and an explanation of what group work offers and requires of the members individually and as a group.

3. Maximizing member choice and minimizing coercive processes by members or worker to the extent possible. Emphasizing member self-determination and empowerment of the group.

4. Discussion of the importance, limits and implications of privacy and confidentiality with the members.

5. Helping the group to maintain the purposes for which it was formed, allowing for changes as mutually agreed upon.

6. Each member is given the help she/he requires within the parameters of the group's purpose, including individual meetings when appropriate.

7. Clarifying the decision-making process.

8. Clarifying how members may be chosen for or excluded from the group.

9. Maintaining group records and storing them in a secure location.

B. Ethical Issues in the Use of New Techniques

As new techniques are used, such as those based on electronic communications, workers should pay attention to ethical issues, practice skills and knowledge and evaluation of these techniques. The following is a general statement with reference to electronic communications:

Increasingly, practice with groups of all kinds is being done by utilizing technologies such as computer and telephone facilities, and professional associations are assessing both effectiveness and ethical issues. Issues such as member interaction, decision-making, group structure, mutual aid and, particularly, confidentiality are of vital concern. Worker competency may require new skills and knowledge, not only in technology use, but also in communication techniques.

Clearly these technologies are likely to be valuable for all persons seeking resources, as well as for the profession's ability to share information about practice, including emerging approaches. In the meantime, workers contemplating the use of such technologies should consider the appropriate codes of ethics as a guide and document processes related to such work.

Notes

1. The terms "social group work," "social work with groups" and "group work" are used interchangeably in these Standards.

2. In the NASW Code current at the time of approval of these Standards these sections include the Preamble and Ethical Principles 1.01, 1.02, 1,05 1.06, 1.07, 2.06, 3.02, 3.07, 3.09, and 4.01.

References

National Association of Social Workers (approved 1996, revised 1999) *Code of Ethics for Social Workers,* Washington, DC: NASW.

Canadian Association of Social Workers/Association canadienne des travailleuses et travailleurs sociaux (2005) *Code of Ethics,* Ottawa. CASW/ACTS.

January 2006.

Copyedited July 15, 2010.

Standards reprinted with permission of the Association for the Advancement of Social Work With Groups (http://www.aaswg.org).

Read more stories of social work practice!

Days in the Lives of Social Workers, 4th Ed.
edited by Linda May Grobman

Did you ever wish you could tag along with a professional in your chosen field, just for a day, observing his or her every move? The fourth edition of DAYS IN THE LIVES OF SOCIAL WORKERS allows you to take a firsthand, close-up look at the real-life days of 58 professional social workers as they share their stories. Join them on their journeys, and learn about the rewards and challenges they face.

ISBN: 978-1-929109-30-2 Publication date: 2012 $21.95

More Days in the Lives of Social Workers
edited by Linda May Grobman

Using the same first person narrative format as the popular DAYS IN THE LIVES OF SOCIAL WORKERS, this volume allows the reader to spend a day with 35 professional social workers, each in a different setting. This book provides more of a focus on macro social work roles than in the first, although this volume also includes micro-level stories, and illustrates ways in which social workers combine macro, mezzo, and micro level work in their everyday practice.

ISBN: 1-929109-16-4 Publication date: 2005 $16.95

Days in the Lives of Gerontological Social Workers
edited by Linda May Grobman and Dara Bergel Bourassa

This collection of first person narratives focuses on social workers' experiences with older adults. It brings to life the variety of ways in which social workers work with and on be-half of this growing population, and it will transform readers' thinking about what this type of work entails. Stunning pho-tographs by social worker/photographer Marianne Gontarz York are featured to expand the reader's visual images of real people as they grow older.

ISBN: 978-1-929109-21-0 Publication date: 2007 $19.95

$8.50/shipping (to U.S. addresses) for first book, $1.50 shipping each additional book. Contact us for shipping rates outside the U.S.

Order these books from:
WHITE HAT COMMUNICATIONS
P.O. Box 5390, Dept. D4 • Harrisburg, PA 17110-0390
Questions? Call 717-238-3787.
*Credit card orders: call 717-238-3787 or fax 717-238-2090
or order online at http://shop.whitehatcommunications.com
or use order form in the back of this book.*

THE FIELD PLACEMENT SURVIVAL GUIDE
What You Need to Know to Get the Most From Your Social Work Practicum
2nd Edition
edited by Linda May Grobman

Field placement is one of the most exciting and exhilarating parts of a formal social work education. It is also one of the most challenging. Considered by the Council on Social Work Education to be the "signature pedagogy" of social work, it allows students to put into practice the concepts, theories, and skills they have learned in the classroom, and it gives them room to explore and grow as budding social work professionals.

This book brings together in one volume more than 30 field placement-related writings from THE NEW SOCIAL WORKER magazine on issues related to choosing a field placement, getting ready, coping with challenges, supervision and evaulation, off and running, and moving on. It is a goldmine of practical information that will help social work students take advantage of all the field placement experience has to offer.

288 pages • 5 1/2 x 8 1/2 • ISBN 978-1-929109-26-5 • 2011
$22.95 plus shipping

Is It Ethical? 101 Scenarios in Everyday Social Work Practice: A Discussion Workbook
by Thomas Horn

What would you do if you were asked to be your hairdresser's social worker? How about if you developed a crush on a client? Or if you un-

expectedly received a $100 check in the mail from an agency to whom you had referred a client? Social work is filled with these kinds of questions. This workbook provides students and professional social workers with 101 different everyday scenarios and challenges them to think about what the ethical and unethical choices might be in each situation.

118 pages 5 1/2 x 8 1/2 ISBN 978-1-929109-29-6 2011
$14.95 plus shipping

Order from White Hat Communications, P.O. Box 5390, Dept. D4, Harrisburg, PA 17110-0390 with order form in the back of this book.

ORDER FORM

I would like to order the following:

Qty.	Item	Price
_____	Riding the Mutual Aid Bus @ $22.95	_____
_____	Days in the Lives of Social Workers @ $21.95	_____
_____	More Days in the Lives of SW @ $16.95	_____
_____	Days in the Lives of Geron. SW @ $19.95	_____
_____	Field Placement Survival Guide @ $22.95	_____
_____	Is It Ethical @ $14.95	_____
_____	The Nonprofit Handbook @ $34.95	_____

Please send my order to:

Name _____

Organization _____

Address_____

City_____ State____ Zip _____

Telephone_____

Please send me more information about ❑social work and ❑nonprofit management publications available from White Hat Communications.

Sales tax: Please add 6% sales tax for books shipped to Pennsylvania addresses.

Shipping/handling:
❑Books sent to U.S. addresses: $8.50 first book/$1.50 each add'l book.
❑Books sent to Canada: $13.00 per book.
❑Books sent to addresses outside the U.S. and Canada: Contact for rates.

Payment:
Check or money order enclosed for $_____
U.S. funds only.

Please charge my: ❑MC ❑Visa ❑AMEX ❑Discover
Card #: _____
Expiration Date _____ 3- or 4-digit CVV_____
Name on card: _____
Billing address (if different from above): _____
_____
Signature: _____

Mail this form with payment to:
WHITE HAT COMMUNICATIONS, P.O. Box 5390, Dept. DGR
Harrisburg, PA 17110-0390
Questions? Call 717-238-3787.
Credit card orders: call 717-238-3787 or fax 717-238-2090
or order online at http://shop.whitehatcommunications.com